POLICIES ON
FACULTY APPOINTMENT

POLICIES ON FACULTY APPOINTMENT

Standard Practices and Unusual Arrangements

Cathy A. Trower

Editor

Harvard University

ANKER PUBLISHING COMPANY, INC.
Bolton, Massachusetts

POLICIES ON FACULTY APPOINTMENT
Standard Practices and Unusual Arrangements

ISBN 1-882982-38-X

Composition by Keller & Keller *Designs in Print*
Cover design by Deerfoot Studios

Anker Publishing Company, Inc.
176 Ballville Road
P. O. Box 249
Bolton, MA 01740-0249

CONTENTS

ABOUT THE EDITOR

Cathy A. Trower is a researcher at the Harvard University Graduate School of Education, Project on Faculty Appointments. She earned a PhD in higher education administration at the University of Maryland in 1996. Her dissertation is titled "The Junior Faculty Experience: Work Life On the Tenure Track, Off the Tenure Track, and at Institutions Without Tenure Systems."

She is the author of several articles including "Alleviating the Torture of the Tenure Track" (1999), "Employment Practices in the Professions: Fresh Ideas Inside and Outside the Academy" (1998), and "Tenure Snapshot" (1996). She is coauthor of "Build It and Who Will Come?" (1998) and "Where Tenure Does Not Reign: Campuses With Contract Systems" (1997). She has written a case study on the University of Minnesota tenure situation and on the University of the South's performance appraisal system.

Previously, she served as a senior level administrator of business degree programs at Johns Hopkins University and was a member of the faculty at Mount Mercy College in Cedar Rapids, Iowa. There, she also served as chair of the business division. She has consulted with numerous colleges on tenure policies and with corporations and colleges on high-performance teams, organizational culture and change, and strategic planning. She holds a bachelor's and a master's of business administration from the University of Iowa.

About the Contributors

Jared L. Bleak is a doctoral candidate in Administration, Planning, and Social Policy at the Harvard University Graduate School of Education. Prior to coming to Harvard, he was the director of school relations at Southern Utah University and most recently worked in the office of the chancellor of the Massachusetts Board of Higher Education. He holds a BS in sociology from Brigham Young University and an EdM from Harvard. His research interests include governing boards, administrative leadership, and faculty worklife.

Lara K. Couturier is project manager of The Futures Project: Policy for Higher Education in a Changing World at Brown University. She previously worked as a consultant and global marketing manager for Andersen Consulting. She holds an EdM from the Harvard Graduate School of Education and a BS in business administration and Japanese from the University of Richmond.

William T. Mallon has authored seven case studies and other book chapters, journal articles, and reports on various higher education issues, including organizational change, faculty employment policy, and business–higher education partnerships. He has served as a program associate at the American Council on Education, associate editor of the Harvard Education Bulletin, and assistant director of admissions at the University of Richmond. He is nearing completion of an EdD in higher education policy and administration from the Harvard Graduate School of Education, where he also earned an EdM. He holds an MA and BA in English from the University of Richmond.

KerryAnn O'Meara is coordinator of the Project on Faculty Appointments at Harvard University. She received her master's degree in higher education from the Ohio State University and recently finished her dissertation on the evaluation of service for promotion and tenure to complete her PhD in education policy from the University of Maryland. KerryAnn has presented, written, and published on reward systems for faculty service.

Cheryl Sternman Rule is a research assistant for the Project on Faculty Appointments at Harvard. She has written several case studies, including one on presidential leadership at the University of Central Arkansas and another chronicling innovations at Georgia State University. She formerly served as a Peace Corps volunteer in Eritrea and worked for the Civil Rights Division of the US Department of Justice. She holds an EdM from the Harvard Graduate School of Education and a BA in philosophy from Haverford College.

Frances L. Shavers is a second year doctoral candidate at the Harvard Graduate School of Education in Administration, Planning, and Social Policy. Previously, she served in two administrative capacities at the University of Notre Dame, where she also completed undergraduate and master's studies. Her research interests include faculty worklife, organizational leadership, and athletic administration.

PREFACE

PRESSING SITUATIONS, COMMON QUESTIONS

A state legislature holds several million dollars in abeyance pending tenure code reform at the flagship university. The Board of Regents has to decide what to do.

- ◆ What areas of policy should be changed?
- ◆ What are typical practices elsewhere?

A vice president for academic affairs has to implement post-tenure review mandated by the state legislature.

- ◆ What are the policy provisions for performance evaluation at other institutions?
- ◆ What sanctions are there for poor performance?
- ◆ How should outstanding performance be rewarded?

Heading into a period of contract negotiations with the faculty union, administrators at a comprehensive university wonder about intermediate sanctions, short of dismissal, for faculty who fail to meet the terms of the contract.

- ◆ What other policies exist for dismissal for cause?
- ◆ How often is dismissal for cause tied to poor performance?

A faculty senate is asked to rethink the promotion and tenure process in light of Boyer's Scholarship Reconsidered *(1990).*

- ◆ How might scholarship and research be redefined?
- ◆ How important is service in obtaining promotion?
- ◆ How are these criteria measured?

Institutions across the country are hiring new faculty onto nontenure-track lines.

♦ What titles are there for full-time faculty who are not on a tenure track?

♦ What roles do nontenure-track faculty play?

♦ What about contract systems—what are the policy provisions for faculty at institutions without tenure?

PURPOSE OF THIS BOOK

Pressures to reinvent academic careers, reformulate academic appointments, and broaden the spectrum of faculty employment arrangements are intense and steadfast nationwide. All too often, legislators, board members, administrators, and faculty discuss faculty appointment policy changes in a vacuum, with little or no data about employment provisions at other institutions.

♦ What's normative?

♦ What's nonstandard?

♦ What policy changes would put an institution outside of the mainstream?

♦ Against what/whom should an institution benchmark?

Prior to the release of this book, and the accompanying CD-ROM archive (FAPA, 1999), answering questions about faculty employment such as "Who else does . . .?," "Does any other institution . . .?," or responding to statements that assert "No other major research institution would . . ." or "No one else has a policy that . . ." was difficult, if not impossible. Now, with the click of a mouse, answers to questions that previously required phone calls, surveys, site visits, web site searches, requests for copies of faculty handbooks, and weeks of research, are at your fingertips.

This book was written with policymakers and other higher education constituent groups in mind. Since one volume cannot possibly address the full range of faculty employment provisions, we concentrated on the topics that have been most discussed in recent years—areas of faculty employment that seem to be foremost on the minds of academic policymakers. In nine key areas of faculty employment policy, *Policies on Faculty Appointment: Standard Practices and Unusual Arrangements* catalogs the range of provisions denoting norms by Carnegie classification and highlighting unusual and/or "unorthodox" policies.

THE BOOK'S ORGANIZATION

Each chapter follows a similar format: 1) an overview of key provisions; 2) a description of standard, or normative, language provided by the American Association of University Professors; 3) notable variations from standard policy language; and 4) summary data and charts.

Policies covered include academic freedom (Chapter One), probationary periods (Chapter Two), the definition and locus of tenure (Chapter Three), faculty ranks and titles including titles and roles for nontenurable faculty at institutions with tenure (Chapter Four), promotion policies (Chapter Five), post-tenure review (Chapter Six), dismissal for cause and lesser sanctions (Chapter Seven), financial exigency and program discontinuance (Chapter Eight), and employment provisions at institutions without tenure (Chapter Nine).

DATA SOURCE

The chapters in the book are based on a CD-ROM that contains the faculty employment provisions from 217 four-year institutions in the United States and software that allows users to search the archive by key words or phrases. Users may search by 1) terms (e.g., *academic freedom, financial exigency*), 2) Carnegie classification (e.g., Research 1 [R1], Baccalaureate 2 [B2]), 3) state, or 4) collective bargaining agreements (CBA).

The CD's primary purpose is to assist decision-makers in answering questions like, "At other institutions . . ."

◆ How is academic freedom protected?

◆ Where is the locus of tenure?

◆ Is there a quota on the percentage of tenured faculty that may be employed?

◆ What happens to tenured faculty in the event of program discontinuance?

◆ What are the criteria, standards, and procedures for tenure reviews?

◆ How is financial exigency defined?

◆ What rewards are available for faculty who are rated as outstanding in a post-tenure review process?

Policies derive from faculty appointment practices at the institutions included, and we often cite policies as they appear in an institution's faculty handbook. Complete information is available on the FAPA CD-ROM. While we do not provide formal bibliographic citations for these policies, the institution is always cited. Readers who do not have access to the CD and would like more specific or complete information on a particular institution's policies should contact that institution's chief academic officer (usually the provost) or visit their web site. In those instances when an institutional policy is cited that does not appear on the FAPA CD-ROM, bibliographic information is provided at the end of the chapter.

FAPA BACKGROUND

In 1998, the Project on Faculty Appointments requested the faculty appointment policies from a random sample of 1,380 US four-year institutions, stratified by Carnegie classification. Table 1 shows the population and Table 2 shows the sample numbers; the sample is representative of the population of four-year institutions in the United States.

MATERIALS REQUESTED

We requested policy statements, provisions, terms, and conditions in the following areas:

Table 1   FAPA Population

Carnegie Classification	Public		Private		Total	
	Number	Percent*	Number	Percent*	Number	Percent**
Research 1	59	67%	29	33%	88	6%
Research 2	26	70%	11	30%	37	3%
Doctoral 1	28	55%	23	45%	51	4%
Doctoral 2	37	63%	22	37%	59	4%
Master's 1	247	58%	177	42%	424	31%
Master's 2	25	27%	66	73%	91	7%
Baccalaureate 1	6	4%	159	96%	165	12%
Baccalaureate 2	75	16%	390	84%	465	34%
TOTAL	503	36%	877	64%	1,380	100%

Table 2   FAPA Sample

Carnegie Classification	Public		Private		Total	
	Number	Percent*	Number	Percent*	Number	Percent**
Research 1	14	67%	7	33%	21	10%
Research 2	11	69%	5	31%	16	7%
Doctoral 1	5	50%	5	50%	10	5%
Doctoral 2	12	71%	5	29%	17	8%
Master's 1	37	63%	22	37%	59	27%
Master's 2	3	23%	10	77%	13	6%
Baccalaureate 1	2	8%	24	92%	26	12%
Baccalaureate 2	9	16%	46	84%	55	25%
TOTAL	93	43%	124	57%	217	100%

NOTE: * denotes % of Carnegie Class; ** denotes % of total

Academic Freedom

Academic Tenure[1]
   Definition of tenure
   Locus of tenure
   Probationary period
   Decision-making process
   Post-tenure review
   Dismissal for cause and lesser sanctions

Annual Evaluation
   Standards, criteria, process, sources of evidence

Financial Exigency

Initial Appointments, Ranks, and Titles

LIMITATIONS

While we intended to gather all of the above materials from each institution in the sample, the policies contained on the CD-ROM and subsequently analyzed and discussed in the chapters that follow may not include every single provision from each institution. In some cases, we were given specific pages from policy handbooks, in other cases, entire collective bargaining agreements were provided, and in still other cases, relevant materials were downloaded from institutional web sites. We attempted to gather as much relevant information as possible in the data collection process, but may not have all faculty employment provisions in their entirety from every institution.

Therefore, it does not necessarily follow that an institution's omission from a particular list in a chapter means that the institution does not have such a provision. It merely means that we did not have access to all institutional policies in all areas in all instances.

Such omissions, however, are quite few.

GRATITUDE

We are especially grateful to Dr. Christine Licata, Senior Associate with the American Association for Higher Education New Pathways II Project and Associate Dean, Rochester Institute of Technology/NTID, whose thoughtful analysis and national perspective on post-tenure review policies on the CD-ROM were essential for Chapter Six.

In addition, we are grateful to The Pew Charitable Trusts for funding our research, to JBL Associates, Inc. for creating the CD-ROM, to Vimi Coca and Jordan Bach for downloading data, and to the authors—Jared Bleak, Lara Couturier, Bill Mallon, KerryAnn O'Meara, Cheryl Sternman Rule, and Frances Shavers—for their countless hours of work and painstaking attention to detail in analyzing the policies.

A special note of thanks to Cheryl Sternman Rule for blazing the trail by writing the first chapter that served as a prototype for all those that follow, familiarizing everyone else with the common format, and for superb editing skills that polished every chapter.

And last, but certainly not least, I am grateful to Richard Chait for sedulous editing of style, sage advice on matters of substance, leadership on this project, and kind and patient mentorship.

Cathy A. Trower
Cambridge, Massachusetts
December 1999

NOTES

1. Policies from some institutions without tenure are included in this research archive. For such institutions, "contract renewal" or "continuous appointment" are more appropriate or accurate terms.

REFERENCES

Boyer, E. L. (1990). *Scholarship reconsidered: Priorities of the professoriate.* Princeton, NJ: Carnegie Foundation for the Advancement of Teaching.

Harvard Project on Faculty Appointments. (1999). *Faculty Appointment Policy Archive [CD-ROM].* Boston, MA: Harvard Graduate School of Education. (Distributed by Anker Publishing Company.)

1

FREEDOM IN THE ACADEMY: ACADEMIC FREEDOM EXPLORED

Cheryl Sternman Rule

HIGHLIGHTS

- 196 (90%) of the institutions in the Faculty Appointment Policy Archive grant tenure.
- 180 (92%) of these institutions provided a statement of academic freedom.

Of the 180 Academic Freedom Statements

- 87 (48%) explicitly cite the *1940 Statement of Principles on Academic Freedom and Tenure* (AAUP Policy Documents & Reports, 1995 Edition, pp. 3-4).
- 42 (23%) use some or all of the American Association of University Professors' (AAUP) language on academic freedom, but neither cite the 1940 statement nor mention the AAUP by name.
- 51 (28%) borrow little to no language from the AAUP and instead offer an original statement of academic freedom.
- 55 (31%) codify the academic freedom of students.

◆ 34 (19%) explicitly mention probationary and/or
  nontenured faculty.

◆ 10 (6%) explicitly mention adjunct and/or part-time faculty.

◆ 9 (5%) explicitly protect the academic freedom of librarians
  and/or library materials.

◆ 24 (13%) mention religion or an institution's religious
  affiliation in the statement of academic freedom.

Sample:

The Project on Faculty Appointments' 1998 Faculty Appointment Policy Archive (FAPA) CD-ROM contains policy provisions from the faculty handbooks of 217 randomly selected
four-year colleges and universities stratified by Carnegie classification. Of these 217 institutions, 196 grant tenure. Of these 196,
180 (92%) provided academic freedom statements for the CD-
ROM. The material provided by 16 tenure-granting institutions
did not include an academic freedom statement. We would not
infer, however, that these institutions lack an academic freedom
policy.

Table 1–1 The Sample

Carnegie Classification	217 Policy Provisions	196 Grant Tenure	180 Provided Academic Freedom Statements	
			# of Academic Freedom Statements	% of Academic Freedom Statements
R1	21	21	19	90%
R2	16	16	15	94%
D1	10	10	9	90%
D2	17	17	17	100%
M1	59	56	50	89%
M2	13	13	11	85%
B1	26	25	21	84%
B2	55	38	38	100%

Key to Carnegie classification abbreviations: R1 = Research 1; R2 = Research 2; D1 = Doctoral 1;
D2 = Doctoral 2; M1 = Master's 1; M2 = Master's 2; B1 = Baccalaureate 1; B2 = Baccalaureate 2
institutions.

INTRODUCTION

Throughout the 20th century, academic freedom has been a central concept of American higher education, arguably the single most important principle of the academy. The key provisions of academic freedom were formally codified in the 1940 *Statement of Principles* by the American Association of University Professors (AAUP). While many institutions have incorporated the AAUP's statement verbatim, a surprisingly large number of colleges and universities have adopted modified versions or altogether different policies in order to meet local needs and concerns. In some instances, the protection of academic freedom has been extended to students, librarians, guest speakers, and the larger community.

This chapter summarizes the academic freedom policies of 180 four-year institutions and answers the following questions:

◆ To what extent do academic freedom policies use AAUP language, and to what extent do policies vary from this standard?

◆ To whom do the protections of academic freedom extend?

◆ Are there notable differences between how religiously-affiliated and nonsectarian institutions define academic freedom?

◆ In what ways is academic freedom linked with tenure?

THE AAUP STANDARD

The 1940 *Statement of Principles on Academic Freedom and Tenure* serves as the standard to which institutions subscribe or from which they deviate. This statement intends "to promote public understanding and support of academic freedom and tenure and agreement upon procedures to assure them in colleges and universities" (AAUP, 1995, p. 3). Its three main components, and those most often replicated verbatim in institutional academic freedom policies, are

a) Teachers are entitled to full freedom in research and in the publication of the results, subject to the adequate performance of their other academic duties, but research for pecuniary return should be based on an understanding with the authorities of the institution.

b) Teachers are entitled to freedom in the classroom in discussing their subject, but they should be careful not to introduce into their teaching controversial matter which has no relation to their subject. Limitations of academic freedom because of religious or other aims of the institution should be clearly stated in writing at the time of the appointment.

c) College and university teachers are citizens, members of a learned profession, and officers of an educational institution. When they speak or write as citizens, they should be free from institutional censorship or discipline, but their special position in the community imposes special obligations. As scholars and educational officers, they should remember that the public may judge their profession and their institution by their utterances. Hence they should at all times be accurate, should exercise appropriate restraint, should show respect for the opinions of others, and should make every effort to indicate that they are not speaking for the institution (AAUP, 1995, pp. 3-4).

Eighty-seven of the 180 (48%) academic freedom statements in the Faculty Appointment Policy Archive explicitly cite and/or quote extensively from the 1940 Statement. Another 42 institutions (23%) crafted academic freedom policies that use some or all of the AAUP's language, but neither cite the 1940 statement nor mention the AAUP by name in the section on academic freedom. The remaining 51 institutions (28%) have written what we will call "original" academic freedom statements; that is, they borrowed little or no language from the 1940 statement. See Table 1-2 for a summary of these results categorized by Carnegie classification.

Clearly, then, far more institutions have chosen to support the 1940 statement in some form than to write an academic freedom statement from scratch.

Table 1-2   Breakdown of Standard and Local Language

Carnegie Classification	Explicitly Cite AAUP/AAC 1940 Statement on Academic Freedom and Tenure		Use Some Language from the 1940 Statement without Citation		Use Locally Crafted Language	
	#	%	#	%	#	%
R1	5	26	4	21	10	53
R2	7	47	2	13	6	40
D1	3	33	2	22	4	44
D2	10	59	3	18	4	24
M1	20	40	17	34	13	26
M2	10	91	0	0	1	10
B1	14	67	3	14	4	19
B2	18	47	11	29	9	24
Total	87	48	42	23	51	28

The Tried and True

Among the 87 institutions that cite the association's statement are, for example, Northwestern University (R1) and Albertson College of Idaho (B2). Aside from the addition of gender-neutral language, Northwestern (1993) offers a straightforward endorsement of the AAUP, choosing not to add any local flourishes to its academic freedom statement:

> Northwestern University subscribes to the principles of academic freedom stated by the American Association of University Professors (AAUP) as follows: a) The teacher is entitled to full freedom in research . . . b) The teacher is entitled to freedom in the classroom . . . c) The college or university teacher is a citizen . . .

While Albertson College of Idaho also endorses the AAUP, it adds local flavor in the form of a preamble that begins:

> Freedom in the context of this document means the opportunity for teachers to examine and reexamine their tasks in light of methodologies established by and evolving in their academic disciplines. It means the critical analysis of the teaching role according to the standards of judgment appropriate to the various academic fields. Hence, responsibility means the accountable

application of these standards of judgment. Without the freedom to employ these standards, creative teaching cannot flourish . . .

The writers of Albertson's preamble hope it "will serve as testament to those who will follow."

In addition to Northwestern and Albertson, 85 other institutions explicitly endorse the AAUP's statement of academic freedom. An additional 42 institutions (23%) use some or all of the association's language without citing its source. When these figures are combined, it becomes quite evident that a solid majority, 129 of 180 institutions (71%), have adopted what can fairly be characterized as the standard language of academic freedom.

THE ROAD LESS TRAVELED

Only one institution, the Richard Stockton College of New Jersey (B1), underscores that it does not subscribe to the 1940 statement: "Neither the state nor the college has endorsed the AAUP 1940 Statement on Academic Freedom and Tenure." Such explicit repudiations are unusual; the other 50 institutions that deviate from the standard do so without mentioning the AAUP at all. Rather, they crafted academic freedom statements on their own.

Brown University (R1), for example, not only affirms "full freedom in . . . teaching, learning, and research" to faculty and students, but also adds significantly more freedoms and protections to its statement on academic freedom:

Brown University also affirms that faculty and students shall have the freedom of religious belief, of speech, of press, of association and assembly, of political activity inside and outside the university, the right to petition the authorities, public and university, to invite speakers of their choice to the campus, and that students and faculty as such should not be required to take any oath not required of other citizens. The time, place, and manner of exercising these rights on the campus shall be subject to reasonable regulation only to prevent interference with the normal functions of the university (1998).

In a similar vein, Texas Woman's University (D1) also chose to craft an academic freedom statement that varies, somewhat, from the standard:

> Membership in the academic community imposes on students, faculty members, administrators, and trustees an obligation to respect the dignity of others, to acknowledge their right to express differing opinions, and to foster and defend intellectual honesty, freedom of inquiry and instruction, and free expression on and off campus. . . .

Also offering some originality are the academic freedom statements of San Francisco State University and the University of Detroit Mercy. At San Francisco State University (M1), academic freedom for faculty members must, among other things, include "the right of both faculty and students to seek censure of faculty members by complaint, petition, or seeking discipline for incompetence or unprofessional behavior." The University of Detroit Mercy (D2) offers "scholars" the right "to study, discuss, investigate, teach, publish, and for artists, freely to create and exhibit their works of art."

These examples just begin to touch upon the broad array of nonstandard academic freedom policies. It should be noted that while these institutions neither cite the AAUP nor use the association's language in their statements of academic freedom, they may endorse AAUP policies elsewhere in their faculty handbooks.

NOT JUST FOR TENURED FACULTY

The question of who is covered under an academic freedom policy is a tricky one. Seventy institutions (39%) use the generic terms "faculty members," "teachers," and "instructors" and do not explicitly extend policy coverage to other groups. Yet, because many institutions award faculty rank and status to librarians and academic administrators, the lines of coverage become more than a bit blurry.

Librarians

Nine institutions (5%) extend the protections of academic freedom to librarians explicitly. The University of Indiana, Bloomington (R1) ensures that "[n]o censorship shall be imposed on the librarian's freedom to select and make available any materials supporting the teaching, research, and general learning functions of the academic community." The University of Detroit Mercy (D2) extends the protections of academic freedom to "professional library service." And California Lutheran University (M1) affords such freedom to librarians "because they are often present at the point of student contact with ideas." The University of Toledo (D1) even goes so far as to protect the library's materials:

> In no case shall materials be excluded from university libraries because of their author(s) or their scientific, economic, social, political, or religious views. No library materials shall be proscribed or removed from the libraries because of partisan or doctrinal disapproval.

Several institutions, then, deem both librarians and library books worthy of mention in statements of academic freedom (see Appendix 1-A).

Students

Fifty-five (31%) of the academic freedom policies specifically mention students, protecting their freedom to learn, speak, and question authority. The University of Louisville (R2) codifies students' "right to their own views on matters of opinion, rather than fact, and a right to express those views in an appropriate way without fear of arbitrary reaction . . ." At East Carolina University (M1), faculty and students alike "share in the responsibility for maintaining an environment where academic freedom flourishes." And Haverford College (B1) protects students' rights to "engage in discussion, to exchange thought and opinion . . . to speak or write freely on any subject . . . [and] to found new, or to join existing organizations on or off campus" not simply as a general prerogative, but as part of the institution's policy on academic freedom. (See Appendix 1-D for a complete list of academic freedom policies that mention students' rights.)

Tenure-Ineligible Faculty

Adjunct, part-time, probationary, and nontenure-track faculty are also, at times, explicitly mentioned in academic freedom policies. Mentioning these groups separately—while perhaps redundant since many policies cover "faculty members" or "all faculty members"—highlights the institutional intention to assure that such faculty members also enjoy the protections of academic freedom. Ten academic freedom statements (6%) specifically include adjunct and/or part-time faculty, and 34 (19%) mention probationary, tenure-track, and/or nontenure-track faculty. The most frequently recurring phrase on this point can be credited to the AAUP (1995), which notes that academic freedom applies "not only to the full-time probationary as well as to the tenured teacher, but also to all others, such as part-time and teaching assistants, who exercise teaching responsibilities" (*1970 Interpretive Comments*, p. 6). Thus, one may reasonably assume that institutions that endorse the association's stance on academic freedom implicitly extend coverage to the above-mentioned groups. (See Appendix 1-B and Appendix 1-C for a list of institutions that explicitly mention part-time, adjunct, probationary, and nontenure-track faculty members in their academic freedom statements.)

And Beyond . . .

Finally, several institutions extend the protections of academic freedom beyond the scope of faculty members, librarians, and students altogether. North Carolina State University (R1), Smith College (B1), and the North Dakota State Board of Higher Education, for example, all offer protection to visiting speakers in their statements of academic freedom. The North Dakota State Board of Higher Education extends protection to "guest speakers, movies, and programs." Auburn University (R2) offers academic freedom to "prospective faculty to whom Auburn has extended an offer of appointment." And nine institutions (5%) guarantee academic freedom to "all members" of the academic or university community, omitting any mention of rank, status, or position within the institution.

A QUESTION OF FAITH

The FAPA CD-ROM contains the policies of both denominational and nonsectarian institutions. The academic freedom statements of some religiously affiliated institutions offer language somewhat at variance with their nondenominational counterparts. Twenty-four (13%) of the institutions in the sample mention religion or their religious heritage in their statement of academic freedom (there are several additional denominational institutions in the FAPA archive, but only 24 mention religion in the context of academic freedom). Of the 24, none of them is a Research 1 institution, and 12 (50%) are Baccalaureate 2. The breakdown by Carnegie classification appears in Table 1-3. (For a complete list, see Appendix 1-E.)

A spectrum of religious institutions emerges: Some institutions explicitly prohibit faculty members from advocating particular viewpoints, others require a demonstrated respect for a doctrinal position, and still others ask that faculty members exercise caution in their speech while nonetheless permitting outsiders to speak on a variety of controversial subjects.

The policy at Walsh University (M2), a Roman Catholic institution in Ohio, states:

> The mission of the university is to provide a Catholic, liberal arts education, while encompassing an international or global perspective, promoting critical thinking. While this places no obligation on faculty members with regard to their personal beliefs or religious practices, it does require of the faculty members a respect for Catholic beliefs and practices. Although faculty members are entitled to freedom in the classroom in discussing their subject and exposing students to diverse points of view, they are expected to refrain from promoting doctrines opposed

Table 1-3   Academic Freedom Policies Mentioning Religious Affiliation

R1 n=19		R2 n=15		D1 n=9		D2 n=17		M1 n=50		M2 n=11		B1 n=21		B2 n=38	
#	%	#	%	#	%	#	%	#	%	#	%	#	%	#	%
0	0	2	13	0	0	1	6	3	6	3	27	3	14	12	32

to the essentials of the Catholic faith or which are inimical to the aims and purposes of the university as a Catholic institution committed to the upholding of Christian faith and morality. The very nature of religious belief requires free, uncoerced consent, just as the nature of the University requires a respect for evidence, for investigation, for reason, and for enlightened assent. . . .

Similarly, Aquinas College (M2) notes the following:

Aquinas College declares its sole limitation of the academic freedom of its faculty shall be the prohibition of any intentional espousal of positions contrary to the defined *de fide* teaching of the Catholic Church.

While such policies may be regarded by some as conditional academic freedom, the limitations are clearly delineated and mission-related.

Some religious institutions, while mentioning their affiliation with a particular faith or doctrine, nonetheless choose not to limit speech on their campuses. Agnes Scott College (B1) and Mount Mercy College (B2) are two such examples. The penultimate sentence of Agnes Scott's academic freedom statement reads:

While the charter of the college states that the program of the college shall be carried out "under auspices distinctly favorable" to the Christian faith, no limitations of academic freedom are thereby intended.

Similarly, Mount Mercy College, a Roman Catholic institution, welcomes controversial speakers because "it is congruent with the belief in academic freedom and freedom of speech that all views be allowed."

The AAUP (1995) notes, "Most church-related institutions no longer need or desire the departure from the principle of academic freedom implied in the 1940 *Statement*, and we do not now endorse such a departure" (p. 6).

THE TENURE LINK

Tenure and academic freedom are often mentioned in the same clause. The AAUP certainly regards these concepts as inextricable, as evidenced by the appellation "1940 Statement of Principles on Academic Freedom and Tenure." Thus, when institutions cite the 1940 statement in their academic freedom policy, they implicitly acknowledge the inseparability of these concepts as well. As noted in Chapter Three, a total of 130 institutions link tenure and academic freedom either in the tenure clause, the academic freedom statement, or both.

For example, the trustees at the University of Rochester (R1) "are fully conscious of the role that tenure plays in protecting academic freedom." At Middle Tennessee State University (D2), "tenure is adopted as a means to protect" academic freedom "while promoting" academic responsibility. Central Connecticut State University (M1) recognizes that "tenure is granted for the purpose of protecting and nurturing academic freedom." Creighton University (M1) "recognizes that there is a close relationship between academic freedom and tenure." And Albertson College of Idaho (B2) asserts that "the necessary protection of academic freedom is tenure."

SUMMARY

Academic freedom is codified in faculty handbooks across institutional types—from the largest research institutions to the smallest religious, nontenure-granting, baccalaureate institutions and everywhere in between. The 1940 *Statement of Principles on Academic Freedom and Tenure* continues to reign supreme 59 years after it was promulgated, with a full 71% of academic freedom statements either explicitly citing it or borrowing its language. And the extent of coverage of these academic freedom policies varies as widely as the institutions themselves: Students, librarians, administrators, and even guest speakers may receive protections similar to those afforded to the traditional class of faculty members. Academic freedom, not only for the elite, extends its reach throughout the academy.

REFERENCES

American Association of University Professors. (1995). *Policy documents and reports* (8th ed.). Washington, DC: AAUP.

Brown University. (1998). *Brown University faculty rules and regulations* [On-line]. Available: http://facgov.brown.edu/facgov/facrulesfolder/part4/sect10/Sect10.html#RTFToC307.

Northwestern University. (1993). *Northwestern University faculty handbook*. Evanston, IL: Northwestern University, University Relations.

APPENDIX 1-A
Academic Freedom Policies That Expressly Cover Librarians and/or Library Materials

Research 1 Institutions
 1. University of Indiana, Bloomington (public)

Doctoral 1 Institutions
 2. University of Toledo (public)

Doctoral 2 Institutions
 3. University of Detroit Mercy (private)

Master's 1 Institutions
 4. California Lutheran University (private)
 5. Central Connecticut State University (public)
 6. Saint Mary's University (private)

Master's 2 Institutions
 7. Lincoln University of Pennsylvania (public)

Baccalaureate 1 Institutions
 8. Hiram College (private)
 9. Ohio Wesleyan University (private)

APPENDIX 1-B

Institutions Whose Academic Freedom Statements
Explicitly Mention Adjunct and/or Part-Time Faculty*

Research 1 Institutions
  1. Columbia University (private)
  2. West Virginia University (public)

Doctoral 1 Institutions
  3. Texas Woman's University (public)

Master's 1 Institutions
  4. Baldwin-Wallace College (private)
  5. Drake University (private)
  6. Pittsburg State University (public)
  7. Springfield College (private)

Baccalaureate 1 Institutions
  8. Wofford College (private)

Baccalaureate 2 Institutions
  9. Greensboro College (private)
  10. Saint Vincent College (private)

APPENDIX 1-C

Institutions Whose Academic Freedom Statements Explicitly
Mention Probationary, Tenure-Track, or Nontenure-Track Faculty

Research 1 Institutions
  1. Columbia University (private)
  2. West Virginia University (public)

Research 2 Institutions
  3. University of Mississippi (public)

Doctoral 1 Institutions
  4. Texas Woman's University (public)

Doctoral 2 Institutions
  5. Middle Tennessee State University (public)

Master's 1 Institutions
  6. Arkansas Tech University (public)
  7. Baldwin-Wallace College (private)
  8. Creighton University (private)
  9. Delta State University (public)
  10. Drake University (private)
  11. Emporia State University (public)

*Many additional institutions use the generic terms "all faculty," "faculty members," or "a faculty member" when describing who is covered by an academic freedom policy. These institutions are not included in the above list.

12. James Madison University (public)
13. Pittsburg State University (public)
14. Russell Sage College (private)
15. Saint Mary's University (private)

Master's 2 Institutions

16. Aquinas College (private)
17. Drury College (private)
18. Lincoln University of Pennsylvania (public)
19. Pacific University (private)
20. Union College (private)
21. Weber State University (public)
22. West Virginia Wesleyan College (private)

Baccalaureate 1 Institutions

23. Agnes Scott College (private)
24. Birmingham-Southern College (private)
25. Illinois Wesleyan University (private)
26. Ohio Wesleyan University (private)
27. Sweet Briar College (private)

Baccalaureate 2 Institutions

28. Albertson College of Idaho (private)
29. Bethel College (private)
30. Carroll College (private)
31. Culver-Stockton College (private)
32. Dakota Wesleyan University (private)
33. Mount Mercy College (private)
34. North Park College (private)

APPENDIX 1-D

Institutions That Explicitly Mention Students' Academic Freedom

Research 1 Institutions

1. Brown University (private)
2. Emory University (private)
3. Florida State University (public)
4. North Carolina State University (public)
5. West Virginia University (public)

Research 2 Institutions

6. Auburn University (public)
7. George Washington University (private)
8. Saint Louis University (private)
9. University of Idaho (public)
10. University of Louisville (public)
11. University of Notre Dame (private)
12. University of Rhode Island (public)

Doctoral 1 Institutions
13. Illinois State University (public)

Doctoral 2 Institutions
14. Middle Tennessee State University (public)
15. North Dakota State University (public)
16. University of North Dakota (public)

Master's 1 Institutions
17. Butler University (private)
18. California Lutheran University (private)
19. California State University, Los Angeles (public)
20. Central Connecticut State University (public)
21. College of Charleston (public)
22. Creighton University (private)
23. East Carolina University (public)
24. Fitchburg State College (public)
25. Holy Names College (private)
26. Pittsburg State University (public)
27. Saint Mary's University (private)
28. San Francisco State University (public)
29. University of North Alabama (public)
30. Valparaiso University (private)

Master's 2 Institutions
31. MidAmerica Nazarene University (private)
32. Union College (private)
33. Weber State University (public)
34. West Virginia Wesleyan College (private)

Baccalaureate 1 Institutions
35. Agnes Scott College (private)
36. Haverford College (private)
37. Hiram College (private)
38. Illinois Wesleyan University (private)
39. The Richard Stockton College of New Jersey (public)
40. Southwestern University (private)

Baccalaureate 2 Institutions
41. Albertson College of Idaho (private)
42. Carroll College (private)
43. Colby-Sawyer College (private)
44. Dickinson State University (public)
45. Fairmont State College (public)
46. Glenville State College (public)
47. Greensboro College (private)
48. Langston University (public)
49. Mayville State University (public)

50. Millikin University (private)
51. Mount Mercy College (private)
52. North Park College (private)
53. University of Southern Colorado (public)
54. Virginia Intermont College (private)
55. Western Montana College (public)

APPENDIX 1-E

Academic Freedom Policies That Mention Religion Or an Institution's Religious Affiliation

Research 2 Institutions
  1. Saint Louis University (private)
  2. University of Notre Dame (private)

Doctoral 2 Institutions
  3. Duquesne University (private)

Master's 1 Institutions
  4. California Lutheran University (private)
  5. Holy Names College (private)
  6. Salve Regina University (private)

Master's 2 Institutions
  7. Aquinas College (private)
  8. MidAmerica Nazarene University (private)
  9. Walsh University (private)

Baccalaureate 1 Institutions
  10. Agnes Scott College (private)
  11. Southwestern University (private)
  12. Wofford College (private)

Baccalaureate 2 Institutions
  13. Asbury College (private)
  14. Bethel College (private)
  15. Cedarville College (private)
  16. McMurry University (private)
  17. Mount Mercy College (private)
  18. North Park College (private)
  19. Paine College (private)
  20. Saint Anselm College (private)
  21. Saint Joseph's College (private)
  22. Saint Vincent College (private)
  23. Taylor University (private)
  24. University of the Ozarks (private)

2

On Probation: The Pre-tenure Period

Jared L. Bleak

HIGHLIGHTS

♦ 196 (90%) of the 217 four-year colleges and universities in the Faculty Appointment and Policy Archive (FAPA) CD-ROM grant tenure and require that faculty complete a probationary period.

Of the 196 tenure–granting institutions requiring a probationary period

♦ 72 (37%) offer a one-year initial tenure-track appointment at the assistant professor rank.

♦ 105 (54%) mandate a maximum probationary period of seven years while 54 (28%) require a six-year probation. Seven (4%) institutions, five in the Research 1 and 2 categories, maintain an eight-year probationary period.

♦ 75 (38%) grant up to three years probationary period credit for prior teaching experience in a university or college, while 27 (14%) grant up to two years' credit for prior experience.

- 38 (19%) allow scholarly leave during the probationary period that counts toward the completion of probation.

- 26 (13%) allow up to two years' leave that counts toward the probationary period, while 20 (10%) allow one year.

- 44 (22%) explicitly allow medical- or health-related leave during the probationary period, but do not count such leave toward completion of the probation.

- 92 (47%) conduct annual reviews of tenure-track faculty. 58 (30%) conduct a major pre-tenure review at the midpoint of the probationary period.

- 37 (19%) list teaching as the most heavily weighted criterion in the tenure review, five (3%) cite "teaching and one other," and five (3%) cite research. The remainder do not specify weights.

- 16 (8%) solicit letters from current students as part of the tenure review.

- Nine (5%) solicit letters from alumni or recent graduates as part of the tenure review.

- 45 (23%) solicit reviews/evaluation letters from faculty outside the institution as part of the tenure review.

- 29 (15%) require observation of the candidate's teaching as part of the tenure review.

- 23 (12%) allow the tenure candidate to either meet with the entire tenure review committee or be interviewed by a member of the committee.

- Nine (5%) allow faculty to remain at the institution even after a negative tenure decision has been rendered and the probationary period has ended.

- 67 (34%) allow "early tenure," that is, a tenure decision before the end of the stated probationary period.

- Nine (5%) allow a faculty member a second tenure review if tenure is not granted after consideration for "early tenure." In the other cases, a negative decision leads to a one-year terminal contract.

◆ Three (2%) allow the tenure candidate to select an advocate from the faculty to speak on the candidate's behalf before the tenure review committee.

◆ Four (2%) allow student participation on the departmental tenure review committee.

◆ Five (3%) grant tenure to part-time faculty.

INTRODUCTION

This chapter examines the probationary period policies of the 196 tenure-granting institutions on the Faculty Appointment Policy Archive (FAPA) CD-ROM and answers the following questions:

◆ What is the length of the probationary period, and in what year are tenure-track faculty reviewed for tenure?

◆ What is the initial term of appointment for a tenure-track position? How does this vary across institutions?

◆ How many years of credit for prior teaching experience are given to new faculty members?

◆ What provisions are made for extending the probationary period or for "stopping the tenure clock"?

◆ What evaluative criteria are most prevalent in the tenure review?

◆ What provisions are made for periodic evaluation and feedback during the probationary period?

◆ What unique or innovative policy provisions are followed during the probationary period?

The probationary period gives a college or university time to evaluate carefully the performance and potential of a new faculty member with respect to teaching, research, and service. In turn, this period allows tenure-track faculty to establish research programs, publish results, demonstrate teaching skills, and contribute as colleagues to their academic department, in particular, and to the institution in general. The American Association of

University Professors (AAUP) underscores the importance of the probationary period:

> Frequently, young faculty members have had no training or experience in teaching, and their first major research endeavor may still be uncompleted at the time they start their careers as college teachers. Under these circumstances, it is particularly important that there be a probationary period . . . before tenure is granted. Such a period gives probationary faculty members time to prove themselves, and their colleagues time to observe and evaluate them on the basis of their performance in the position rather than on the basis only of their education, training, and recommendations. (1995, p. 16)

DEFINITIONS OF THE PROBATIONARY PERIOD

Institutions define the probationary period in two ways. First, there are technical or legal definitions that specify a faculty member's employment relationship to the institution. The following is an example:

> A probationary appointment is an appointment other than fixed-term, adjunct, or tenured. A probationary appointment means that the individual holding such an appointment holds it for a stated term but that during such term the faculty member is being evaluated for purposes of determining whether at some fixed time an appointment with tenure shall be offered. (United States International University, D1)

A slight variation provides, instead, a rationale for the pretenure probationary period consisting of two basic elements: 1) a description of the faculty member's responsibility to demonstrate ability and 2) competence and a delineation of the institution's role in making the judgment on awarding tenure. Illinois State University (D1) broadly defines its rationale for the probationary period and indicates its purpose:

The probationary appointment is that period of professional service during which a faculty member does not hold tenure and is carefully and systematically observed by colleagues for the purpose of evaluation of his professional qualifications. By the end of this period, the faculty member either receives tenure or is not reappointed.

A statement on the probationary period from Bethel College (B2), among others, illustrates the dual nature of probation and mirrors the AAUP's (1995, p. 16) description of probation as a time for "faculty to prove themselves," and for colleagues "to observe and evaluate them on the basis of their performance in the position . . ." Further, Bethel College asserts:

The probationary status gives individuals time to demonstrate their ability and also gives the college time to observe and evaluate them on the basis of their performance in a faculty position.

Similarly, Holy Names College (M1) states:

A probationary period of faculty appointment is desirable because it provides the faculty members with time to evaluate their experience at Holy Names College, while the college makes an assessment of their value to its educational enterprise.

The University of Texas, Pan American (M1) gives slightly more detail in its policy:

The purpose of the probationary period is to allow reasonable time for tenure-track faculty members to establish their academic performance, for adequate peer and administrative evaluations, and for recommendations concerning reappointment, nonrenewal, and tenure.

Finally, the University of Missouri, Columbia (R1) speaks to the dual nature of probation in light of tenure's long-range implications:

The purpose of a probationary period is to allow reasonable time for faculty members to establish their academic

Table 2-1   Term of Initial Tenure-Track Appointment at Assistant Professor Rank

	R1 n=21		R2 n=16		D1 n=10		D2 n=17		M1 n=56		M2 n=13		B1 n=25		B2 n=38		Total n=196	
	#	%	#	%	#	%	#	%	#	%	#	%	#	%	#	%	#	%
1 year	7	33	5	31	4	40	6	35	20	36	3	23	8	32	19	50	72	37
2 years	2	14	2	13	1	10	0	0	0	0	0	0	5	20	1	3	11	6
3 years	3	10	1	6	1	10	1	6	1	2	0	0	1	4	1	3	9	5
4 years	3	14	2	13	0	0	0	0	0	0	0	0	0	0	0	0	5	3
Variable	5	24	1	6	1	10	3	18	4	7	2	15	2	8	0	0	18	9
Unstated	1	5	5	31	3	30	7	41	31	55	8	62	9	36	17	45	81	41

performance and for their departments to evaluate performance and potential performance in the long-range future in order to validate recommendations for continuous or terminal appointments.

The Initial Appointment

The AAUP (1995) makes no definitive recommendation on the length of the initial appointment for probationary period faculty, but suggests that "the precise terms and conditions of every appointment" be clearly stated before the appointment begins (p. 16).

When making an appointment to the tenure track, 72 institutions (37%) typically offer a one-year initial appointment (see Table 2-1). Eleven institutions (6%) normally offer new tenure-track faculty a two-year initial appointment, while nine (5%) usually offer a three-year appointment and five (3%) a four-year initial appointment. All five institutions offering a four-year initial appointment, and four of the nine offering a three-year appointment, have research Carnegie classifications.

Eighteen institutions (9%) offer initial appointments for varying terms, including one institution, the University of Georgia (R1), which permits a five-year initial appointment. These varying terms include a period of "up to three years," which is offered by nine (5%) institutions: Brown University (R1), University of Missouri, Columbia (R1), George Mason University (D2), University of New Orleans (D2), Bowie State University

(M1), Central Connecticut State University (M1), Philadelphia College of Textiles and Science (M2), Lake Forest College (B1), and Agnes Scott College (B1).

The Massachusetts Institute of Technology (R1) offers an initial contract for new tenure-track faculty of "up to five years," while George Washington University (R2) and the University of Indiana, Bloomington (R1) provide for an initial appointment of "not more than three years." Wake Forest University (D2), California State University, Los Angeles (M1), and American University (D1) provide for either a one-or two-year initial appointment, while Butler University (M1) grants either a two- or three-year appointment initially. Finally, Drury College (M2) states its initial appointment term as "for one year, or for other stated periods."

Michigan State University's (R1) policy for initial appointments is unique. A faculty member appointed to the tenure track at the rank of instructor is appointed for one three-year probationary period. If the person is not promoted to assistant professor at the conclusion of this period, he or she is ineligible for reappointment. However, if during the three-year probationary period the instructor is promoted, the next appointment period will be for three years if promoted after one year as an instructor, two years if promoted after two years, or one year if promotion occurs after three years as an instructor. If the faculty member is then reappointed, he or she will receive another three-year appointment that will complete the probationary period. However, this type of appointment is the exception at Michigan State, where most faculty are appointed at the rank of assistant professor "for a probationary period of four years and may be reappointed for an additional probationary period of three years. If an assistant professor is appointed beyond the two probationary periods, tenure is granted."

Columbia University (R1) makes a one-year initial appointment and then grants another one-year contract upon reappointment. Following these two one-year appointments, the faculty member receives a three-year appointment which ends in a major review, called the "critical review." A successful review earns the faculty member another three-year appointment

Table 2-2   Maximum Length of the Probationary Period

	R1 n=21		R2 n=16		D1 n=10		D2 n=17		M1 n=56		M2 n=13		B1 n=25		B2 n=38		Total n=196	
	#	%	#	%	#	%	#	%	#	%	#	%	#	%	#	%	#	%
8 years	4	19	1	6	0	0	0	0	0	0	0	0	0	0	2	5	7	4
7 years	15	71	9	56	10	100	10	59	29	52	6	46	13	52	13	34	105	54
6 years	2	10	5	31	0	0	5	29	17	30	5	38	4	16	16	42	54	28
5 years	0	0	0	0	0	0	0	0	9	16	0	0	2	8	1	3	12	6
Variable	0	0	0	0	0	0	0	0	1	2	0	0	1	4	0	0	2	1
Unstated	0	0	1	6	0	0	2	12	0	0	2	15	5	20	6	16	16	8

which takes him or her into the eighth year and review for tenure.

The Probationary Period: Maximum Length

Concerning the length of the probationary period, the AAUP (1995) asserts, "Beginning with appointment to the rank of full-time instructor or a higher rank, the probationary period should not exceed seven years . . . " (p. 90). One hundred five institutions (53%) in the sample follow this recommendation for the maximum length of the probationary period (see Table 2-2 and Appendix 2-A). Fifty-four institutions (28%) mandate a six-year probation, while 12 institutions (6%) require a five-year probation.

Listed in Table 2-2 in the "Variable" category, Haverford College (B1) allows either a six- or seven-year probationary period, while Youngstown State University (M1) allows either a five-, six-, or seven-year probationary period. The timing of the tenure review at Haverford depends on whether the faculty member took a junior faculty leave of one year for research and scholarship in year four of the probationary period. If this leave was taken, the review occurs in year seven. Youngstown State University (M1) allows the faculty member to choose in which year the tenure review will occur.

Seven (4%) institutions, five in the Research 1 and 2 categories, maintain an eight-year probationary period, including Columbia University (R1), the Massachusetts Institute of Technology (R1), North Carolina State University (R1), the University of California, Irvine (R1), the University of California, Santa Cruz (R2), Asbury College (B2), and Wiley College (B2).

Across Carnegie classifications, 77% of Research or Doctoral institutions have maximum probationary periods of either seven or eight years, while only 48% of Master's and Baccalaureate institutions stipulate either a seven- or eight-year probation. Most Master's and Baccalaureate institutions require either a seven-year (46%) or a six-year probation (32%). Those institutions mandating a five-year probationary period are exclusively in the Master's and Baccalaureate classifications.

Tenure Review Year: Variability

Though most institutions (130; 66%) list the final year for the tenure review as year five, six, or seven of the probationary period, 12 institutions (6%) allow flexibility in the timing of the review. For example, at Emory University (R1) a candidate can choose to be reviewed for tenure at any time, though the review normally occurs in year five or six. The University of Central Florida (D2) normally reviews in year five, but "at the option of the faculty member, and with concurrence of the appropriate administrative officials," the review can be made in year six. Idaho State University (D2) allows the tenure review to be in either year five or year six of the probationary period, while Elon College (M2) conducts the tenure review in either year four or year five. Rice University (R2) allows the candidate to apply for tenure at any time during the probationary period, but the review normally occurs in year six or seven. Saint Louis University (R2) normally reviews in year six, except in the medical school where the tenure review is conducted in year eight.

Three institutions (2%), all Baccalaureate 2, allow multiple tenure reviews. Dana College (B2) first conducts a review in year four of the probationary period; if tenure is not granted, then another review is conducted in year five. If the candidate is still unsuccessful, he or she is reviewed again in year six. If tenure is not granted in year six, the candidate is given a one-year terminal contract. Langston University (B2) and Central State University (B2) review tenure-track faculty in year five of the probationary period; if tenure is not granted, a second review in year six is conducted. If unsuccessful in year six, the candidate is given a one-year terminal contract.

Colby-Sawyer College (B2) requires probationary faculty to either apply for tenure or a three- or one-year rolling contract in year six. The faculty member is informed as to the type of contract available in year five: "The type of contract offered will be determined by the academic vice president and dean of faculty, after consultation about institutional need criteria." The tenure review is then conducted in year six.

Youngstown State University (M1) allows the tenure candidate to decide the tenure review year, either year four, five, or six. Hunter College, City University of New York (M1) begins its tenure review in the spring semester of year four.

McMurry University (B2) conducts the tenure review in year six of the probationary period; however, a probationary faculty may defer the tenure review twice, pushing it back to year eight.

Columbia University (R1) allows a "ninth-year exception" or postponement of the tenure review until year nine of the probationary period in special circumstances. Columbia normally considers candidates for tenure no later than the end of year seven but can postpone the review until year eight. The ninth-year exception requires prior special permission of the provost and is possible only if the tenure clock has not been stopped. The exception is made during year six if 1) there is substantial evidence of excellence; 2) there are specific, compelling reasons for deferring tenure (generally, the only acceptable grounds are that scholarly publications or accomplishments are expected during the forthcoming year that will have a material effect on the outcome of the ad hoc review); and 3) the department or school includes a statement that a positive recommendation is expected from an internal review of the candidate.

Credit for Prior Teaching Experience

The AAUP (1995) makes provisions for probationary period credit for a faculty member's prior teaching experience elsewhere:

Beginning with appointment to the rank of full-time instructor or a higher rank, the probationary period should not exceed seven years, including within this period full-time service in all institutions of higher education; but subject to the proviso that when, after a term of probationary service of more than three years in one or more institutions, a teacher is called to another institution, it may be agreed in writing that the new appointment is for a probationary period of not more than four years, even though thereby the person's total probationary period in the academic profession is extended beyond the normal maximum of seven years. (p. 90)

In making the recommendation that up to three years of prior credit be allowed, the AAUP (1995) maintains that its purpose is to guard against "excessive probation" if a professor has experience at several institutions, and also to recognize "university teaching as a profession" in which experience is largely transferable. However, the AAUP also recognizes that experience in teaching and research may not be interchangeable across the broad array of higher education institutions and "that an institution may properly wish to determine whether an individual meets its standards for permanent appointment by on-the-spot experience" (p. 90).

Seventy-five institutions (38%) award up to three years of credit for prior teaching experience in a university or college toward the completion of the probationary period. Twenty-seven institutions (14%) grant a maximum of two years of credit for prior experience, while six institutions (3%) award a maximum of four years of credit (see Table 2-3 below and Appendix 2-B). Eighteen institutions in the sample (9%) expressly allow the faculty member to negotiate the amount of credit for prior experience.

Across Carnegie classifications, of the institutions granting up to two years of prior credit, 22 (81%) institutions are in the Master's 1 and 2 or Baccalaureate 1 and 2 classifications. Fifteen (20%) of the 75 institutions granting up to three years of prior credit are in the Research 1 and 2 classifications.

Table 2-3   Maximum Number of Years Credit Granted for Prior
Teaching Experience

	R1 n=21		R2 n=16		D1 n=10		D2 n=17		M1 n=56		M2 n=13		B1 n=25		B2 n=38		Total n=196	
	#	%	#	%	#	%	#	%	#	%	#	%	#	%	#	%	#	%
2 years	3	14	1	6	1	10	0	0	6	11	2	15	5	20	9	24	27	14
3 years	11	52	4	25	2	20	8	47	21	38	4	31	11	44	14	37	75	38
4 years	0	0	1	6	2	20	0	0	3	5	0	0	0	0	0	0	6	3
Nego-tiable	1	5	0	0	2	20	2	12	8	14	0	0	4	16	1	3	18	9

Three institutions (2%), Culver-Stockton College (B2), Dana
College (B2), and North Park College (B2), allow a faculty
member to receive credit toward the completion of the probationary period for teaching experience in an elementary or secondary school or for other work experience. All three institutions give one year of probationary period credit for every two
years of teaching.

STOPPING THE TENURE CLOCK: PROBATIONARY PERIOD LEAVE

Rice University (R2) defines the tenure clock as "the schedule
for the probationary period during which a person in the professorial ranks becomes eligible for tenure review." This clock
starts when a faculty member begins the probationary period
and ends with the tenure review, counting all time served
toward completion of the probationary period unless special
allowance is made. This special allowance could include scholarly leave, medical leave, or other personal leave.

Scholarly Leave

The AAUP (1995) states:

Leaves of absence are among the most important means
by which the teaching effectiveness of faculty members
may be enhanced, their scholarly usefulness enlarged,
and an institution's academic program strengthened and

Table 2-4   Institutions Allowing Scholarly Leave Toward the Completion
of the Probationary Period

R1 n=21		R2 n=16		D1 n=10		D2 n=17		M1 n=56		M2 n=13		B1 n=25		B2 n=38		Total n=196	
#	%	#	%	#	%	#	%	#	%	#	%	#	%	#	%	#	%
2	10	6	38	1	10	4	24	8	23	4	31	7	28	6	16	38	19

enhanced. A sound program of leaves is therefore of vital importance to a college or university . . . (p. 242)

The association further maintains, "Scholarly leave of absence for one year or less will count as part of the probationary period as if it were prior service at another institution" (p. 22).

Thirty-eight institutions (19%) in the sample state clearly that scholarly leave is available during the probationary period and is counted toward the completion of probation, without stopping the tenure clock (see Table 2-4 and Appendix 2-C).

However, four of these 38 institutions provide probationary faculty with structured opportunities for scholarly leave before the tenure review. For instance, Davidson College (B1) provides sabbatical leaves in year five of the probationary period for all assistant professors. This leave immediately precedes the tenure review year and is meant to "provide probationary faculty with early research and writing opportunities before, rather than after, a tenure decision is made." Haverford College (B1) employs a similar program, but gives "special junior faculty leave" in year four of the probation and also gives faculty the option of not including this year in the probationary period. To qualify for this leave, a faculty member at Haverford "must demonstrate significant effort." Upon reappointment following a four-year initial contract, all assistant professors at Rice University (R2) may take a paid, one semester junior leave "devoted entirely to research, scholarship, or creative work." This leave usually occurs in year four or five. The University of Rochester (R1) also provides "Junior Leave," which neither delays the tenure decision nor prevents the probationary faculty from applying for a "Bridging Fellowship." These allow a faculty member to spend a semester in a department other than his or

Table 2-5   Institutions Explicitly Allowing up to Two Years Leave for Health or Family-Related Reasons

R1 n=21		R2 n=16		D1 n=10		D2 n=17		M1 n=56		M2 n=13		B1 n=25		B2 n=38		Total n=196	
#	%	#	%	#	%	#	%	#	%	#	%	#	%	#	%	#	%
12	57	10	63	3	30	6	35	7	13	0	0	4	16	2	13	44	22

her own and "permits the acquisition of knowledge and methods in a quite different field."

Medical Leave

The AAUP (1995) does not elaborate on medical leave during the probationary period; however, on family leave, it asserts, "An institution's policies on faculty appointments should be sufficiently flexible to permit faculty members to combine family and career responsibilities in the manner best suited to them as professionals and parents" (p. 245).

Forty-four institutions (22%) give an allowance for health- or family-related leave during the probationary period that does not count toward completion of probation (see Table 2-5 and Appendix 2-D). Twenty-two (50%) of these institutions are in the Research 1 and 2 classifications.

There are several examples of policy provisions for health- or family-related leave during the probationary period. Michigan State University (R1) allows a tenure candidate to stop the tenure clock for childbirth; adoption; care of an ill and/or disabled child, spouse, or parent; or for personal reasons. North Carolina State University (R1) allows leave for "compassionate reasons of health, or requirements of childbirth or child care, or similar compelling reasons." And Northwestern University (R1) allows for such circumstances as "parental responsibilities relating to the birth, adoption or rearing of a child; personal or family emergencies, for example, chronic illness of the faculty member or a member of the immediate family . . ." The University of Arizona (R1) and American University (D1) allow for two one-year periods of "parental delay" in the probationary period.

Table 2-6   Maximum Number of Years Leave Allowed During the
             Probationary Period

	R1 n=21		R2 n=16		D1 n=10		D2 n=17		M1 n=56		M2 n=13		B1 n=25		B2 n=38		Total n=196	
	#	%	#	%	#	%	#	%	#	%	#	%	#	%	#	%	#	%
1 year	4	19	2	13	0	0	0	0	6	11	2	15	4	16	2	5	20	10
2 years	7	33	5	31	3	30	4	24	4	7	1	8	0	0	2	5	26	13

The faculty policy for Marquette University (D1) reads as
follows:

Upon the request of a tenure-track faculty member who
becomes the parent of a child (either by birth or adoption), he or she shall be granted a one-year extension of
the time period for conferral of tenure.

Similarly, Northern Arizona University (D1) allows the following:

Extension of the probationary period for good cause:
serious illness; disability; exceptional family care responsibilities such as pregnancy, childbirth, adoption; less
than full-time service, etc.; and any other good cause that
is shown to interfere with a faculty member's efforts to
perform duties necessary to meet the criteria for tenure.

Leave: Years Allowed

Twenty-six institutions (13%) allow a maximum of two years'
"stop the clock" leave during the probationary period. Another
20 institutions (10%) allow one year of leave that is not credited
toward completion of the probationary period (see Table 2-6
above and Appendix 2-E).

Perhaps because of greater research demands, 73% of the
institutions allowing two years of leave are in the Research 1
and 2 and Doctoral 1 and 2 Carnegie classes; only seven of the 26
institutions are Master's 1 and 2 and Baccalaureate institutions.
Conversely, 70% of those allowing one year of leave are in the
Master's 1 and Baccalaureate 2 categories.

Table 2-7   Frequency and Nature of Periodic Review During the
            Probationary Period

	R1 n=21		R2 n=16		D1 n=10		D2 n=17		M1 n=56		M2 n=13		B1 n=25		B2 n=38		Total n=196	
	#	%	#	%	#	%	#	%	#	%	#	%	#	%	#	%	#	%
Annual Review	11	52	7	44	5	50	9	53	28	50	6	46	7	28	19	50	92	47
Major Mid-term Review	7	33	4	25	2	20	4	24	17	30	4	31	9	36	11	29	58	30

PROBATIONARY PERIOD PERFORMANCE REVIEWS

The AAUP (1995) calls for interim evaluations during the probationary period to "review a faculty member's situation" (p. 16). The AAUP (1995) further states:

> Nontenured faculty members should have available to them the advice and assistance of their senior colleagues, and the ability of senior colleagues to make a sound decision on renewal or tenure will be enhanced if an opportunity is provided for a regular review of the candidate's qualifications. (p. 16)

The AAUP (1995) contends that periodic review during the probationary period "should minimize the likelihood of reasonable complaint if nontenured faculty members are given notice of nonreappointment" (p. 17).

Ninety-two institutions (47%) conduct an annual review of probationary tenure-track faculty members (see Table 2-7) and 58 institutions (30%) conduct a major review at the mid-point of the probationary period regardless of whether an annual review occurs (see Appendix 2-F).

Purpose of Periodic Review

Though the primary purpose of periodic review is to assist the faculty member in his or her development toward tenure, this is stated quite differently among the institutions in the FAPA sample. For example, Agnes Scott College (B1) asserts that the purpose of its periodic review is to "provide constructive criticism of probationary faculty members, acquaint them with department needs and expectations, encourage them to develop their particular talents as teachers and scholars, and in general to build good working relationships within departments." Hiram College (B1) states plainly that in its review, "Faculty members' strengths and weaknesses will be assessed and areas for improvement identified."

The University of Texas, Pan American's (M1) policy states:

Nontenured tenure-track faculty are expected to demonstrate consistent progress toward the achievement of tenure. To facilitate this, the faculty member's immediate supervisor or administrative equivalent shall hold a conference with the faculty member at the conclusion of the annual evaluation process to discuss perceived strengths/weaknesses, possible means of improvement, and prospects for reappointment and tenure.

At the University of Arkansas (R2), annual reviews are occasions for the faculty member to receive feedback concerning progress to tenure, and "the primary basis for the chairperson's recommendations relating to salary, promotion, granting of tenure, successive appointment, nonreappointment, and dismissal."

A central purpose of periodic review is to give the faculty member an opportunity to receive feedback on his or her progression toward tenure. Illinois Wesleyan University (B1) states the following:

The faculty member should strive at this point to place her or his accomplishments to date in the context of her or his larger goals and strategies for continuing development toward tenure. The Promotion and Tenure Committee has time to give constructive feedback to the candidate so that he or she can develop further before having to make a case for tenure.

In much the same spirit, Auburn University's (R1) policy states:

The particular focus of the review is the faculty member's progress toward achieving tenure. The review therefore must address the criteria for tenure set forth in this document . . . the review shall involve the entire tenured faculty . . . it shall conclude with a vote on whether or not, in the judgment of the tenured faculty, the candidate is making appropriate progress toward tenure.

Probationary period reviews at Southwestern University (B1) fulfill two purposes: First, they assist Southwestern University "in identifying faculty members with the strongest credentials for tenure." Second, they provide feedback that "promotes enhanced teaching skills and professional growth."

Periodic review is also a time when institutions may choose not to renew the contracts of poor performing tenure-track faculty. The University of Rhode Island (R2) asserts that "no system of tenure will work unless the administration acts with firmness in not renewing contracts of those who are not adapted by training, experience, or temperament to the institution."

Whitworth College (M1) lists some of the distinct outcomes of the periodic review:

1) "provides a mutual understanding of the faculty member's role in meeting college, departmental, and specific instructional goals,"

2) "helps the faculty member to improve teaching performance,"

3) "provides information which will assist the faculty person to make career decisions,"

4) provides information to the college "to make staffing decisions such as contract renewal, promotion, and tenure, and to develop strategies for faculty retention and development."

Northwestern University's (R1) periodic reviews not only afford a chance to give feedback to a faculty member on his or her progress toward tenure, but also offer an appropriate time for a nonreappointment decision when a faculty member is not performing adequately.

> In the present job market, younger members of the faculty are not well served if they are retained by Northwestern without having a genuine chance to obtain tenure here. To be let go by an institution at the brink of tenure is to face the problem of relocating at one of its most difficult points. Accordingly, recommendations to reappoint are treated with the utmost seriousness by the dean and should be so taken by the departments.

The University of Iowa's (R1) policy echoes Northwestern University's (R1):

> Only if an institutional need is found likely to exist for a person with the faculty member's substantive background, and only if the faculty member's teaching effectiveness and research productivity and potential are deemed of such a quality that an affirmative tenure decision is likely to be made three years later, should something other than a terminal appointment be tendered.

An unusual provision at Birmingham-Southern College (B1) permits the transfer of probationary faculty members from the tenure track to a nontenure track until sufficient progress toward tenure is exhibited, whereupon the faculty member may be reinstated to his or her original position. The policy reads as follows:

> When a member of the faculty is on a tenure track and is making progress toward achieving tenure but will not achieve tenure within the prescribed probationary period, that faculty member will be removed from the tenure track until such time as the provost and the Promotion and Tenure Committee deem it appropriate to reinstate the faculty member on the tenure track.

Though the main purpose of periodic review, as stated in most policies, is to provide feedback to the candidate on his or her progress toward tenure, reviews also give the tenure-track faculty member an "explanation of the department's, program's, or division's needs" (Brown University, R1) so far as they affect the faculty member. In this sense, the review gives the unit a chance to discuss its needs and priorities with the faculty member.

THE TENURE DECISION

The importance of the tenure decision to the institution's quality and vitality is highlighted in most policies. Though the significance of this decision is articulated in various ways, policies stress the importance of the review not only for the institution but also for the faculty member.

Auburn University (R2) links the importance of the tenure decision to its goal of maintaining a high-quality faculty:

> Auburn University recognizes that its success as an educational institution depends largely upon its ability to attract and retain well-educated, talented, and dedicated faculty members. Thus, within available resources, it rewards individuals who demonstrate high quality performance in its primary activities-teaching, research/creative work, and extension—by . . . tenure . . .

The University of Louisville (D1) underscores the importance of the tenure decision as a means to encourage "the development of a faculty of high quality." The nature of the tenure decision and gravity of the institution's tenure commitment are underscored by the University of New Hampshire (D2):

> Tenure decisions are enormously important, both for the faculty member and for the university. Tenure shall not be recommended routinely; rather, tenure is granted to those who, by reason of their excellent performance and promise of long-range contribution to the educational purposes of the institution, are deemed worthy of this important commitment.

In light of the commitment the institution makes when awarding tenure, Wake Forest University (D2) asserts that "the decision to grant or withhold tenure is the most important decision, as a rule, that the university makes about a faculty member." And Michigan State University (R1) recognizes that "the reputation and prominence of MSU for many years to come will be determined in large measure by these decisions." In the same vein, the University of Iowa (R1) maintains that "the tenure decision is the most important quality control available to the university" while Rice University (R2) states that for faculty, the tenure review is "the most important review of their academic career."

The University of Indiana, Bloomington (R1) stresses the forward-looking nature of the tenure decision: "The granting of tenure is not only recognition of past achievement but a sign of confidence that the individual is capable of greater responsibilities and accomplishments." The University of Nebraska, Lincoln (R1) maintains, "The tenure decision ultimately is based on an evaluation of the quality and quantity of work accomplished during the probationary period and is an expectation and prediction of the quality and quantity of a faculty member's future performance." Dakota Wesleyan University (B2) states, "The tenure decision must be made very selectively with an eye toward the institutions' obligations to its future students." San Jose State University (M1) highlights its expectations of faculty after a positive tenure decision:

> The granting of tenure is not solely a reward for services performed during the probationary years, but also represents an explicit expectation that a faculty member will continue to be a valued colleague; a good teacher and an active scholar, artist, or leader in his or her profession; and a contributor to the university's mission, including collegial governance of the university.

To guide both faculty and administrators in the tenure review, and also to make tenure expectations explicit for new faculty, several institutions include in their policies an overall question that encapsulates the essence of the tenure review. For example, the University of Rochester (R1) asks:

But of course the central concern in tenure is with future expectations, and the primary use of the record of the past is to answer the question "Is this individual likely to be an important teacher and scholar (or artist) for the many years ahead, as in the past?"

In much the same way, Rice University (R2) states:

The award of tenure represents a major commitment on the part of the university and is a concrete demonstration of its confidence that the individual will be a productive and valuable member of the community throughout her/his working life. Thus, the central question being asked at all levels of the tenure review process is "What does performance to date lead us to predict in terms of lifetime achievement and contribution to the overall goals of Rice University?"

Illinois Wesleyan University (B1) is guided in its tenure decisions by this question: "Has it been established that the university will benefit from entering into a binding commitment to that person, a commitment potentially lasting for a professional lifetime?"

Tenure Quotas

The AAUP (1995) clearly opposes the use of quotas to limit the number of tenured faculty either in a department or in the institution as a whole. The association asserts that "a quota system is a crude and unjust substitute for more equitable methods of academic planning" and that "imposing a numerical limit on the percentage of tenured faculty disregards a range of other ways to attain a desired mix of senior and junior faculty" (p. 47).

In spite of this position, eight institutions (4%) set a quota or limit on the number of tenured faculty. These institutions include George Washington University (R2), the University of Idaho (R2), Idaho State University (D2), California Lutheran University (M1), Springfield College (M1), Elon College (M2), Lake Forest College (B1), and Colby-Sawyer College (B2). No institutions in the Research 1 or Doctoral 1 categories impose quotas.

Idaho State University (D2) stipulates that only 75% of its faculty may be tenured, while California Lutheran University (M1) sets its tenure quota at 66% of the university's full-time faculty. Springfield College (M1) attempts "to maintain the college-wide percentage of full-time faculty who are tenured at 67% or above." However, Springfield also sets a lower limit quota, requiring that at least 55% of full-time faculty must be tenured or all full-time faculty appointments will be tenure-track "until the percentage of tenured faculty reaches or exceeds 67%." Elon College (M2) "seeks to appoint and maintain a faculty that is between 1/2 and 3/4 tenured" and states that "no department will be 'tenured in.'" Colby-Sawyer College (B2) allows only 50% of its full-time faculty to be tenured and prohibits any department from having its faculty fully tenured.

Santa Clara University (M1) has an interesting tradeoff for not having a tenure quota:

> The university does not limit by quota the percentage of tenured faculty either in individual departments or in the university as a whole. Yet, as the percentage of tenured faculty increases, the application of criteria inevitably becomes more rigorous.

Thus, though no quota is applied, the number of faculty receiving tenure may be limited by the rising standards for tenure as the percentage of tenured faculty increases.

Tenure Criteria

Thirty-seven institutions (19%) explicitly list teaching as the highest priority in the tenure review; none are in the Research or Doctoral classifications (see Appendix 2-G). Five institutions (3%), all in the research categories, explicitly cite research as the most heavily weighted criterion. Eight institutions (4%) state that "teaching and one other" criterion, either research or service, must be performed exceptionally well for a positive tenure decision, and 11 institutions (6%), including Brown University (R1), the Georgia Institute of Technology (R1), North Dakota

Table 2-8   Criterion Receiving Highest Priority in Tenure Review

Highest Priority Criterion	R1 n=21		R2 n=16		D1 n=10		D2 n=17		M1 n=56		M2 n=13		B1 n=25		B2 n=38		Total n=196	
	#	%	#	%	#	%	#	%	#	%	#	%	#	%	#	%	#	%
Teaching	0	0	0	0	0	0	0	0	14	25	1	8	7	28	15	39	37	19
Research	4	19	1	6	0	0	0	0	0	0	0	0	0	0	0	0	5	3
Teaching and one other Criterion	0	0	0	0	0	0	2	12	5	9	0	0	1	4	0	0	8	4
Determined by Unit	3	14	1	6	1	10	2	12	3	5	1	8	0	0	0	0	11	6

State University (D2), and the University of New Orleans (D2), allow the tenure candidate's department to determine the criteria for tenure (see Table 2-8). No institution considers service as the highest priority in the tenure review; however, three institutions, Indiana State University (D2), Saint Vincent College (B2), and the University of the Ozarks (B2), mention service as having significant weight in their review.

Criteria: Teaching effectiveness.   On the importance of teaching, the AAUP (1995) states:

> Colleges and universities properly aspire to excellence in teaching. Institutional aspirations, however, have not often led to practices which clearly identify and reward teaching excellence, and the quality of teaching is not in fact the determining consideration in many decisions on retention, promotion, salary, and tenure. (p. 133)

In this vein, only 37 institutions (19%) expressly cite teaching as the highest priority criterion in the tenure review; however, its importance is highlighted in the policy language of a number of institutions, including several research universities (see Appendix 2-G), for example, Brown University (R1):

> Candidates for tenure must show evidence of outstanding scholarship. They must also be highly effective teachers and be positive contributors to faculty governance as

well as to the intellectual life of their department, university, and profession.

Columbia University (R1) maintains that a candidate must show "the highest effectiveness as a teacher" for a positive tenure review, yet asserts that this alone "is not a sufficient basis for tenure." The University of California, Irvine (R1) elevates teaching by asserting, "Under no circumstances will a tenure commitment be made unless there is clear documentation of ability and diligence in the teaching role."

The University of Iowa (R1) recognizes teaching as a threshold consideration for tenure, a necessary but not sufficient qualification for tenure:

> The first step in a tenure decision should be an evaluation of teaching effectiveness. Only after an affirmative judgment as to effectiveness has been made can serious consideration be given to an evaluation for scholarship and of professional service. Unless a determination is made that the candidate is an effective teacher—whether at the departmental or interdisciplinary level—tenure is not and should not be granted.

> The university is committed to the proposition that neither teaching nor research standing alone justifies the granting of tenure. In the absence of research, it is believed that teaching effectiveness will not be maintained for a lifetime career. Thus, while teaching effectiveness is the condition precedent to a consideration of the quality of research, in the absence of quality research, teaching effectiveness alone will not permit the granting of tenure.

> In summary, The University of Iowa is both a teaching and research institution, as all good universities are. Unless both tasks are accomplished, the university's vitality will be sapped and neither function will be performed well. As noted, the two functions cannot be separated.

The University of Rochester's (R1) policy language parallels the University of Iowa's (R1):

There are two thresholds that must be crossed on the path to tenure. The first is of excellence in teaching. No matter how good the scholarly or artistic work, nobody belongs in a university unless he or she is a good teacher. The second threshold is of scholarship or artistic work.

Other institutions are more straightforward about the importance of teaching in the tenure decisions. For example, the American University (D1) states, "The quality of teaching is a primary consideration in the selection, retention, and promotion of faculty members." San Jose State University (M1) maintains that teaching is the highest weight in the tenure review and that candidates must "show increasing effectiveness in teaching, or consistent effectiveness in the case of individuals whose teaching is fully satisfactory from the start."

Criteria: Research/scholarship. Only five institutions (3%) explicitly cite research as the most heavily weighted criterion in the tenure decision. These institutions, all either Research 1 or 2 universities, include Brown University (R1), Columbia University (R1), the Massachusetts Institute of Technology (R1), the University of Georgia (R1), and Rice University (R2).

Columbia University (R1) states: "The essential requirement . . . is scholarly achievement testifying to an unusually critical or original mind. In assessing especially a young scholar's record, it should be necessary to point to examples of published work of truly outstanding quality; the quantity . . . of lesser concern." The Massachusetts Institute of Technology (R1) also underscores the preeminence of research and scholarship in its tenure criteria by stating that though teaching and service are important, they "are not a sufficient basis for awarding tenure."

Rice University (R2) stipulates:

Rice has a deep commitment to excellence in scholarship and thus places a primary emphasis on scholarly achievements as judged both by unbiased expert external reviewers in the appropriate scholarly field and by Rice faculty members with similar scholarly interests.

Criteria: Determined by department.   Eleven institutions (6%) explicitly allow the tenuring unit to determine the tenure criteria. The University of Arizona (R1) states:

> Promotion and tenure require excellent performance and the promise of continued excellence in teaching, research and service. Within these general guidelines, promotion and tenure criteria are to be developed by the faculty members and department head in each department and approved by and filed with the dean and the provost.

The Georgia Institute of Technology (R1) allows departments to vary the weighting of the teaching, research, and service criteria with the individual case of the candidate. Kent State University (R2) permits departments to set tenure criteria "in light of collegial and university standards and guidelines, the mission of the unit, and the demands of the discipline."

Illinois State University (D1) grants departments great flexibility in the individual faculty member's case in defining and administering tenure criteria. It states:

> We recognize that provisions are necessary for the balanced individual who may perform well in all three areas but is exceptional in one and for the individual who is contributing significantly to a department but in an unorthodox way.

Criteria: Need for tenured position.   A number of institutions mention institutional need as a criterion in the tenure decision or as a factor in the periodic evaluations of probationary faculty. For example, Brown University (R1) lets faculty request a written statement of the unit's criteria for recommending renewal and promotion and an "explanation of the unit's needs as far as these may affect his or her . . ." prospects. As part of the yearly evaluation of probationary faculty at Brown, the unit chair is also required to provide "an explanation of the department's, program's, or division's needs so far as these may affect the appointee."

In its policy on institutional need for a tenured position, Columbia University (R1) states:

Appointments to tenure . . . are offered only to the most able scholars and in those areas of research which are most promising and in which the needs of the university are most pressing. Nomination to tenure is the occasion for a department or school to consider its condition and to restate its objectives, both within its discipline and the university.

However, Columbia maintains that "not even the most stringent financial constraints should preclude the offer of tenure to an individual of truly exceptional merit. . . ."

Emory University (R1) is quite clear on the importance of need as a consideration for a tenured appointment: "Since all appointments are contingent upon the needs of the department and the college and the resources of the university, eligibility for renewal of appointment does not guarantee reappointment."

The definition of need is not only financial, but includes "the fit" of the candidate within the goals and mission of the department and college. The Georgia Institute of Technology (R1) asserts, "The primary criterion for tenure is the compatibility of the individual's performance and interests with the objectives for the unit, the college and the institute."

Classroom observation. The AAUP (1995) criticizes most evaluation procedures for teaching effectiveness. "Casual procedures, a paucity of data, and unilateral judgments by department chairs and deans too often characterize the evaluation of teaching in American colleges and universities" (p. 134). However, "because of the usefulness of having first-hand information about an individual's teaching effectiveness, some institutions have adopted a program of classroom visitation" (AAUP 1995, p. 135).

Twenty-nine institutions (15%) expressly permit direct classroom observation as part of the teaching evaluation for tenure (see Table 2-9 and Appendix 2-H). Of these 29 colleges and universities, 86% (25) are in the Master's 1 and 2 and Baccalaureate 1 and 2 categories. In the Research and Doctoral categories, only four institutions (2%) (no Research 1 institutions), explicitly encourage classroom observation.

Table 2-9   Use of Direct Classroom Observation to Evaluate Teaching

R1 n=21		R2 n=16		D1 n=10		D2 n=17		M1 n=56		M2 n=13		B1 n=25		B2 n=38		Total n=196	
#	%	#	%	#	%	#	%	#	%	#	%	#	%	#	%	#	%
0	0	1	6	1	10	2	12	4	7	2	15	8	32	11	29	29	15

Observation procedures also vary widely. For example, at Arkansas Tech University (M1), classroom observation can only be conducted at the candidate's request, while at Beloit College (B1) the observation is conducted at the discretion of the departmental tenure review committee. Eight of the 29 institutions explicitly require an observation, while the remainder either recommend it or leave it as an option in the review.

The individuals making the classroom visit also vary from institution to institution. The AAUP (1995) states that "faculty members should have the primary though not exclusive role in evaluating an individual faculty member's performance as teacher" (p. 136). At Shepherd College (B1), the college president or other administrators observe the faculty member, while at Asbury College (B2) the department chair and faculty colleagues make the observation and evaluation of teaching. Dakota Wesleyan University's (B2) policy states that the observation may be made by the "division chair, department chair, vice president for academic affairs, faculty peers, or outside professionals." (See Appendix 2-H for a full list of institutions employing this practice.)

External review. As part of the tenure review, 45 institutions (23%) solicit evaluation letters from faculty outside the institution (see Table 2-10 below and Appendix 2-I). Twenty-five of the 45 institutions (55%) following this practice are in the Research or Doctoral classification.

To guide the external referees, Brown University (R1) asks "whether they would be prepared to recommend the candidate for a position such as the one contemplated at Brown at their own institution, or at other major research universities, based on the candidate's scholarly ability and achievement." Columbia University (R1) requests a comparison of the candidate "with

Table 2-10   Institutions Using External Evaluation in the Tenure Review

R1 n=21		R2 n=16		D1 n=10		D2 n=17		M1 n=56		M2 n=13		B1 n=25		B2 n=38		Total n=196	
#	%	#	%	#	%	#	%	#	%	#	%	#	%	#	%	#	%
10	48	8	50	2	20	5	30	6	11	1	8	9	36	4	11	45	23

the leading scholars in the field" while the University of Rochester (R1) asks for comparisons with other individuals of similar standing in the field.

Southwestern University (B1) leaves the decision of whether to conduct an external review solely to the tenure candidate. Its policy states, "The decision whether or not to request an outside evaluation rests solely with the faculty member, and no implications shall be drawn from the presence or absence of such a request."

Student/alumni participation in tenure review. The AAUP (1995) does not comment on student participation in the review for tenure, other than allowing for the use of "student opinion" in the teaching evaluation (p. 136). The FAPA institutions solicit student opinions in varying ways (see Appendix 2-J). Sixteen institutions (8%) either seek evaluation letters from current students or conduct student interviews, and nine institutions (5%) request evaluation letters from alumni or recent graduates.

Emory University (R1) uses notes from department faculty's conversations with former students in the tenure evaluation, and the University of Georgia (R1) obtains comments on a faculty member's tenure candidacy by administering a student questionnaire. Auburn University (R2) requires that letters from three of the tenure candidate's graduate students be included in the review. At Creighton University (M1), the tenure candidate provides the names of six student references to the unit chair who then solicits evaluation letters.

Austin College (B1) allows the dean to interview students as part of the tenure review. Central College (B1) and Coe College (B1) also permit students to be interviewed in order to evaluate the faculty candidate for tenure. At Hamilton College (B1), the college registrar randomly solicits 30 to 35 evaluation letters from former students of the candidate. Beloit College (B1) conducts a survey of students who have completed one course with the tenure candidate, and Millikin University (B2) conducts a student opinion survey of the candidate.

Student participation on the tenure review committee. Four institutions (2%) allow students to participate as members of the tenure review committee. The University of Idaho (R2) mandates that students comprise "no less than 25% and no more than 50%" of the departmental tenure review committee. These students, with full voting rights, must "have had experience in the department with which the faculty member being evaluated is associated." Idaho State University (D2) also requires student participation on the departmental tenure review committee.

The University of Wisconsin, Superior (M1) requires one student major to sit on the departmental review committee, but without vote, and Beloit College (B1) mandates departmental committee membership for two student majors.

Two other institutions (1%) do not allow students to sit on the tenure review committee, but mandate formal participation by students in the review. Pace University (D2) requires that procedures be established within departments that allow students to "assess individual faculty members" and make their views known during the tenure review process. The University of New Hampshire (D2) gives its departments the option of conducting student interviews as part of the departmental tenure review.

Candidate interviews and the use of an advocate. Twenty-three institutions (12%) have a provision allowing the tenure candidate to either meet with or be interviewed by the tenure review committee (see Table 2-11 and Appendix 2-K). Twenty of these 23 institutions are in the Master's 1 and 2 or Baccalaureate 1 and 2 classifications.

Both Brown University (R1) and Millersville University of Pennsylvania (M1) give the candidate the right to appear before the tenure committee. Virginia Polytechnic Institute and State University (R1) gives the tenure candidate the option of not only "presenting oral arguments" to the tenure review committee, but also of submitting written material. Auburn University (R2)

Table 2-11   Institutions That Allow Tenure Candidates to Appear Before or Be Interviewed by the Tenure Review Committee

R1 n=21		R2 n=16		D1 n=10		D2 n=17		M1 n=56		M2 n=13		B1 n=25		B2 n=38		Total n=196	
#	%	#	%	#	%	#	%	#	%	#	%	#	%	#	%	#	%
2	10	1	6	0	0	0	0	9	16	2	15	5	20	4	11	23	12

allows the candidate to present his or her qualifications for tenure to the department faculty. Beloit College (B1) and Asbury College (B2) reserve the right, at the committee's discretion, to allow the tenure candidate to speak on his or her own behalf before the committee.

Three institutions (2%) allow the tenure candidate to select an "advocate" from the faculty who can speak on his or her behalf before the tenure review committee. These institutions are Emory University (R1), Rice University (R2), and Hiram College (B1). Rice University's (R1) policy reads:

> During the process of reviewing the candidates' dossiers, the tenured members of the [university] council invite the departmental chairmen to speak on behalf of their department's recommendations. In addition, every candidate is given the option of naming an advocate familiar with the candidate's qualifications who is invited to present the candidate's case to the council.

Columbia University (R1) does not allow the selection of an advocate, but grants the provost the option of calling for "the personal testimony of witnesses" to be heard by the tenure review committee.

OTHER POLICY PROVISIONS

Four other areas of probationary period policy were identified. These include provisions for 1) faculty to remain on term contract even after a negative tenure decision; 2) the granting of tenure before the completion of the probationary period; 3) a second tenure review, with no prejudice, after an unsuccessful early tenure consideration; and 4) tenure for part-time faculty.

No "Up or Out"

Nine institutions (5%) allow faculty to remain at the institution even after a negative tenure decision has been rendered. This relaxation of the traditional "up or out" policy applies only at institutions in the Doctoral 1 to Baccalaureate 1 categories.

The United States International University (D1) either gives a terminal appointment after a negative tenure decision or a seven-year term appointment. Russell Sage College (M1) has the option of a renewable, nontenure-track faculty position for faculty who are deemed worthy but not granted tenure due to institutional need. West Virginia Wesleyan College (M2) allows faculty who choose not to apply for tenure to "negotiate ongoing term contracts with the college if the interests of the college are effectively served thereby."

The University of Hartford (M1), Weber State University (M2), Saint Olaf College (B1), Greensboro College (B2), Saint Vincent College (B2), and Langston University (B2) also allow a faculty member to continue on term contract, at the discretion of the institution, following a negative tenure decision.

Early Tenure

Sixty-seven institutions (34%) explicitly allow a candidate to apply or be considered for tenure before the end of the probationary period (see Table 2-12 below and Appendix 2-L).

In its policy on early tenure, the University of Detroit Mercy (D2) requires that department faculty "meet, confer, and vote" on whether to support a candidate's request for early tenure. The University of Rochester (R1) allows an individual to be "recommended for promotion and tenure at any time that the chair and the dean are persuaded that it is in the university's interest to do so." At West Virginia University (R1), "faculty members who have records of achievement substantially beyond that normally expected for the awarding of tenure may be considered at an earlier date." While allowing early consideration for tenure, Lake Forest College (B1) calls for an "even more rigorous application of the [tenure] criteria than is normally the case."

Table 2-12   Institutions That Allow an Early Tenure Review before the
              Conclusion of the Probationary Period

R1 n=21		R2 n=16		D1 n=10		D2 n=17		M1 n=56		M2 n=13		B1 n=25		B2 n=38		Total n=196	
#	%	#	%	#	%	#	%	#	%	#	%	#	%	#	%	#	%
9	43	9	56	4	40	6	35	21	38	1	8	9	36	8	21	67	34

Second Consideration

After an unsuccessful early consideration for tenure, nine institutions (5%) explicitly allow the tenure candidate to reapply and be considered at least one more time (see Appendix 2-M for a complete list). For example, Kent State University (R2) states, "Unsuccessful candidates for early tenure shall be reevaluated without prejudice at the normal time." The University of Toledo's policy (D1) reads:

If the faculty member so requests, he or she may be considered for tenure, if otherwise eligible, in any year of the probationary period. A faculty member may be considered early for tenure only once. Denial of tenure prior to the last year of the probationary period shall not prejudice subsequent application for tenure and in no case shall be construed per se as a ground for termination.

In contrast, several institutions explicitly state that after a negative early tenure decision, the tenure candidate is given a terminal contract. For example, Southern Illinois University, Carbondale (R2) states, "The decision emanating from such a request [for early tenure] shall be considered as final. If the decision is negative, the faculty member will be notified in writing that the following contract year will be terminal." Cedarville College (B2) permits faculty to apply for early tenure consideration, but then asserts that "if a candidate who is considered for early tenure is denied early tenure by the Board of Trustees, then the same provision will apply as for any candidate who is denied tenure," that is, the issuance of a terminal contract.

Tenure for Part-time Faculty

Concerning part-time faculty, the AAUP (1995) recommends that colleges and universities should "consider creating a class of regular part-time faculty members," and that these faculty "should have the opportunity to achieve tenure and the rights it confers" (p. 54). In accordance with this recommendation, three institutions (2%) grant tenure to part-time faculty. These include the University of Iowa (R1), the University of Alaska (M1), and the University of Wisconsin, Superior (M1).

The University of Iowa (R1) provides an example of a policy statement on part-time tenure:

> Tenure shall be awarded to part-time faculty members who are found to meet university standards for granting tenure, with the performance expectations to be identical with those required of full-time faculty members. The length of service of part-time faculty members will be calculated by adding together part-time service. Thus, 12 years of 50% service will be deemed the equivalent of six years of fulltime service.

The University of Wisconsin, Superior (M1), allows tenure appointments to be "granted to any ranked faculty member who holds or will hold a 50% appointment or more" and stipulates a maximum probationary period of 14 years for part-time faculty.

SUMMARY

This analysis shows the wide variety of practices involved in the probationary period. Though the AAUP recommends a seven-year probationary period, only 54% (105 institutions) explicitly follow this recommendation. Only 38% (75 institutions) award three years' probationary period credit for prior experience, which is the maximum credit the AAUP recommends, while the others offer between two and four years or allow the faculty member to negotiate credit.

The AAUP (1995) urges institutions to "provide for a regular review of the candidate's qualifications" in order to enhance the "decision on renewal or tenure" (p. 16). Many institutions (92 or 47%) conduct annual reviews of tenure-track faculty during the probationary period and advocate the nonrenewal of the appointment if the candidate is not making sufficient progress toward tenure. Often this is done following a major mid-term review, conducted by 58 institutions (30%), in the spirit of concern for the faculty member's welfare and also for the future of the university or college.

Contrary to the public's perception that teaching is not valued in higher education, 37 institutions (19%) in the sample cite teaching as the highest weighted criterion in the tenure review. Another five institutions (3%) assert that teaching and one other criterion must be met exceptionally well by the candidate for tenure to be awarded. Even the Research 1 institutions are quite clear about the importance of teaching in the tenure review.

Finally, this chapter highlights other interesting and innovative policy provisions dealing with the probationary period and the award of tenure. Many institutions (67 or 34%) allow tenure to be awarded before the completion of the probationary period, either following the candidate's application or through action by the institution. Following an early tenure bid resulting in a negative decision, nine institutions (5%) give the candidate a second chance for tenure later in the probationary period. And five institutions (3%) offer tenure to part-time faculty.

The probationary period is a crucial time for both faculty and institutions, a time of hard work, stress, careful evaluations, and momentous decisions. Yet this chapter illustrates that though most probationary period policies fall within the mainstream, some are quite flexible in providing for the interests of faculty, allowing the tenure clock to be stopped for various leaves, giving early tenure, allowing faculty to negotiate prior credit, and even providing for part-time tenure. However, these policies also effectively address the concerns of the institution, for example, setting tenure quotas, recognizing institutional need, and conducting interim probationary period reviews. This attempt to balance the needs of faculty with the needs of the institution is a salient quality of probationary period policies.

REFERENCE

American Association of University Professors. (1995). *Policy documents and reports* (8th ed.). Washington, DC: AAUP.

APPENDIX 2-A
Probationary Period Length

8 Years

Research 1 Institutions
  1. Columbia University
  2. Massachusetts Institute of Technology
  3. North Carolina State University
  4. University of California, Irvine

Research 2 Institutions
  5. University of California, Santa Cruz

Baccalaureate 2 Institutions
  6. Asbury College
  7. Wiley College

7 Years

Research 1 Institutions
  1. Brown University
  2. Emory University
  3. Florida State University
  4. Georgia Institute of Technology
  5. Johns Hopkins University
  6. Michigan State University
  7. Northwestern University
  8. University of Arizona
  9. University of Georgia
  10. University of Hawaii, Manoa
  11. University of Indiana, Bloomington
  12. University of Iowa
  13. University of Nebraska, Lincoln
  14. University of Rochester
  15. West Virginia University

Research 2 Institutions
16. Auburn University
17. George Washington University
18. Rice University
19. University of Arkansas
20. University of Idaho
21. University of Louisville
22. University of Mississippi
23. University of Notre Dame
24. University of Rhode Island

Doctoral 1 Institutions
25. American University
26. Claremont Graduate University
27. Illinois State University
28. Marquette University
29. Northern Arizona University
30. Saint John's University (Jamaica, NY)
31. Texas Woman's University
32. United States International University
33. University of Texas, Arlington
34. University of Toledo

Doctoral 2 Institutions
35. Cleveland State University
36. Idaho State University
37. Indiana State University
38. Montana State University
39. Pace University
40. University of Central Florida
41. University of Detroit Mercy
42. University of Massachusetts, Lowell
43. University of New Orleans
44. Wake Forest University

Master's 1 Institutions
45. Baldwin-Wallace College
46. Butler University
47. California State University, Los Angeles
48. Central Connecticut State University
49. Creighton University
50. Delta State University
51. Drake University
52. East Carolina University
53. Emporia State University
54. Georgia College and State University
55. Holy Names College

56. James Madison University
57. Keene State College
58. Manhattan College
59. Northern Kentucky University
60. Salve Regina University
61. San Francisco State University
62. San Jose State University
63. Santa Clara University
64. Southeastern Oklahoma State University
65. University of Alaska
66. University of Colorado, Colorado Springs
67. University of Hartford
68. University of Texas, El Paso
69. University of Texas, Pan American
70. University of Wisconsin, Superior
71. Valdosta State University
72. Valparaiso University
73. Villanova University

Master's 2 Institutions
74. Aquinas College
75. Drury College
76. Lincoln University of Pennsylvania
77. Pacific University
78. Philadelphia College of Textiles and Science
79. Weber State University

Baccalaureate 1 Institutions
80. Austin College
81. Birmingham-Southern College
82. Coe College
83. Connecticut College
84. Davidson College
85. Drew University
86. Illinois Wesleyan University
87. Lake Forest College
88. Ohio Wesleyan University
89. Saint Olaf College
90. Shepherd College
91. Southwestern University
92. Sweet Briar College

Baccalaureate 2 Institutions
93. Carroll College
94. Dakota Wesleyan University
95. Dana College
96. Greensboro College

97. Mayville State University
98. McMurry University
99. Mount Mercy College
100. North Park College
101. Paine College
102. Saint Anselm College
103. Saint Joseph's College
104. Taylor University
105. University of the Ozarks

6 Years

Research 1 Institutions
1. University of Missouri Columbia
2. Virginia Polytechnic Institute and State University

Research 2 Institutions
3. Kent State University
4. Lehigh University
5. Oklahoma State University
6. Saint Louis University
7. Southern Illinois University, Carbondale

Doctoral 2 Institutions
8. Clarkson University
9. Duquesne University
10. George Mason University
11. North Dakota State University
12. University of North Dakota

Master's 1 Institutions
13. Bowie State University
14. California Lutheran University
15. Chicago State University
16. College of Charleston
17. College of Saint Rose
18. Eastern Illinois University
19. Fitchburg State College
20. Hunter College, City University of New York
21. Norwich University
22. Russell Sage College
23. Saginaw Valley State University: 3 yr. "probation" period, 3 yr. "pre-tenure" period
24. Saint Mary's University
25. Southeastern Louisiana University
26. Springfield College
27. University of Northern Iowa
28. University of Southern Maine

58 Policies on Faculty Appointment

29. Whitworth College

Master's 2 Institutions
30. Elon College
31. Southern Arkansas University
32. Union College
33. Walsh University
34. West Virginia Wesleyan College

Baccalaureate 1 Institutions
35. Agnes Scott College
36. Beloit College
37. Hendrix College
38. Hiram College

Baccalaureate 2 Institutions
39. Albertson College of Idaho
40. Bethel College
41. Bridgewater College
42. Central State University
43. Coker College
44. Colby-Sawyer College
45. Dickinson State University
46. Dillard University
47. Fairmont State College
48. Glenville State College
49. Le Moyne College
50. Millikin University
51. Saint Norbert College
52. Saint Vincent College
53. University of Southern Colorado
54. Virginia Intermont College

5 Years

Master's 1 Institutions
1. Arkansas Tech University
2. Bemidji State University
3. Bloomsburg University of Pennsylvania
4. Mankato State University
5. Millersville University of Pennsylvania
6. Pittsburg State University
7. Texas Wesleyan University
8. University of North Alabama
9. West Chester University of Pennsylvania

Baccalaureate 1 Institutions
10. Richard Stockton College of New Jersey, The
11. Wofford College

Baccalaureate 2 Institutions
12. Culver-Stockton College

APPENDIX 2-B

Probationary Period Credit for Prior Teaching Experience

3 Years at the Assistant Professor Rank
Research 1 Institutions
 1. Georgia Institute of Technology
 2. Michigan State University
 3. North Carolina State University
 4. Northwestern University
 5. University of Georgia
 6. University of Hawaii, Manoa
 7. University of Indiana, Bloomington
 8. University of Iowa
 9. University of Missouri, Columbia
 10. University of Nebraska, Lincoln
 11. Virginia Polytechnic Institute and State University

Research 2 Institutions
 12. Auburn University
 13. Saint Louis University
 14. University of Louisville
 15. University of Rhode Island

Doctoral 1 Institutions
 16. Illinois State University
 17. Saint John's University (Jamaica, NY)

Doctoral 2 Institutions
 18. Cleveland State University
 19. Duquesne University
 20. Indiana State University
 21. Montana State University
 22. North Dakota State University
 23. Pace University
 24. University of Massachusetts, Lowell
 25. University of North Dakota

Master's 1 Institutions
 26. Baldwin-Wallace College
 27. Butler University
 28. California Lutheran University
 29. Central Connecticut State University
 30. College of Charleston
 31. College of Saint Rose

32. Drake University
33. East Carolina University
34. Emporia State University
35. Georgia College and State University
36. Manhattan College
37. Pittsburg State University
38. Russell Sage College
39. Saint Mary's University
40. Southeastern Oklahoma State University
41. Texas Wesleyan University
42. University of Colorado, Colorado Springs
43. University of Hartford
44. Valdosta State University
45. Valparaiso University
46. Villanova University

Master's 2 Institutions
47. Lincoln University of Pennsylvania
48. Philadelphia College of Textiles and Science
49. Walsh University
50. Weber State University

Baccalaureate 1 Institutions
51. Agnes Scott College
52. Beloit College
53. Birmingham-Southern College
54. Connecticut College
55. Davidson College
56. Drew University
57. Hamilton College
58. Hendrix College
59. Illinois Wesleyan University
60. Lake Forest College
61. Saint Olaf College

Baccalaureate 2 Institutions
62. Albertson College of Idaho
63. Asbury College
64. Carroll College
65. Central State University
66. Dakota Wesleyan University
67. Dickinson State University
68. Greensboro College
69. Mayville State University
70. Saint Anselm College
71. Saint Joseph's College
72. Saint Norbert College
73. Taylor University

74. University of the Ozarks
75. Western Montana College

2 Years at the Assistant Professor Rank
Research 1 Institutions
   1. Emory University
   2. Florida State University
   3. University of Arizona

Research 2 Institutions
   4. Kent State University

Doctoral 1 Institutions
   5. American University

Master's 1 Institutions
   6. California State University, Los Angeles
   7. Keene State College
   8. Norwich University
   9. Salve Regina University
   10. San Francisco State University
   11. San Jose State University

Master's 2 Institutions
   12. Elon College
   13. West Virginia Wesleyan College

Baccalaureate 1 Institutions
   14. Austin College
   15. Bethany College
   16. Shepherd College
   17. Smith College
   18. Sweet Briar College

Baccalaureate 2 Institutions
   19. Bethel College
   20. Coker College
   21. Culver-Stockton College
   22. Millikin University
   23. Mount Mercy College
   24. North Park College
   25. Saint Vincent College
   26. Shawnee State University
   27. Virginia Intermont College

Negotiable at the Assistant Professor Rank
Research 1 Institutions
   1. West Virginia University

Doctoral 1 Institutions
   2. Northern Arizona University
   3. University of Toledo

Doctoral 2 Institutions
 4. George Mason University
 5. University of New Orleans: credit given at discretion of president

Master's 1 Institutions
 6. Bloomsburg University of Pennsylvania
 7. Millersville University of Pennsylvania
 8. Northern Kentucky University
 9. Southeastern Louisiana University
 10. University of Southern Maine
 11. University of Wisconsin, Superior
 12. West Chester University of Pennsylvania
 13. Whitworth College

Baccalaureate 1 Institutions
 14. Haverford College
 15. Hiram College
 16. Ohio Wesleyan College
 17. Wofford College

Baccalaureate 2 Institutions
 18. McMurry University

APPENDIX 2-C

Scholarly Leave

Research 1 Institutions
 1. North Carolina State University: candidate can take off-campus
    scholarly assignment
 2. University of California, Irvine

Research 2 Institutions
 3. George Washington University
 4. Kent State University
 5. Rice University
 6. Saint Louis University: allow leave counting toward probation for
    scholarly, political, or public activity
 7. University of California, Santa Cruz
 8. University of Louisville

Doctoral 1 Institutions
 9. University of Toledo

Doctoral 2 Institutions
 10. University of Central Florida
 11. University of New Hampshire
 12. University of North Dakota
 13. Wake Forest University

Master's 1 Institutions
14. College of Charleston
15. College of Saint Rose
16. Drake University
17. Emporia State University
18. Pittsburg State University
19. Saint Mary's University
20. Southeastern Oklahoma State University
21. University of Alaska

Master's 2 Institutions
22. Drury College
23. Pacific University
24. Southern Arkansas University
25. Weber State University

Baccalaureate 1 Institutions
26. Agnes Scott College: paid scholarly leave possible after three years of service
27. Davidson College
28. Haverford College
29. Hendrix College
30. Lake Forest College
31. Smith College
32. Sweet Briar College

Baccalaureate 2 Institutions
33. Cedarville College: "educational leave" counts toward probation
34. Dickinson State University: two years' leave available for "development"
35. Millikin University
36. North Park College: leave available for three years to obtain doctorate
37. St. Francis College (Brooklyn): allow leave due to the award of prestigious grant or fellowship
38. University of Southern Colorado: developmental leave available for one year

APPENDIX 2-D

Probationary Period Leave Allowed for Health, Personal, or Family Reasons

Research 1 Institutions
1. Brown University: for any medical reason
2. Columbia University: for childbirth or adoption for either men or women
3. Florida State University: six months leave for childbirth/adoption

4. Johns Hopkins University: parental leave
5. Michigan State University: maternity leave; adoption; care of an ill and/or disabled child, spouse, or parent; or personal illness
6. North Carolina State University: can go to part-time status for "compassionate reasons of health"
7. Northwestern University: for birth/adoption, family reasons
8. University of Arizona: "parental delay" can be taken twice for one year each time
9. University of California, Irvine: for childcare or birth
10. University of Missouri, Columbia: for pregnancy, serious illness, care of spouse or other family
11. University of Rochester: for health or "if personal problems impede progress"
12. Virginia Polytechnic Institute and State University: for birth or other nonprofessional concerns

Research 2 Institutions
13. Auburn University: leave granted according to Family Medical Leave Act
14. George Washington University: for family or medically related purposes
15. Lehigh University: for maternity or health reasons
16. Rice University: for medical and childbirth
17. Saint Louis University: for medical or family matters
18. Southern Illinois University, Carbondale: for sickness and disability
19. University of Arkansas: leave granted according to Family Medical Leave Act
20. University of California, Santa Cruz: for childcare or birth
21. University of Louisville: for "medical conditions"
22. University of Notre Dame: leave granted to primary caregivers

Doctoral 1 Institutions
23. Marquette University: for childbirth or other medical concern
24. Northern Arizona University: for "adverse circumstances"
25. University of Toledo: sickness

Doctoral 2 Institutions
26. Clarkson University: for medical conditions
27. Montana State University: for "good cause"
28. North Dakota State University: continual service requirement may be waived for medical condition
29. University of Central Florida: leave granted according to Family Medical Leave Act
30. University of North Dakota: for maternity, disability, or family concerns
31. Wake Forest University: for birth or adoption

Master's 1 Institutions
32. College of Charleston: leave granted according to Family Medical Leave Act
33. Creighton University: for childbirth

34. East Carolina University: for health
35. Eastern Illinois University: "fractional leaves" are granted only after three years of probation
36. University of Hartford: for "illness or exceptional situations"
37. University of Texas, Pan American: for birth, child, illness, ill family, etc.
38. University of Wisconsin, Superior: childbirth, dependent care, illness, or disability

Baccalaureate 1 Institutions
39. Agnes Scott College: for parental or medical leave
40. Beloit College: for parental leave or for Family Medical Leave Act
41. Davidson College: for childbirth or for Family Medical Leave Act (candidate can count leave at his or her discretion)
42. Smith College: for illness or personal

Baccalaureate 2 Institutions
43. McMurry University: for medical or other extenuating circumstances
44. St. Francis College (Brooklyn): for ill health, accident, etc.

APPENDIX 2-E
Countable Leave

1 Year
Research 1 Institutions
1. Columbia University
2. Johns Hopkins University
3. Northwestern University
4. University of Rochester

Research 2 Institutions
5. University of Arkansas
6. University of Louisville

Master's 1 Institutions
7. California State University, Los Angeles
8. San Francisco State University
9. San Jose State University
10. University of Hartford
11. University of Texas, Pan American
12. University of Wisconsin, Superior

Master's 2 Institutions
13. Pacific University
14. Southern Arkansas University

Baccalaureate 1 Institutions
15. Beloit College
16. Davidson College
17. Haverford College

18. Smith College

Baccalaureate 2 Institutions
19. Saint Francis College
20. University of Southern Colorado

2 Years
Research 1 Institutions
 1. Georgia Institute of Technology
 2. Michigan State University
 3. University of Arizona
 4. University of California, Irvine
 5. University of Georgia
 6. University of Missouri, Columbia
 7. Virginia Polytechnic Institute and State University

Research 2 Institutions
 8. Auburn University
 9. Rice University
10. Saint Louis University
11. University of California, Santa Cruz
12. University of Notre Dame

Doctoral 1 Institutions
13. American University
14. Claremont Graduate University
15. University of Texas, Arlington

Doctoral 2 Institutions
16. Montana State University
17. North Dakota State University
18. University of North Dakota
19. Wake Forest University

Master's 1 Institutions
20. College of Charleston
21. East Carolina University
22. Georgia College and State University
23. Valdosta State University

Master's 2 Institutions
24. Weber State University

Baccalaureate 2 Institutions
25. Dickinson State University
26. McMurry University

APPENDIX 2-F

Midpoint Review

Research 1 Institutions
 1. Brown University

2. Emory University
3. Georgia Institute of Technology
4. North Carolina State University
5. Northwestern University
6. University of Georgia
7. University of Iowa

Research 2 Institutions
8. Auburn University
9. Kent State University
10. Rice University
11. University of Idaho

Doctoral 1 Institutions
12. American University
13. Claremont Graduate University

Doctoral 2 Institutions
14. Duquesne University
15. Montana State University
16. University of New Hampshire
17. University of North Dakota

Master's 1 Institutions
18. Arkansas Tech University
19. Baldwin-Wallace College
20. California Lutheran University: reviewed in year two and year four by promotion and tenure committee
21. California State University, Los Angeles: reviewed in year two and year four by promotion and tenure committee
22. College of Charleston
23. Holy Names College
24. James Madison University: major review comes in second semester of year one
25. Russell Sage College
26. Saginaw Valley State University: review in year three for "pre-tenure" status
27. Saint Mary's University: reviewed by Faculty Advancement and Tenure Committee
28. San Francisco State University: reviewed in year two and year four by promotion and tenure committee
29. San Jose State University: reviewed in year two and year four by promotion and tenure committee
30. Santa Clara University
31. Southeastern Louisiana University
32. Springfield College
33. University of Colorado, Colorado Springs
34. Valdosta State University

Master's 2 Institutions
35. Elon College
36. Union College
37. Weber State University
38. West Virginia Wesleyan College

Baccalaureate 1 Institutions
39. Agnes Scott College
40. Austin College
41. Birmingham-Southern College
42. Hiram College
43. Illinois Wesleyan University
44. Lake Forest College
45. Shepherd College
46. Southwestern University
47. Sweet Briar College

Baccalaureate 2 Institutions
48. Albertson College of Idaho: mid-term evaluation at discretion of tenure committee
49. Asbury College
50. Bethel College
51. Carroll College
52. Cedarville College: reviewed in year two and year four by academic vice president
53. Colby-Sawyer College
54. Culver-Stockton College: major review of progress to tenure in year four
55. McMurry University
56. Saint Joseph's College: preliminary tenure review in year four
57. Saint Vincent College: major review in year two and year four
58. Virginia Intermont College

APPENDIX 2-G
Highest Weighted Criterion in Tenure Review

Teaching
Master's 1 Institutions
1. Arkansas Tech University
2. California Lutheran University
3. California State University, Los Angeles
4. Central Connecticut State University
5. Chicago State University
6. College of Charleston
7. College of Saint Rose
8. Eastern Illinois University

9. Saginaw Valley State University
10. San Francisco State University
11. San Jose State University
12. Southeastern Oklahoma State University
13. Springfield College
14. Valdosta State University

Master's 2 Institutions
15. Philadelphia College of Textiles and Science

Baccalaureate 1 Institutions
16. Austin College
17. Coe College
18. Hamilton College
19. Illinois Wesleyan University
20. Lake Forest College
21. Richard Stockton College of New Jersey, The
22. Shepherd College

Baccalaureate 2 Institutions
23. Asbury College
24. Cedarville College
25. Culver-Stockton College
26. Dakota Wesleyan University
27. Dana College
28. Dickinson State University
29. Dillard University
30. McMurry University
31. Millikin University
32. Mount Mercy College
33. Saint Anselm College
34. Saint Vincent College
35. Shawnee State University
36. Taylor University
37. University of the Ozarks

Teaching and One Other Criterion
Master's 1 Institutions
   1. Chicago State University
   2. Eastern Illinois University
   3. Southeastern Oklahoma State University
   4. Springfield College

Baccalaureate 1 Institutions
   5. Agnes Scott College

Research
Research 1 Institutions
   1. Brown University

2. Columbia University
3. Massachusetts Institute of Technology
4. University of Georgia

Research 2 Institutions
5. Rice University

APPENDIX 2-H
Classroom Observation for Tenure Review

Research 2 Institutions
1. Auburn University: classroom observation not required but is an option

Doctoral 1 Institutions
2. University of Texas, Arlington: observation can occur with candidate's permission

Doctoral 2 Institutions
3. George Mason University: class observation procedure and use determined by department
4. University of New Hampshire

Master's 1 Institutions
5. Arkansas Tech University: classroom observation is conducted only by candidate's request
6. California State University, Los Angeles: classroom observation is conducted only by candidate's request
7. Saint Mary's University: unit chair makes at least one classroom visit with prior notice to candidate
8. University of Northern Iowa: classroom observation performed by faculty colleagues

Master's 2 Institutions
9. MidAmerica Nazarene University
10. West Virginia Wesleyan College: at least two classroom observation visits are conducted per year during the probationary period

Baccalaureate 1 Institutions
11. Beloit College: classroom observation conducted at discretion of review committee
12. Coe College
13. Davidson College: observation conducted by vice president for academic affairs, unit chair, and one other faculty member
14. Illinois Wesleyan University: observation conducted by faculty colleagues
15. Lake Forest College: observation arranged in advance and conducted by department chair
16. Saint Olaf College: department chair and at least one other faculty member conducts observation

17. Shepherd College: college president or other administrators may visit classes at their discretion
18. Southwestern University: Faculty Status Committee in whole or part may visit classes at their discretion

Baccalaureate 2 Institutions

19. Asbury College: classroom observation conducted by department chair and by faculty colleagues
20. Carroll College: classroom observations conducted by three colleagues
21. Cedarville College: tenure candidate chooses class and time of observation
22. Dakota Wesleyan University: observation conducted by division chair, department chair, vice president for academic affairs, faculty peers, or outside professionals
23. McMurry University: at least two classroom observations are conducted during the review year
24. Millikin University: observation not required but is recommended
25. Mount Mercy College: department chair makes classroom observation
26. North Park College: probationary faculty member is observed twice during their first four terms of employment
27. Saint Francis College: classroom observation made by department chair and vice president for academic affairs
28. Saint Vincent College
29. Taylor University

APPENDIX 2–I

External Evaluation Letters

Research 1 Institutions

1. Brown University: list of external references supplied by candidate, tenure committee chooses five reviewers from list
2. Emory University: six external evaluators—two from candidate's list, two chosen by dean, two chosen by committee
3. Florida State University: two external evaluators
4. Georgia Institute of Technology: external reference list developed by candidate and department chair; department chair and faculty committee solicit review letters
5. Northwestern University: five outside evaluation letters solicited, no more than half of reviewers can be recommended by candidate
6. University of California, Irvine: outside evaluators chosen by department chair
7. University of Georgia: minimum of three reviewers—two selected from candidate's list, one chosen by department head (candidate submits list of three reviewers who cannot be used)

8. University of Indiana, Bloomington: candidate submits list of possible external evaluators
9. University of Nebraska, Lincoln: department committee decides outside review procedure
10. University of Rochester: 12 external reviews are solicited—five or six from candidate's list, others chosen by unit chair

Research 2 Institutions
11. Auburn University: external reviewers chosen from list compiled by department head
12. Kent State University: three external reviews chosen by candidate
13. Lehigh University: three external reviews selected by candidate, department chair, and dean
14. Rice University: reviewers suggested by candidate and approved by dean
15. University of Arkansas: the policy is not explicit on this issue
16. University of California, Santa Cruz: outside evaluators chosen by department chair
17. University of Louisville: unit may require external evaluation, but it is not mandatory
18. University of Mississippi: unit may require external evaluation, but it is not mandatory

Doctoral 1 Institutions
19. Claremont Graduate University: five reviews solicited—two from candidate's list, others chosen by chair
20. University of Texas, Arlington: five reviews solicited

Doctoral 2 Institutions
21. Clarkson University
22. Cleveland State University: external reviews solicited by Peer Review Committee
23. Duquesne University: four reviews solicited by department chair
24. George Mason University: department determines procedure for external review
25. Montana State University: three reviews solicited, department determines procedure for external review

Master's 1 Institutions
26. California Lutheran University: outside review is not mandatory, department determines procedure if used
27. College of Charleston
28. Creighton University: at least two reviews solicited—suggested by candidate and then requested by dean
29. Santa Clara University: external reviewers selected by review committee

30. Southeastern Louisiana University: provost has option to seek outside evaluation
31. University of Hartford: three external evaluations agreed upon by candidate and dean/department head; candidate can also solicit additional external evaluations

Master's 2 Institutions
32. Philadelphia College of Textiles and Science: two external reviews solicited by academic vice president

Baccalaureate 1 Institutions
33. Austin College: candidate provides ten names, dean can add to this list—the vice president for academic affairs solicits evaluations
34. Beloit College: external evaluations can be solicited at the discretion of the department chair
35. Davidson College: external evaluators selected by vice president for academic affairs from candidate's list
36. Drew University: two names submitted by candidate as external evaluators
37. Hamilton College: external evaluators selected by department chair and dean from list submitted by candidate
38. Lake Forest College: candidate submits list from which dean solicits external reviews
39. Shepherd College: external review encouraged but not mandatory
40. Smith College: external evaluators selected by tenure and promotion committee from candidate's and department chair's list
41. Southwestern University: candidate may request external review; candidate submits list of five possible evaluators and dean solicits reviews

Baccalaureate 2 Institutions
42. Colby-Sawyer College: candidate suggests reviewers
43. Dakota Wesleyan University: external review may be conducted, but is not mandatory
44. Le Moyne College: external review conducted by promotion and tenure committee; candidate can waive or not waive access to the review letters
45. Millikin University: external review may be used as approved by the provost

APPENDIX 2-J
Student/Alumni Involvement in Tenure Review

Student Participation on Departmental Tenure Review Committee
Research 2 Institutions
1. University of Idaho: committee must comprise no less than 25% students but no more than 50%

Doctoral 2 Institutions
  2. Idaho State University: mandates "equitable student representation"
  3. Pace University: requires procedures to be established that allow students to "assess individual faculty members" and make their views known to department
  4. University of New Hampshire: department tenure committee has option of conducting student interviews as part of review

Master's 1 Institutions
  5. University of Wisconsin, Superior: at least one student major can participate on review committee but cannot vote

Baccalaureate 1 Institutions
  6. Beloit College: two student majors sit on committee

Letters from Students or Alumni Included in Dossier or in Tenure Review
Research 1 Institutions
  1. Brown University
  2. Emory University: uses notes on conversations with candidate's former students as part of evaluation
  3. Northwestern University: also solicits written comments on candidate from former students/alumni
  4. University of California, Irvine: opinions of both students and alumni used to evaluate teaching effectiveness
  5. University of Georgia: student comments from student questionnaires used in tenure review

Research 2 Institutions
  6. Auburn University: three letters from thesis/dissertation students included in tenure review
  7. University of California, Santa Cruz: opinions of both students and alumni used to evaluate teaching effectiveness

Doctoral 1 Institutions
  8. Claremont Graduate University: student letters solicited by unit chair

Master's 1 Institutions
  9. College of Charleston: evaluations solicited from alumni
  10. Creighton University: candidate provides six student references to unit chair for tenure review
  11. Saint Mary's University: review committee solicits evaluations of faculty performance from selected students
  12. University of Hartford: letters from ex-student/alumni are used to attest to quality teaching
  13. University of Northern Iowa: formal assessment of faculty candidate's teaching conducted by students

Baccalaureate 1 Institutions
  14. Austin College: dean may interview students as part of tenure review

15. Beloit College: survey of students who have completed one course with tenure candidate is performed
16. Bethany College: student and alumni letters are solicited
17. Central College: students are interviewed by unit chair/review committee
18. Coe College: students may be interviewed as part of review
19. Davidson College: three letters from former students are solicited for review
20. Hamilton College: 30 to 35 student letters are solicited randomly by registrar; candidate submits the names of 10 to 15 student references
21. Hiram College: candidate provides list of student references; other student references are randomly selected
22. Illinois Wesleyan University: alumni comments/letters collected for tenure review

Baccalaureate 2 Institutions
23. Albertson College of Idaho: student and alumni letters are an optional part of tenure review
24. Millikin University: student opinion survey conducted as part of tenure review
25. North Park College: candidate is formally evaluated by present and former students

APPENDIX 2-K
Institutions That Allow Tenure Candidate to Either Meet with the Entire Tenure and Promotion Committee or Be Interviewed by a Member of the Committee as Part of the Candidate's Review for Tenure

Research 1 Institutions
1. Brown University: candidate has the right to appear before the committee
2. Virginia Polytechnic Institute and State University: candidate has the option of presenting oral arguments to the committee as well as written

Research 2 Institutions
3. Auburn University: candidate may make presentation to department faculty

Master's 1 Institutions
4. Arkansas Tech University
5. Bloomsburg University of Pennsylvania: candidate has option of appearing before committee
6. Bowie State University: provost and senior vice president for academic affairs may meet with candidate
7. Millersville University of Pennsylvania: candidate has option of appearing before committee

8. Saint Mary's University: Faculty Advancement and Tenure Review Committee interviews all tenure candidates
9. Southeastern Louisiana University: dean and provost can interview candidate
10. University of Wisconsin, Superior: tenure candidate can attend all committee meetings due to open meeting law
11. West Chester University of Pennsylvania: candidate has option of appearing before committee
12. Youngstown State University: candidate meets with department chair and with tenured department faculty

Master's 2 Institutions
13. Lincoln University of Pennsylvania: candidate has option of appearing before committee
14. Weber State University: candidate can have hearing before College Committee

Baccalaureate 1 Institutions
15. Agnes Scott College: candidate can confer with committee
16. Beloit College: candidate may appear before committee at its discretion
17. Bethany College: Faculty Personnel Committee meets with candidate
18. Coe College: unit chair interviews candidate
19. Lake Forest College: candidate meets with tenure subcommittee

Baccalaureate 2 Institutions
20. Asbury College: committee can interview candidate at its discretion
21. Colby-Sawyer College: department chair meets with candidate at request of personnel committee
22. North Park College: Faculty Personnel Committee explains committee's evaluation and recommendation to candidate
23. Taylor University: Faculty Personnel Committee interviews candidate

APPENDIX 2-L
Institutions That Allow an Early Tenure Review
Before the Conclusion of the Probationary Period

Research 1 Institutions
1. Brown University
2. Emory University
3. University of Arizona
4. University of Indiana, Bloomington
5. University of Iowa
6. University of Nebraska, Lincoln: if unsuccessful, candidate may be reviewed again
7. University of Rochester
8. Virginia Polytechnic Institute and State University: if unsuccessful, candidate may be reviewed again
9. West Virginia University

Research 2 Institutions

10. Auburn University: if unsuccessful, candidate may be reviewed again
11. Kent State University: if unsuccessful, candidate may be reviewed again
12. Lehigh University
13. Oklahoma State University
14. Rice University
15. Southern Illinois University, Carbondale
16. University of Idaho
17. University of Louisville
18. University of Mississippi

Doctoral 1 Institutions

19. American University
20. Saint John's University (Jamaica, NY)
21. United States International University
22. University of Toledo

Doctoral 2 Institutions

23. Clarkson University
24. George Mason University
25. North Dakota State University
26. University of Detroit Mercy: after year two, candidate may apply annually until probationary period is complete
27. University of Massachusetts, Lowell
28. University of North Dakota

Master's 1 Institutions

29. Bemidji State College
30. Butler University
31. California State University, Los Angeles
32. Central Connecticut State University: if unsuccessful, candidate may apply for tenure again
33. Creighton University: if unsuccessful, candidate may be reviewed again
34. East Carolina University
35. Fitchburg State College
36. Hunter College, City University of New York
37. James Madison University
38. Keene State College
39. Northern Kentucky University: if unsuccessful, candidate may be reviewed again
40. Saginaw Valley State University: if unsuccessful, candidate may be reviewed again
41. San Francisco State University
42. San Jose State University
43. Southeastern Louisiana University

44. Southeastern Oklahoma State University
45. University of Alaska
46. University of Northern Iowa
47. Valdosta State University
48. Valparaiso University
49. Youngstown State University

Master's 2 Institutions
50. Weber State University

Baccalaureate 1 Institutions
51. Agnes Scott College
52. Beloit College
53. Central College
54. Coe College
55. Connecticut College
56. Davidson College
57. Lake Forest College
58. Richard Stockton College of New Jersey
59. Shepherd College

Baccalaureate 2 Institutions
60. Bethel College: college may grant early tenure, but candidate can't apply
61. Cedarville College
62. Fairmont State College
63. Glenville State College
64. Le Moyne College
65. North Park College
66. University of Southern Colorado
67. Western Montana College

APPENDIX 2-M

Institutions Granting More Than One Tenure Review

Research 1 Institutions
   1. University of Nebraska, Lincoln
   2. Virginia Polytechnic Institute and State University

Research 2 Institutions
   3. Auburn University
   4. Kent State University

Doctoral 2 Institutions
   5. University of Detroit Mercy

Master's 1 Institutions
   6. Central Connecticut State University
   7. Creighton University
   8. Northern Kentucky University
   9. Saginaw Valley State University

3

THE TIE THAT BINDS: MEANING, PURPOSE, AND LOCUS OF TENURE

Cathy A. Trower

HIGHLIGHTS

◆ 196 (90%) of the institutions in the Faculty Appointment Policy Archive grant tenure.

◆ 190 (97%) of the institutions that grant tenure define the term in policy statements.

◆ 36 (19%) of the institutions in the Faculty Appointment Policy Archive that define tenure discuss the locus of tenure in policy statements.

Of the 190 Institutions That Define Tenure

◆ Tenure means permanency of employment at all institutions.

  ▪ 165 (87%) refer to tenure as "permanent" or "continuous" employment until retirement, barring dismissal for cause.

- 27 (14%) refer to tenure as an expectation of annual contracts until retirement.

- Ten (5%) refer to tenure as a "contractual right to continuing appointment." (These percentages do not sum to 100 because some institutions use multiple descriptions of tenure.)

◆ 99 (52%) explicitly link tenure to academic freedom in the tenure clause.

  - An additional 32 (17%) link tenure and academic freedom in the academic freedom clause by explicitly endorsing the AAUP guidelines for academic freedom and tenure, but do not restate the linkage in the tenure clause.

  - Thus, 131 (69%) link academic tenure and academic freedom.

◆ 62 (33%) explicitly link tenure to economic security for faculty.

◆ 61 (32%) have policy provisions that either limit or enhance the standard meaning and protection of tenure.

◆ 52 (27%) use some or all of the AAUP's language on tenure from the *1940 Statement on Academic Freedom and Tenure* (AAUP Policy Documents & Reports, 1995 Edition, pp. 3-4) when defining tenure.

  - 17 (33%) of these institutions are collectively bargained by the AAUP. Eight of these use standard AAUP language in the tenure definition. Nine of these do not use standard AAUP language in the tenure definition.

  - 15 (8%) use some or all of the AASCU's language on tenure from The American Association for State Colleges and Universities statement on "Academic Freedom and Responsibility, and Academic Tenure" (1988).

Of the 36 Policies with Locus of Tenure Language

◆ 19 (53%) locate tenure in the department or unit.

◆ 11 (31%) locate tenure at the institution level.

Table 3-1   The Sample

Carnegie Classification	217 Policy Provisions	196 Grant Tenure	190 Define Tenure in Policy Statements	
			# that Provide a Tenure Definition	% that Provide a Tenure Definition
R1	21	21	21	100%
R2	16	16	16	100%
D1	10	10	8	80%
D2	17	17	17	100%
M1	59	56	54	95%
M2	13	13	12	92%
B1	26	25	24	96%
B2	55	38	38	100%

Key to Carnegie classification abbreviations: R1 = Research 1; R2 = Research 2; D1 = Doctoral 1; D2 = Doctoral 2; M1 = Master's 1; M2 = Master's 2; B1 = Baccalaureate 1; B2 = Baccalaureate 2 institutions.

Sample:

The Project on Faculty Appointments' 1998 Faculty Appointment Policy Archive (FAPA) CD-ROM contains policy provisions from the faculty handbooks of 217 randomly selected four-year colleges and universities stratified by Carnegie classification. Of these 217 institutions, 196 grant tenure. Of these 196, 190 (97%) define academic tenure in the policy statements on the CD-ROM.

THE DEFINITION AND MEANING OF TENURE

Much that has been written about academic tenure offers a definition followed by a defense or a critique. *The Case For Tenure* (Finkin, 1996) devotes 61 pages to "The Meaning of Tenure," described in brief:

At the end of a period of probation, commonly not to exceed six years of full-time service, a faculty member is either to be accorded "tenure" or to be given a terminal appointment for the ensuing academic year. Thereafter, the professor can be discharged only for "just cause" or other permissible circumstance and only after a hearing before a body of his or her academic peers. (p. 3)

Finkin then cites William Van Alstyne to explain "what that really means."

Tenure, accurately and unequivocally defined, lays no claim whatever to a guarantee of lifetime employment. Rather, tenure provides that no person continuously retained as a full-time faculty member beyond a specified lengthy period of probationary service may thereafter be dismissed *without adequate cause* . . . tenure is translatable principally as a statement of formal assurance that . . . the individual's professional security and academic freedom will not be placed in question without . . . full academic due process. (p. 4)

Thus, tenure means that faculty shall expect academic freedom and lifetime employment in the absence of just cause for dismissal, and when just cause is present, faculty shall expect due process procedures to determine the validity of those allegations.

This chapter:

♦ Defines the meaning and purpose of tenure according to the American Association of University Professors (AAUP)

♦ Defines the meaning and purpose of tenure according to the American Association of State Colleges and Universities (AASCU)

♦ Analyzes policy language that defines the meaning and purpose of tenure at specific institutions

♦ Examines the locus of tenure at institutions that explicitly state where one's tenure is located

Tenure as Defined by the American Association of University Professors

Fifty-two (27%) institutions use AAUP language (see Appendix 3-A) to define tenure. AAUP language appears most commonly

Table 3-2 AAUP Language to Define Tenure

R1 n=21		R2 n=16		D1 n=8		D2 n=17		M1 n=54		M2 n=12		B1 n=24		B2 n=38		Total n=190	
#	%	#	%	#	%	#	%	#	%	#	%	#	%	#	%	#	%
4	19	6	38	3	38	6	35	13	24	3	25	8	33	9	24	52	27

in Research 2 and Doctoral 1 policies (38%) and least often among Research 1 (19%) institutions.

The AAUP (1995) states: "Tenure is a means to certain ends; specifically: 1) freedom of teaching and research and of extramural activities, and 2) a sufficient degree of economic security to make the profession attractive to men and women of ability" (p. 3). To this statement, the AAUP adds a presumptive declaration: "Freedom and economic security, hence, tenure, are indispensable to the success of an institution in fulfilling its obligation to its students and to society" (p. 3). The AAUP statement continues:

> After the expiration of a probationary period, teachers or investigators should have permanent or continuous tenure, and their service should be terminated only for adequate cause, except in the case of retirement for age, or under extraordinary circumstances because of financial exigencies. (p. 4)

For the AAUP, then, academic tenure and academic freedom are inextricably linked. Tenure is defined as continuous employment barring just cause for dismissal and academic due process; tenure's purpose is to provide academic freedom and employment security to faculty members.

Of the 52 institutions that use standard AAUP language to define tenure, 17 have the AAUP as a bargaining agent. Nine of the 17 are collectively bargained by the AAUP but do not use standard AAUP language when defining tenure in the collective bargaining agreement; that is, these policies do not define tenure by linking it to both academic freedom and economic security (see Appendix 3-B).

Tenure as Defined by the American Association of State Colleges and Universities

While only 15 (8%) institutions use some or all of the AASCU language (see Appendix 3-C) to define the meaning and purpose of tenure, the distinctions between the AASCU and AAUP guidelines are important enough to highlight here.

AASCU published its own statement on Academic Freedom and Responsibility and Academic Tenure, in 1988, in an effort "to clarify and promote understanding" (p. 1). The AASCU statement presents a definition and meaning for tenure that, unlike the AAUP's, decouples academic tenure from academic freedom and, instead, links academic freedom with responsibility.

> Academic tenure is not prerequisite to academic freedom, for academic freedom is the right of all members of the academic community, as is responsibility the obligation of all. Rather, tenure, where recognized, is a specific provision of employment that is accorded to certain specified members of the academic community who qualify for it, as a means of providing institutional stability and strength through its faculty. Tenure, therefore, contributes to the success of an institution in fulfilling its obligations to its students and to society. (p. 3)

The distinction between the AAUP and AASCU statements is not insignificant.

The AASCU statement further asserts that "academic freedom and responsibility are inseparable and must be considered simultaneously. . . . Tenure is a specific provision of employment. . . . Therefore, academic tenure should be considered separately from academic freedom and responsibility" (p. 2). Moreover, "Tenure is not a shield for mediocrity, incompetence, or academic irresponsibility, nor does it provide freedom from regular and constructive reviews of professional performance" (p. 3). Tenure is an employment provision to provide institutional stability and strength.

Four institutions (Hiram College (B1), Saint Joseph's College (B2), Texas Woman's University (D1), and West Virginia Univer-

Table 3-3   AASCU Language to Define Tenure

R1 n=21		R2 n=16		D1 n=8		D2 n=17		M1 n=54		M2 n=12		B1 n=24		B2 n=38		Total n=190	
#	%	#	%	#	%	#	%	#	%	#	%	#	%	#	%	#	%
2	10	0	0	1	13	0	0	4	7	0	0	3	13	5	13	15	8

sity (R1)) use both AAUP and AASCU language when defining tenure. These institutions use AAUP language that describes tenure as a means to an end (academic freedom and employment security) and add AASCU language stating that tenure and academic freedom should not be used as shields for professional incompetence or professional irresponsibility.

The Meaning of Tenure: Policy Statements

Tenure: A right to expect permanency (a continuing contract). With the AAUP's and AASCU's definitions of tenure as a backdrop, we next explore institutional policy surrounding the meaning of tenure. Although policy statements may not cite the AAUP or AASCU, or even use language directly from AAUP or AASCU guidelines, all institutions define tenure as an assurance that, after a probationary period, faculty shall have permanent employment until retirement barring dismissal for cause (see Chapter 7), bona fide financial exigency, or program discontinuance (see Chapter 8). The majority (165, 87%) of institutions refer to tenured status as "permanent," "continuous," or "guaranteed" employment.

The language of permanent employment (tenure) is much the same across the academy:

◆ "A tenured appointment may not be terminated by the corporation except for adequate cause and after the appointment holder has been accorded the rights of due process. It [tenure] conveys both a status and a contingent right, the assurance of continuous academic employment until retirement . . ." (Brown University, R1)

◆ "Tenure is the right to continuous employment." (University of Arkansas, R2)

Table 3-4   Tenure: Permanent Employment

R1 n=21		R2 n=16		D1 n=8		D2 n=17		M1 n=54		M2 n=12		B1 n=24		B2 n=38		Total n=190	
#	%	#	%	#	%	#	%	#	%	#	%	#	%	#	%	#	%
19	90	14	88	7	88	15	88	54	100	12	100	18	75	26	68	165	87

- ◆ "Tenure is the right of a member of the university faculty to continuous employment by the university." (University of Toledo, D1)

- ◆ "Tenure shall mean the right of a faculty member to hold his/her position and not to be removed therefrom except for just cause . . ." (Bloomsburg University, M1)

- ◆ "Tenure grants the teaching faculty member the contingent right to retain his/her appointment without term until retirement." (Walsh University, M2)

- ◆ "Permanent tenure means the college guarantees the faculty member academic freedom and continuing faculty appointments" except for just cause for dismissal. (Saint Norbert College, B2)

Contractual right to an annual contract. A variation in the permanency policy language found on the CD-ROM at 27 (14%) institutions is that tenured faculty are, as a procedural matter, issued an annual contract rather than a continuous one, until retirement, resignation, or dismissal for cause. Such policies are most prevalent at the Master's 2 and Baccalaureate 2 institutions and not used at Research 1, Doctoral 1, or Doctoral 2 institutions. For example, the University of Mississippi (R2) provides that "The award of tenure . . . assures the faculty having such status that they will be automatically recommended each year . . . except under extraordinary circumstances" (e.g., financial exigencies, termination or reduction of programs, malfeasance, inefficiency, or contumacious conduct, for cause), and Bethany College (B1) stipulates that "The granting of tenure assures the faculty member of the privilege of being issued an annual contract until retirement or resignation . . ., until relieved of duties for physical or mental disability, bona fide financial exigency,

Table 3-5   Tenure: Annual Contract

R1 n=21		R2 n=16		D1 n=8		D2 n=17		M1 n=54		M2 n=12		B1 n=24		B2 n=38		Total n=190	
#	%	#	%	#	%	#	%	#	%	#	%	#	%	#	%	#	%
0	0	1	6	0	0	0	0	8	15	4	33	2	8	12	32	27	14

failure to perform . . ." See Appendix 3-D for institutions that offer annual contracts to tenured faculty.

Contractual right to a continuous contract.   Ten (5%) institutions (five baccalaureate, three doctoral, two research—see Appendix 3-E) declare that tenure is a "contractual right to continuous appointment" unless the faculty member resigns or is dismissed for cause, financial exigency, or program discontinuance. Such language typically reads like Austin College's (B1) statement: "Tenure, as a contractual relationship with the college, is understood as a commitment to continued appointment until retirement unless the faculty member resigns or is dismissed for cause" or "Tenure is a contractual recognition of the faculty member's right to continuing employment that is subject to termination only by resignation, retirement, . . . or for one of the causes for termination . . ." at St. Louis University (R2).

A commitment.   Finally, tenure is referred to as a "commitment" at 30 (16%) institutions (see Table 3-6). In some instances, the commitment refers to the institution's commitment to the faculty member:

- ◆ "Tenure is a commitment by the college that a faculty member will be retained on a full-time basis until the faculty member's employment ends through resignation, retirement, or dismissal or termination for cause." (Lake Forest College, B1)

- ◆ "Tenure is a commitment made by the university to an individual . . ." (California Lutheran University, M1)

- ◆ A department and school make a career commitment when the award of tenure is recommended. The Institute as a whole . . . joins in this commitment when tenure is awarded." (Massachusetts Institute of Technology, R1)

Table 3-6   Tenure: A Commitment

R1 n=21		R2 n=16		D1 n=8		D2 n=17		M1 n=54		M2 n=12		B1 n=24		B2 n=38		Total n=190	
#	%	#	%	#	%	#	%	#	%	#	%	#	%	#	%	#	%
4	19	0	0	1	13	3	18	11	20	2	17	6	25	3	8	30	16

In other cases, it is a two-way commitment between the institution and the faculty member:

◆ "Tenure is a mutual commitment between the college and the faculty member for a continuing relationship . . ." (Asbury College, B2)

◆ Tenure "assumes a strong moral commitment between the parties involved." (Pace University, D2)

◆ "Tenure is a relationship of continuing commitment between the university and the employee benefiting both." (Chicago State University, M1)

◆ "By granting tenure, the university assures a member of the faculty" academic freedom. "By accepting tenure, the faculty member reaffirms his or her continuous commitment to the purposes and goals of the university." (Valparaiso University, M1)

◆ "Granting tenure implies a commitment by the university. Likewise, the faculty member who is granted tenure makes an equally strong commitment to serve students, colleagues, their discipline and the university in a manner befitting an academic person." (Weber State University, M2)

Tenure: Its Purpose and Intent

The primary purpose of academic tenure is to protect academic freedom, evidenced in the policy language of 99 (52%) FAPA institutions. A secondary purpose is to provide economic security, demonstrated in the policy language of 62 (33%) institutions on the CD-ROM. The third most commonly cited purpose of tenure is to provide institutional stability, mentioned in the policy provisions of 15 (8%) institutions.

Academic freedom. Over half (99, 52%) of the FAPA institutions explicitly link tenure and academic freedom in the tenure clause by adopting or adapting the AAUP's language on academic freedom and the link to tenure. An additional 32 (17%) institutions (see Appendix 3-F) link tenure and academic freedom in the academic freedom clause by expressly endorsing the AAUP guidelines for academic freedom and tenure, but do not restate this linkage in the statement defining tenure. Thus, a total of 131 (69%) institutions link academic freedom and academic tenure in policy statements.

Where faculty handbooks define tenure, they typically do so in the context of academic freedom and its importance to society, institutions, and individuals. Earlier, we discussed the AAUP's language around the link between tenure and academic freedom. Here we present highlights of policy statements with a similar intent but different language.

Tenure is good for society . . .

♦ "'Academic freedom is the cornerstone of a free society, and it will be scrupulously defended at Southwestern University.' . . . To give assurance to faculty members that they may feel secure in their positions, tenure is established . . .'" (Southwestern University, B1)

♦ "The University of Texas Board of Regents recognizes the time-honored practice of tenure for university faculty as an important protection of free inquiry, open intellectual and scientific debate, and unfettered criticism of the accepted body of knowledge. . . . That is why tenure is so valuable, not merely for the protection of individual faculty members but also as an assurance to society that the pursuit of truth and knowledge commands our first priority. Without freedom to question, there can be no freedom to learn." (University of Texas, Arlington, D1)

♦ "Academic freedom and tenure exist in order that society may have the benefit of honest judgment and independent criticism." (Florida State University, R1)

Tenure benefits institutions . . .

♦ "Academic tenure and academic freedom are distinguishable but linked in the life of a college or university. Tenure is an institutional safeguard for the conditions of academic freedom." (Dakota Wesleyan University, B2, extends academic freedom to all faculty "without regard to rank or tenure.")

♦ "Tenure is the university's most effective guarantee of academic freedom . . ." (Cleveland State University, D2)

Tenure benefits individual faculty members . . .

♦ "A major object of tenure is to protect the faculty from harassment or reprisal within the university community for expression or espousal of unpopular views or principles, and to encourage freedom of inquiry and expression." (Creighton University, M1)

♦ "The purpose of tenure is to promote and protect the academic freedom of members of the faculty." (North Carolina State University, R1)

♦ "Tenure is an institution developed for the protection of the academic freedom of the teaching faculty in institutions of higher education." (Virginia Polytechnic Institute and State University, R1)

Economic security. Although often implied rather than stated, the second most commonly cited purpose of tenure is to provide economic security, included in the policies of one-third (62) of institutions on the CD-ROM. While academic freedom is often cited on the CD-ROM as a primary purpose of tenure without also mentioning employment security, the reverse is not the case. In fact, all of the institutions that mention economic security as a benefit of tenure also cite academic freedom, and only four do so outside of the context of the AAUP or the AASCU language. Policy language linking economic security and tenure but without AAUP or AASCU language verbatim follows.

♦ "Professional security may be a secondary benefit of tenure, but that is not its primary intention, which is the pursuit of knowledge." (Albertson College of Idaho, B2)

Table 3-7   Tenure: Protection for Academic Freedom

R1 n=21		R2 n=16		D1 n=8		D2 n=17		M1 n=54		M2 n=12		B1 n=24		B2 n=38		Total n=190	
#	%	#	%	#	%	#	%	#	%	#	%	#	%	#	%	#	%
14	67	11	69	4	50	9	53	23	43	4	33	13	54	20	53	99	52

- The purpose of tenure, among other reasons stated, is "To protect the academic freedoms of the faculty member . . ." and to "Provide adequate financial security to make the profession attractive to persons of outstanding ability." (Langston University, B2)

- "The tenure system is intended to protect academic freedom, to provide a reasonable measure of employment security . . ." (James Madison University, M1, 1994, p. 23)

- "Academic freedom and professional security, the products of tenure, are needed to assure the success of an institution in fulfilling its obligations." (University of Texas Pan American, M1)

Institutional stability.   A third benefit of tenure is institutional stability achieved by retaining faculty over the long-term. Sixteen (8%) institutions cite this benefit.

- "Tenure, which gives a degree of economic security and professional security to the individual and stability to the faculty as a whole . . ." (Agnes Scott College, B1)

- "The college recognizes the value of tenure as promoting not only academic freedom but also the stability as a community of teachers and scholars dedicated to these ideas." (Bethel College, B2)

- Tenure is "a means of providing institutional stability and

Table 3-8   Tenure: Economic Security

R1 n=21		R2 n=16		D1 n=8		D2 n=17		M1 n=54		M2 n=12		B1 n=24		B2 n=38		Total n=190	
#	%	#	%	#	%	#	%	#	%	#	%	#	%	#	%	#	%
6	29	6	38	3	38	6	35	16	30	3	25	10	42	12	32	62	33

strength through its faculty." (Texas Woman's University, D1)

♦ "For the university, tenure is a major safeguard of academic freedom, of the quality of education offered here, and of the continuity and stability of the institution." (George Mason University, D2)

♦ "The university recognizes the importance of tenure and tenure-track appointments as vehicles for preserving academic freedom, for sustaining continuity in the ranks of the faculty and for affording security . . ." (Texas Wesleyan University, M1)

♦ "The tenured faculty member becomes a leader of the university's community by providing direction, expertise, and stability to the university's academic programs." (Valdosta State University, M1)

♦ "A tenure policy strengthens the capability of a university to attract and retain superior teachers and scholars as members of the faculty." (University of Idaho, R2)

Special Provisions

One-third (61) of the FAPA institutions have developed special language and/or caveats of particular interest. This section explores policy language around additional benefits of tenure, limitations or restrictions placed on tenure, and some comparatively unusual provisions.

Tenure: Additional benefits. Many institutional policies acknowledge that tenure provides a "climate of free inquiry and expression in which students and nontenured faculty may share academic freedom equally with tenured faculty" (Agnes Scott College, B1). In similar statements at Middle Tennessee State University (D2) and Wake Forest University (D2), it is clear that the academic freedom accorded to tenured faculty serves to benefit untenured faculty as well as students.

At 14 institutions, tenure provides additional guarantees beyond lifetime employment. At Lake Forest College (B1), for example, "Tenure is a commitment by the college that a faculty

Table 3-9   Tenure: Institutional Stability

R1 n=21		R2 n=16		D1 n=8		D2 n=17		M1 n=54		M2 n=12		B1 n=24		B2 n=38		Total n=190	
#	%	#	%	#	%	#	%	#	%	#	%	#	%	#	%	#	%
1	5	1	6	1	13	1	6	4	7	0	0	3	13	5	13	16	8

member will be retained on a *full-time* basis" (emphasis added). Likewise, at Georgia College and State University (M1):

> Institutional responsibility for employment of a tenured individual is to the extent of continued employment on a one hundred percent workload basis for three out of every four consecutive academic quarters . . .

Similarly, the tenure policies of Ohio Wesleyan University (B1) and Pacific University (M2) assure full-time employment *and* a salary within a specified range at rank. Tenured faculty "shall not be dismissed or *reduced in compensation* except for inefficiency, unsatisfactory professional performance, incapacity or other just cause and then only in the manner prescribed . . ." (emphasis added) at the Richard Stockton College of New Jersey (B1).

Three policies provide tenured faculty with a guarantee against demotion or reduction in rank: Northern Kentucky University (M1), University of Louisville (R2), North Carolina State University (R1). Tenured faculty at Clarkson University (D2) are entitled to "fair compensation." At Bridgewater College (B2), where tenured faculty receive annual contracts renewable for life, the tenure guarantee means "the college or the faculty member shall give the other party *one year's notice* of any contemplated discontinuance of their contractual relationship."

Faculty on continuing contract (with tenure) at Shawnee State University (B2) enjoy a "reduction in the required number of student evaluations" and "an increase in maximum faculty development funds." At Asbury College (B2), tenure provides faculty "a voice in the formulation of the academic policies of the college." In a unique policy, in addition to "(a) continued employment until retirement barring just cause for dismissal," the privileges of tenured faculty at Rice University (R2) include:

. . . b) equitable compensation and benefits, c) continued institutional support for teaching and scholarship, and d) continued involvement in the academic mission of the university.

Tenure: Limitations.   At the opposite end of the spectrum, several institutions place certain limitations or restrictions on their tenure provisions. Some tenure policy language is clearly designed to afford institutions a degree of flexibility by stating that the terms and conditions of tenured employment may change.

♦ "Permanent status relates to faculty status and not to specific assignments of duties." (Coe College, B1)

♦ "Tenure does not preclude the possibility of legitimate redeployment. . . . tenured faculty members are expected to respond to the needs of the University to maintain educational flexibility." (Drew University, B1, 1969, p. 23)

♦ "Tenure is not a guarantee that the terms and conditions of employment will not change from year to year." (Hiram College, B1)

♦ "A tenure contract is for a contract year and gives the faculty member the contractual right to be reemployed for succeeding years . . . but subject to the terms and conditions of employment which exist from contract year to contract year." (Cedarville College, B2)

♦ "Faculty members employed under a continuous contract are entitled to annual contract renewal and shall be subject to the terms and conditions of employment that exist at the time of each annual renewal . . ." (Millikin University, B2)

♦ "Such reappointment (tenure) shall be subject to the terms and conditions of employment which exist at the commencement of each contract term." (Montana State University, D2)

While unsatisfactory performance may trigger dismissal for cause proceedings at almost all institutions, many policies state that continued employment is subject to performance. (Details regarding post-tenure review of faculty may be found in Chapter 6). Such language reads as follows:

♦ "A faculty member who accepts tenure also accepts continuing responsibility to the institution and to students at a commensurate level of performance." (Mount Mercy College, B2)

♦ "Tenure means continued employment during satisfactory conduct and effective performance." (Millikin University, B2)

♦ "Appointment to tenure does not automatically guarantee employment for life." (University of the Ozarks, B2)

♦ "Tenured faculty members must maintain a level of professional competence that serves as a model for all faculty members . . . According to Board of Regents' policy, this competence must be evaluated periodically throughout each faculty member's career." (Valdosta State University, M1)

♦ "Tenure is an important part of academic freedom, but does not accord freedom from accountability . . . the concept of regular, rigorous review is part of the university's commitment to providing support to all its faculty." (Emporia State University, M1)

♦ ". . . full-time reappointment (analogous to tenure) in the college, [is] subject to continued satisfactory performance, stability in academic program, sufficiency of registration, and financial ability." (City University of New York, Hunter College, M1)

At least two institutions make mention of the need to have money behind tenured appointments. The University of Arizona (R1) policy states:

It is within neither the president's nor the ABOR's power to commit the State of Arizona to an obligation for which an appropriation has not been made. The use of the term "with tenure" neither constitutes nor implies a legal obligation which the president of the board is not empowered to undertake. In practice, renewals of appointments of tenured faculty members have been approved and funds have been allocated annually for these appointments.

In a similar statement, the West Virginia University (R1) asserts:

> The institution, while not maintaining "tenure quotas," shall be mindful of the dangers of losing internal flexibility and institutional accountability to the citizens of the state as the result of an overly tenured faculty. Tenure may be granted only to people in positions funded by monies under the Board of Trustees' control.

Tenure's obligations.   Several institutions make special note of the obligations assumed by both the institution and the individual faculty member. This obligation is so strong at St. Olaf College (B1), for example, that tenured faculty members:

> share responsibility for the total life and program of the institution. They will resign from their positions only after careful consideration of the effect upon the work of the college and only after ascertaining that the college is in a position to continue in a competent manner the work for which they have been responsible.

Other language reads as follows:

- ◆ "Tenure is the university's most effective guarantee of academic freedom and embraces the reciprocal obligation of the faculty member to maintain the highest standards of his or her profession." (Cleveland State University, D2)
- ◆ "When faculty members receive tenure, it means they have acquired a vested interest in the college . . . " (College of Saint Rose, M1)
- ◆ "Tenure as a trust most effectively permits the self-regulation (as in law and medicine) of the teaching profession. Although tenure does involve a degree of professional security, it does not (nor is it intended to) provide a refuge for the incompetent." (Albertson College of Idaho, B2)
- ◆ "The principle of faculty tenure imposes reciprocal responsibilities on the university as a body politic and on a faculty member." (University of Indiana, Bloomington, R1)

Finally, the University of Iowa (R1) has perhaps the most extensive and elaborate discussion of tenure, its meaning, and purpose. Iowa's policy essentially encompasses all aspects of tenure. This policy affirms that "tenure will continue as a cornerstone of the university's relationship with faculty members. Tenure is not only consistent with academic vitality but essential to it." "No system of quotas is contemplated" so that probationary faculty will continue to be hired and they shall receive tenure as merited. The University of Iowa recognizes that it must "revitalize itself" and "retain flexibility to adjust its educational programs to meet the changing needs of students and society and to take into account advances in the world's knowledge base." This section of policy is followed by a lengthy discussion of the necessity of tenure to protect academic freedom and a statement that "the tenure system must continue if the university is to recruit and maintain a distinguished faculty." The policy states that the university's competitive position would be "damaged beyond repair if tenure were abandoned or seriously weakened." Finally, the University of Iowa's policy includes a section about job security for civil servants and state and federal employees, claiming ultimately that "While the job security aspects of tenure bear surface relationship to other job security systems, the primary rationale for tenure is that it is essential to the creation and maintenance of an atmosphere which encourages the free exchange of ideas so necessary to educational vitality."

THE LOCUS OF TENURE

Only 36 (19%) of the institutions that define tenure mention locus of tenure.

While rarely defined in faculty handbooks, the locus of one's tenure directly affects the level of security tenured faculty members enjoy. The higher the level of one's tenure (e.g., system or university-wide versus program-specific), the more secure faculty are with respect to program discontinuance.

Table 3-10   Institutions That Define the Locus of Tenure

R1 n=21		R2 n=16		D1 n=8		D2 n=17		M1 n=54		M2 n=12		B1 n=24		B2 n=38		Total n=190	
#	%	#	%	#	%	#	%	#	%	#	%	#	%	#	%	#	%
10	48	3	19	3	38	2	12	8	15	2	17	0	0	8	21	36	19

Of the 36 policies that mention the locus of tenure, over half (20, 56%) locate tenure in the department or unit and one-third (12) locate tenure at the institution level.

Research institutions are more apt than others to define the locus of tenure; 35% of research, 20% of doctoral, 15% of master's, and 13% of baccalaureate institutions do so. This makes sense intuitively because research institutions are the most structurally complex and the locus of tenure may be more relevant than at smaller institutions. For a list of locus of tenure by institution, see Appendix 3-G.

Tenure at the Campus Level

At the University of Hawaii (R1), tenure is granted at one of the campuses within the university system. The following provisions state that a tenured faculty member at a particular campus may "bump" a less-senior colleague within their locus of tenure (e.g., on the same campus if their program area is closed). However, the same does not apply if the entire campus closes.

> At the Manoa campus, tenure is further limited to a given college, school, or organized research or service unit. At the other campuses, similar distinctions shall be made with tenure granted at a college or major service or program unit.

> A tenured faculty member who is retrenched according to the provisions of this article shall have employment rights to any position within the locus of tenure for which the faculty member is qualified and which is occupied by the faculty member with the least seniority, provided that the provisions of this paragraph shall not be applicable to the faculty member who is displaced.

Table 3-11   Locus of Tenure: Level

System		Campus		Institution		School/College		Department or Unit		Program	
#	%	#	%	#	%	#	%	#	%	#	%
0	0	2	6	12	33	1	3	20	56	1	3

Table 3-12   Locus of Tenure: Level and Carnegie Classification

	R1	R2	D1	D2	M1	M2	B1	B2	Total
Number That Define Locus of Tenure	10	3	3	2	8	2	0	8	36
System	0	0	0	0	0	0	0	0	0
Campus	2	0	0	0	0	0	0	0	2
Institution	5	0	2	1	3	0	0	1	12
School/College	1	0	0	0	0	0	0	0	1
Department/Unit	2	3	1	1	5	2	0	6	20
Program	0	0	0	0	0	0	0	1	1

Similarly, tenure at the University of Indiana, Bloomington (R1) is "specific to the campus . . . in which he/she is serving at the time of acquisition of tenure"; therefore, there is a "geographic limitation to tenure." This suggests that if a particular campus within the system is closed, faculty members may not expect to be moved automatically to another campus in the Indiana system.

Tenure at the Institution Level

Among research universities, tenure is most commonly located at the institutional level. Should a department or program area close, the institution must retain, and in some cases retrain, displaced faculty members. George Mason University's (D2) policy clearly delineates the importance of locus of tenure. It reads:

> Although tenure resides in the university as a whole, probationary and tenured faculty, . . . are appointed directly to one or more local academic units. The status established by such an appointment is called . . . "primary affiliation". . . .

> Tenure, once conferred, resides in the university, and is not affected by the reorganization of academic units. In the event of program discontinuation or financial

exigency, the institution will make a good faith effort to protect and retain its tenured faculty members . . .

Tenure at the School/College Level

Only one institution on the CD-ROM, Northwestern University (R1), maintains tenure at the level of the school or college. In the event of program closure, Northwestern attempts to move a displaced tenured faculty member to another department or program within the school or college in which his/her tenure resides.

Tenure at the Department/Unit Level

Whereas tenure typically resides at the institutional level at research universities, elsewhere tenure resides in the academic department where faculty are based. In over half of the FAPA policies that specify a locus of tenure, the policy language for departmental tenure usually reads quite simply, such as: "All faculty appointments . . . have as the locus of their appointment the department which is stated in their annual letter of appointment." (Bethel College, B2; Langston University, B2; Millikin University, B2; Saint Vincent College, B2; California Lutheran University, M1; Chicago State University, M1; Northern Kentucky University, M1; Saint Mary's University, M1; Pace University, D2; Southern Illinois University, Carbondale, R2; University of Louisville, R2).

Some policy language is slightly more specific and highlights, especially in the case of larger state systems, that tenure is specific to a unit and not to the university or system.

- ◆ "Tenure is with the institution and resides within a specific academic discipline and not with the Montana University System. The academic discipline to which the faculty member is tenurable shall be identified in each faculty member's individual contract." (Western Montana College, B2; a similar statement for Montana State University, D2)

- ◆ "Faculty are tenured within an academic unit or units of a university within the University of Alaska system." (University of Alaska, M1)

- "'Indefinite tenure' is a right of a faculty member to continuous appointment to a professional position of specified locus in the university. Tenure is granted in the unit of instruction, department, or school specified in the appointment. Tenure is granted either at the Kent campus or in the regional campuses system, but not both, as specified in the appointment." (Kent State University, R2)

Other locus of tenure policy language covers faculty who teach in part outside of the department where their tenure resides, faculty who have an interdisciplinary appointment, or whether, how, and under what circumstances one's locus of tenure may change.

- "All faculty appointments to annual, continuous contracts or rolling contracts have as the locus of their appointment the department of the college which is stated in their annual letter of appointment. Faculty members teaching in interdisciplinary programs shall have their locus in one of the academic departments." (Colby-Sawyer College, B2)
- "Contractually, tenure is conferred to a specific departmental appointment. A faculty member under a continuous contract who is involved in a major program change or redirection . . . and who has tenure in one department may have his/her tenure transferred to a new department . . ." (Dakota Wesleyan University, B2)
- "The locus of appointment . . . is the program(s) stated in the contract. It does not, however, preclude part-time teaching in programs outside the locus of appointment. The locus of appointment may be changed by the college to accommodate its changing needs." (West Virginia Wesleyan College, M2)
- "Tenure is granted by the university . . . Tenure appointments shall be held only in academic departments or similar academic units. All changes in the locus of tenure assignment require specific approval of the president." (Illinois State University, D1)

SUMMARY

While specific language varies from policy to policy, tenure's essential meaning does not vary much at all. This chapter demonstrates that the definition of tenure is similar throughout the academy, but that its precise meaning and protections differ somewhat at the local level.

Tenure means permanency of employment at all institutions. Fully 87% of the institutions with tenure refer to it as "permanent" or "continuous" employment until retirement, barring dismissal for cause. Fourteen percent refer to tenure as the expectation of annual contracts until retirement, and ten state that tenure is a contractual right to continuing appointment. Whether through annual contracts for life or a lifelong contract, tenure is a commitment between institution and faculty member.

Tenure's purpose, first and foremost, is to accord faculty members academic freedom in teaching, research, and extramural utterances (52%). A secondary benefit of tenure provides employment security, discussed expressly in the policy provisions of 33% of FAPA institutions. Along with employment security comes institutional stability, mentioned as a benefit of tenure by 8% of institutions.

Some policies include benefits beyond lifetime employment barring just cause for dismissal (7%), while others place some limitations or restrictions on tenure (8%). Additional guarantees include full-time employment, no salary reduction, no demotion in rank, more notice in the event of program discontinuance, an increase in faculty development funds, and fewer course evaluations. Limitations on tenure include duties may change, terms and conditions may change, and permanency of employment may be linked to performance, financial exigency, or program discontinuance.

What would happen to tenured faculty in the event of program discontinuance relates to the locus of tenure which most often resides at the department or unit level at Master's 1, Master's 2, and Baccalaureate 2 institutions and at the institutional level at Research 1 institutions.

REFERENCES

American Association for State Colleges and Universities. (1998). *Academic freedom and responsibility, and academic tenure.* Washington, DC: AASCU.

American Association of University Professors. (1995). *Policy documents and reports* (8th ed.). Washington, DC: AAUP.

Drew University. (1969). *Charter and bylaws and faculty personnel policy.* Madison, NJ: Drew University.

Finkin, M. W. (Ed.) (1996). *The case for tenure.* Ithaca, NY: Cornell University Press.

James Madison University. (1994). *Faculty handbook, 1994–1995.* Harrisonburg, VA: James Madison University.

APPENDIX 3-A
Institutions That Use AAUP Language
When Defining Tenure (in the Tenure Clause)

Research 1 Institutions
1. Emory University (private)
2. University of California, Irvine (public) *
3. University of Missouri, Columbia (public)
4. West Virginia University (public)

Research 2 Institutions
5. Auburn University (public)
6. Rice University (private)
7. University of California, Santa Cruz (public) *
8. University of Delaware (public) *
9. University of Mississippi (public)
10. University of Rhode Island (public) *

Doctoral 1 Institutions
11. Illinois State University (public)
12. Saint John's University, Jamaica, NY (private)
13. Texas Woman's University (public)

Doctoral 2 Institutions
14. Clarkson University (private)
15. Duquesne University (private)
16. Middle Tennessee State University (public)

17. North Dakota State University (public)
18. Pace University (private)
19. University of North Dakota (public)

Master's 1 Institutions
20. Arkansas Tech University (public)
21. Baldwin-Wallace College (private)
22. Butler University (private)
23. College of Charleston (public)
24. Drake University (private)
25. Keene State College (public)
26. Pittsburg State College (public)
27. Santa Clara University (private)
28. Southeastern Louisiana University (public)
29. University of Alaska (public) *
30. University of Hartford (private)
31. University of Northern Iowa (public) *
32. Whitworth College (private)

Master's 2 Institutions
33. Lincoln University of Pennsylvania (public) *
34. MidAmerica Nazarene University (private)
35. Pacific University (private)

Baccalaureate 1 Institutions
36. Agnes Scott College (private)
37. Birmingham-Southern College (private)
38. Connecticut College (private)
39. Davidson College (private)
40. Hiram College (private)
41. Illinois Wesleyan University (private)
42. Ohio Wesleyan University (private)
43. Sweet Briar College (private)

Baccalaureate 2 Institutions
44. Bloomfield College (private) *
45. Carroll College (private)
46. Coker College (private)
47. Dickinson State College (public)
48. Dillard University (private)
49. Mayville State University (public)
50. North Park College (private)
51. Saint Joseph's College (private)
52. Saint Vincent College (private)

---

* Bargained by AAUP

APPENDIX 3-B

Institutions That Are Collectively Bargained by the AAUP But That Do Not Use Standard AAUP Language in Tenure Definition

	Tenure Statement Refers To		
	Academic Freedom	*Economic Security*	*Neither*
Research 2 Institutions			
1. Kent State University	X		
Doctoral 2 Institutions			
2. Cleveland State University	X		
Master's 1 Institutions			
3. Bloomsburg University of PA			X
4. Central Connecticut State University		X	
5. Millersville University of PA			X
6. San Francisco State University			X
7. San Jose State University	X		
8. West Chester University of PA			X
Baccalaureate 2 Institutions			
9. Central State University	X		

APPENDIX 3-C

Institutions That Use AASCU Language When Defining Tenure

Research 1 Institutions
1. Michigan State University (public)
2. West Virginia University (public)

Doctoral 1 Institutions
3. Texas Woman's University (public)

Master's 1 Institutions
4. California Lutheran University (private)
5. Central Connecticut State University (public)
6. Emporia State University (public)
7. Holy Names College (private)

Baccalaureate 1 Institutions
8. Hiram College (private)

9. Richard Stockton College of New Jersey, The (public)
10. Shepherd College (private)

Baccalaureate 2 Institutions
11. Colby-Sawyer College (private)
12. Fairmont State College (public)
13. Glenville State College (public)
14. Saint Joseph's College, IN (private)
15. Saint Vincent College (private)

APPENDIX 3-D
Institutions That Offer Tenured Faculty Annual Contracts

Research 2 Institutions
1. University of Mississippi (public)

Master's 1 Institutions
2. Arkansas Tech University (public)
3. Bemidji State University (public)
4. California Lutheran University (private)
5. Holy Names College (private)
6. Mankato State University (public)
7. Norwich University (private)
8. Saginaw Valley State University (public)
9. Saint Mary's University (private)

Master's 2 Institutions
10. Pacific University (private)
11. Southern Arkansas University (public)
12. Union College (private)
13. West Virginia Wesleyan College (private)

Baccalaureate 1 Institutions
14. Bethany College (private)
15. Hiram College (private)

Baccalaureate 2 Institutions
16. Albertson College (private)
17. Bethel College (private)
18. Bridgewater College (private)
19. Cedarville College (private)
20. Colby-Sawyer College (private)
21. Culver-Stockton College (private)
22. Dakota Wesleyan University (private)
23. Millikin University (private)
24. Saint Vincent College (private)
25. University of Southern Colorado (public)
26. Western Montana College (public)
27. Wiley College (private)

APPENDIX 3-E
Tenure Is a Contractual Right to Continuous Appointment

Research 2 Institutions
 1. Saint Louis University (private)
 2. University of Arkansas (public)

Doctoral 1 Institutions
 3. Northern Arizona University (public)

Doctoral 2 Institutions
 4. George Mason University (public)
 5. Montana State University (public)

Baccalaureate 1 Institutions
 6. Austin College (private)
 7. Davidson College (private)

Baccalaureate 2 Institutions
 8. Cedarville College (private)
 9. Dakota Wesleyan University (private)
 10. University of Southern Colorado (public)

APPENDIX 3-F
Institutions That Endorse the AAUP Tenure and Academic Freedom Linkage in the Academic Freedom Statement (and Not Again in the Tenure Clause)

Research 1 Institutions
 1. Northwestern University (private)

Doctoral 1 Institutions
 2. American University (private)
 3. Marquette University (private)
 4. University of New Hampshire (public)

Doctoral 2 Institutions
 5. Indiana State University (public)
 6. Montana State University (public)
 7. University of Massachusetts, Lowell (public)

Master's 1 Institutions
 8. Central Connecticut State University (public)
 9. Delta State University (private)
 10. Manhattan College (private)
 11. Norwich University (private)
 12. Russell Sage College (public)
 13. Saint Mary's University (private)
 14. Salve Regina University (private)
 15. Springfield College (private)

16. University of Wisconsin, Superior (public)

Master's 2 Institutions
17. Aquinas College (private)
18. Elon College (private)
19. Philadelphia College of Textiles and Science (private)
20. Union College (private)
21. Weber State University (public)
22. West Virginia Wesleyan College (private)

Baccalaureate 1 Institutions
23. Bethany College (private)
24. Drew University (private)
25. Lake Forest College (private)
26. Saint Olaf College (private)

Baccalaureate 2 Institutions
27. Bridgewater College (private)
28. Greensboro College (private)
29. Shawnee State University (public)
30. Saint Anselm College (private)
31. Saint Vincent College (private)
32. University of Southern Colorado (public)

APPENDIX 3-G

Locus of Tenure

Campus
1. University of Hawaii, Manoa	Research 1	Public
2. University of Indiana, Bloomington	Research 1	Public

Institution
3. George Mason University	Doctoral 2	Public
4. Georgia College and State University	Master's 1	Public
5. Georgia Institute of Technology	Research 1	Public
6. Massachusetts Institute of Technology	Research 1	Private
7. Michigan State University	Research 1	Public
8. Russell Sage College	Master's 1	Public
9. Saint John's University (Jamaica, NY)	Doctoral 1	Private
10. Saint Joseph's College	Baccalaureate 2	Private
11. Texas Woman's University	Doctoral 1	Public
12. University of Georgia	Research 1	Public
13. University of Iowa	Research 1	Public
14. Valdosta State University	Master's 1	Public

School/ College

15. Northwestern University	Research 1	Private

Department/Unit

16. Bethel College	Baccalaureate 2	Private
17. California Lutheran University	Master's 1	Private
18. Chicago State University	Master's 1	Public
19. Colby-Sawyer College	Baccalaureate 2	Private
20. Dakota Wesleyan University	Baccalaureate 2	Private
21. Illinois State University	Doctoral 1	Public
22. Kent State University	Research 2	Public
23. Millikin University	Baccalaureate 2	Private
24. Montana State University	Doctoral 2	Public
25. Northern Kentucky University	Master's 1	Public
26. Pacific University	Master's 2	Private
27. Saint Mary's University	Master's 1	Private
28. Saint Vincent College	Baccalaureate 2	Private
29. Southern Illinois University, Carbondale	Research 2	Public
30. University of Alaska	Master's 1	Public
31. University of Louisville	Research 2	Public
32. Virginia Polytechnic Institute and State University	Research 1	Public
33. West Virginia University	Research 1	Public
34. West Virginia Wesleyan College	Master's 2	Private
35. Western Montana College	Baccalaureate 2	Public

Program

36. Greensboro College	Baccalaureate 2	Private

4

ACADEMIC RANKS AND TITLES OF FULL-TIME NONTENURE-TRACK FACULTY

Frances L. Shavers

HIGHLIGHTS

Of the 196 Institutions with Tenure in the FAPA Sample

◆ 183 (93%) provide details and titles for tenure-track faculty appointments, while 13 (7%) did not.

◆ 175 (89%) provide details and titles for tenure-ineligible faculty appointments, ranging from full-time to part-time, indefinite to limited renewal, and internally to externally funded.

Of the 175 Institutions with Tenure–Ineligible Faculty

◆ 101 (58%) make use of full-time, long-term, indefinitely renewable tenure-ineligible faculty.

◆ 41 (23%) appoint research faculty.

◆ 31 (18%) appoint nontenure-track faculty to the lecturer

position.

◆ 30 (17%) appoint nontenure-track faculty only to the instructor level without a terminal degree.

◆ 29 (17%) appoint clinical faculty.

◆ 19 (11%) appoint in-residence faculty.

◆ 15 (9%) appoint nontenure-track faculty to the instructor, assistant professor, and associate professor levels.

◆ 14 (8%) appoint nontenure-track faculty to the instructor, assistant professor, associate professor, and full professor levels.

INTRODUCTION

The majority of postsecondary institutions have a "ladder" system of ranks and titles for tenure-track faculty appointments that extends from untenured instructors to tenured professors. In recent decades, academe has experienced significant growth in the number and types of nontenurable positions (Chronister, Baldwin & Bailey 1992; Leatherman 1999; Gappa 1996).

This chapter answers five questions:

◆ How many institutions supplement their tenure-track appointments with nontenurable, full-time faculty positions?

◆ How do the job titles and responsibilities of these individuals differ from those in tenure-track positions?

◆ What qualifications are required of nontenure-track faculty, and how do they differ, if at all, from tenure-track requirements?

◆ What assignments do nontenure-track faculty assume?

◆ What are the primary employment provisions for nontenure-track faculty?

This chapter does not address the number or distribution of nontenure-track faculty in American higher education. For that purpose, see Chronister, Baldwin, and Bailey (1992).

A SNAPSHOT OF TENURABLE AND TENURED RANKS AND TITLES

As a foundation for the analysis of norms surrounding non-tenure-track appointments, we first provide a brief look at tenurable faculty ranks and titles. Thirteen (7%) of the 196 tenure-granting institutions did not provide explicit details on the ranks and titles for tenured faculty members. Thus, this overview covers 183 institutions.

As Table 4-1 depicts, across all Carnegie classifications, the titles of assistant professor, associate professor, and full professor are consistently and typically used to denote tenurable or tenured faculty. The instructor title is also widely used; however, it sometimes denotes a contingency appointment with limited renewal (essentially nontenure-track) where time-in-rank does not count toward tenure in the probationary period.

Academic Degree Requirements

Faculty title and rank policies commonly refer to two factors that, in part, distinguish one rank from the next: academic degree and prior experience. Almost two-thirds (123, 64%) of the institutions in the sample do not require a terminal degree for the rank of instructor; instead, they accept a master's degree in an appropriate field. As rank advances from assistant to full professor, institutions increasingly require a terminal degree: 78 (43%) require a terminal degree for assistant professors; 121 (66%) for associate professors; and 137 (75%) for full professor. Thirty-one (17%) do not specify degree requirements in the materials reviewed.

Of the institutions that do not require a terminal degree for the associate and full professor ranks, policies often permit prior teaching or comparable work experience to compensate for the lack of the degree.

◆ "The minimum qualifications for appointment to the rank of associate professor are: earned master's degree and ten years of successful college teaching experience in an appropriate field(s) or equivalent experience; *or* a post-graduate degree, other than a doctorate, recognized by the college, as the ter-

Table 4-1   Titles for Tenurable and Tenured Faculty

Carnegie	183	Tenurable and Tenured Faculty Titles							
Classification	Institutions	Instructor		Assistant Professor		Associate Professor		Full Professor	
		#	%	#	%	#	%	#	%
R1	20	18	90	20	100	20	100	20	100
R2	14	8	57	14	100	14	100	14	100
D1	10	10	100	10	100	10	100	10	100
D2	17	13	76	17	100	17	100	17	100
M1	51	39	76	48	94	48	94	48	94
M2	13	13	100	13	100	13	100	13	100
B1	24	20	83	23	96	23	92	23	96
B2	34	31	91	34	100	34	100	34	97
TOTAL	183	152	83	179	98	179	97	179	98

Key to Carnegie classification abbreviations: R1 = Research 1; R2 = Research 2; D1 = Doctoral 1; D2 = Doctoral 2; M1 = Master's 1; M2 = Master's 2; B1 = Baccalaureate 1; B2 = Baccalaureate 2.

minal degree for the faculty member's discipline . . . " (Cedarville College, B2)

♦ "Associate professor: master's degree plus 30 hours of graduate work toward the doctorate from a regionally accredited institution of higher education." (Shepherd College, B1)

♦ "A person who holds the terminal degree, has extensive teaching or professional experience, or has other outstanding professional qualifications may be assigned the rank of professor." (Bethany College, B1)

♦ "Professor: the earned doctorate, plus a minimum of seven years of college teaching, or 90 hours of graduate study, including the master's degree, plus a minimum of ten years of college teaching." (Culver-Stockton College, B2)

♦ "For promotion to the rank of professor, an individual shall have tenure, an earned doctorate from an accredited institution of higher education in a relevant academic field, plus a minimum of six (6) consecutive years of service at YSU at the rank of associate professor immediately prior to the year of application for promotion, *or* a master's degree, *or* its equivalent, from an accredited institution of higher education in a relevant academic field, plus a minimum of eight

(8) consecutive years of service at YSU at the rank of associate professor immediately prior to the year of application for promotion." (Youngstown State University, M1)

Time-in-Rank

Time-in-rank requirements indicate the expected length of time that appointees must serve in an immediately lower rank or position before they may be considered for a higher rank. Appointments as instructor are generally entry-level and seldom require previous teaching or related experience. Of the 183 institutions in the sub-sample, 143 (78%) require less than two years of experience for instructors, and the remaining 40 (22%) do not state specific time-in-rank requirements for instructor-level appointments.

Similarly, assistant professor is commonly considered the entry-level rank for appointees with a terminal degree. Time-in-rank requirements range from zero to three years. At institutions where a master's degree may suffice for appointment to assistant professor, the time-in-rank requirements range from zero to six years of prior work experience.

On average, appointments to associate professor require time-in-rank ranging from three to seven years, with at least three years at the assistant professor rank. In turn, appointments to full professor typically accompany or follow the granting of tenure, and time-in-rank ranges from 7 to 12 years with at least four years served, on average, as an associate professor.

Thus, time-in-rank requirements tend to increase as one advances from the lower ranks of instructor and assistant professor to the higher ranks of associate professor and full professor. Additionally, time-in-rank standards are closely tied to degree requirements.

Other Titles

Other tenure track or tenurable titles include tutors (Saint John's College, B1), assistant instructor (Mount Mercy College, B2), artist-teacher (Sweet Briar College, B1), and various clinical (or professor in practice) and research positions.

DEFINING NONTENURE TRACK

A fairly loose nomenclature for nontenure-track appointments characterizes the 175 institutions that offer such positions. For instance, the commonly used term "adjunct" sometimes describes long-term full-time positions; however, the word typically applies to temporary, part-time appointments.

Most institutions label all nontenurable positions as "nontenure track," from part-time to full-time, visiting to adjunct, and temporary to contingent. The American Association of University Professors (AAUP, 1995) concurs with this definition as applied to three categories of nontenure-track positions:

> The first hold indefinitely renewable appointments: the faculty members are appointed for one or more years and are told that their appointments may be renewed— no limit is placed on the number of possible renewals. The second hold "limited renewable" appointments: the faculty members are told that their (usually one-year) appointments may be renewed so many times only. . . . The third occupy "folding chairs": The faculty member's initial appointments (usually for two or three years) are explicitly terminal—no renewal is possible under any circumstances. (pp. 65-66)

This chapter focuses on the 101 (58%) institutions that permit full-time, continuous nontenure-track appointments (the AAUP's first group defined above). Nontenurable positions with limited renewal (the AAUP's second group) and those "folding chair" appointees (the AAUP's third group) are not classified as nontenure-track in this analysis, although they are often referred to as such within the policies reviewed.

THE AAUP'S POSITION ON NONTENURE–TRACK APPOINTMENTS

The AAUP views nontenure-track positions as a threat to the academy and to appointees:

Nontenure-track appointments do considerable damage both to principles of academic freedom and tenure and to the quality of our academic institutions—not to mention the adverse consequences for the individuals serving in such appointments. (1995, p. 64)

In Regulation 1(b) of the *Association's Recommended Institutional Regulations on Academic Freedom and Tenure*, the AAUP strongly discourages the use of such positions:

[W]ith the exception of special appointments clearly limited to a brief association with the institution, and reappointments of retired faculty members on special conditions, all full-time faculty appointments are of two kinds: 1) probationary appointments; 2) appointments with continuous tenure. (1995, p. 64)

Although nontenure-track appointments may afford financial and programmatic flexibility, the association (and other critics) suggest that these faculty suffer heavier teaching loads, lower compensation, fewer opportunities for research and professional development, and less job security than colleagues in tenurable positions. In fact, the AAUP argues that any flexibility that institutions attain with nontenurable ranks comes at the price of an unstable learning environment, and the system becomes "a divided, two-class faculty [that] erodes collegiality and sound governance practices" (AAUP, 1995, p. 69).

NONTENURE-TRACK APPOINTMENTS

Nontenure-track faculty appointments carry various labels including extended term appointments, term appointments, multiple-year contracts, fixed-length appointments, temporary instructional staff, rolling appointments, at-will contracts, and special appointments.

Of the 196 tenure-granting institutions, 21 (11%) did not provide relevant information on nontenure-track faculty. Of the remaining 175 (89%) institutions with tenure-ineligible faculty appointments, 101 (58%, and 52% of the 196 total tenure-

Table 4-2   Policies for Full-Time Nontenure-Track Positions

R1 n=20		R2 n=9		D1 n=10		D2 n=17		M1 n=47		M2 n=12		B1 n=24		B2 n=36		Total n=175	
#	%	#	%	#	%	#	%	#	%	#	%	#	%	#	%	#	%
18	90	7	78	7	70	10	59	31	55	6	50	7	29	13	36	99	57

granting institutions) explicitly mention full-time, renewable positions (the focus of this chapter) (see Appendix 4-A and Table 4-2).

Long-term, full-time nontenure-track appointments are most common among research and least common at baccalaureate institutions, and are justified under various circumstances:

◆ "Nontenure-track positions may be established for full-time professional personnel employed in administrative positions or to staff research, technical, special, career, and public service programs or programs which are anticipated to have a limited lifespan or which are funded, fully or partially, through non-system resources." (Georgia Institute of Technology, R1)

◆ "Nontenure-track faculty members function on a full-time basis in clinical service or supervision, in research positions supported by grants or contracts from organizations outside the university, as aviation specialists, in research, clinical or teaching positions whose long-term existences are not assured, or under other conditions that make the attainment of tenure . . . a practical impossibility." (Saint Louis University, R2)

Ranks and Titles

Only 15 (9%) institutions assign to nontenure-track faculty those ranks and titles commonly associated with, and typically reserved for, tenure-track and tenured faculty: assistant professor, associate professor, or full professor. (See Table 4-3.)

◆ "In certain specifically designated colleges or schools of the university, or their sub-units, where the provost in consultation with the faculty senate determines and recommends to the president that the practice is vital to the well-being of the university, temporary, renewable, contracts as professor, associate professor, assistant professor, or instructor may be authorized. In exceptional circumstances, after consultation with the faculty senate executive committee, one- or three-year contracts may be issued." (University of Hartford, M1)

♦ "Multiple year contracts are offered to ranked faculty members at the rank of assistant professor or higher who have completed the probationary period and whom the college feels it is unable to grant tenure but who for institutional mission or need it may wish to retain." (Saint Vincent College, B2)

♦ "The office of the provost will endorse appointment recommendations to appoint individuals on a temporary basis (with an ending date) with the rank of instructor, assistant professor, associate professor, and professor only in instances in which the primary recommending unit is an academic department (a department in a college or colleges) and/or a school and/or a college." (Michigan State University, R1)

More institutions tend to appoint nontenure-track faculty as instructors/senior instructors (30 institutions, 17%) or lecturers (31 institutions, 18%); however, these faculty may only be promoted to higher levels at 15 (9%) of the institutions. Where promotions are possible, policies often indicate that the appointee must undergo a performance review:

Lecturers are appointed initially for a period of two years. On successful review during the second year, the lecturer is reappointed for a three-year period. On successful review during the fifth year, the lecturer is reappointed for a five-year period, and may be promoted to the position of senior lecturer. Subsequent reappointments are for five-year periods, subject to review in the tenth year, the fifteenth year, and so on. (Connecticut College, B1)

At the College of Charleston (M1), promotions of nontenure-

Table 4-3   Full-time Nontenure-Track Faculty Across Traditional Ranks and Titles

		175 institutions with full-time nontenure-track appointments								
	N	Lecturer		Instructor		Assistant Professor		Associate Professor		Professor	
		#	%	#	%	#	%	#	%	#	%
R1	20	6	30	5	25	3	15	3	15	3	15
R2	9	3	33	4	44	2	22	2	22	2	22
D1	10	2	20	2	20	0	0	0	0	0	0
D2	17	3	18	3	18	1	6	1	6	1	6
M1	47	11	23	12	26	4	11	4	11	4	11
M2	12	3	25	1	8	1	8	1	8	1	8
B1	24	1	4	1	4	1	4	1	4	1	4
B2	36	2	6	2	6	3	8	3	8	2	6
Total	175	31	18	30	17	15	9	15	9	14	9

track faculty are granted as an indication of a longer-term commitment and to reward a high level of performance:

> Promotion [of instructors] requires substantial evidence of exemplary performance as a teacher and of consistently high professional competence in professional development and service. Promotion to senior instructor is a long-term commitment by the college; it is not merely a reward for work accomplished, but it is an award given with the expectation that consistently high professional competence will continue.

Or as Elon College (M2) demonstrates, promotion may signal higher expectations for performance:

> For faculty on term appointments, promotion will not normally occur prior to the fifth-year review but can occur concurrently. Although fundamental responsibilities of the faculty are qualitatively the same, regardless of rank, faculty who have been rewarded by the college with promotion or appointment to a higher rank and a higher level of compensation are expected to serve the college and to perform at a higher level of responsibility.

Other policies explicitly state the limits of promotion opportunities for nontenure-track faculty:

♦ "Nontenure-track faculty are not eligible for promotion or tenure . . ." (University of North Alabama, M1)

♦ "Promotion for [lecturers] is usually recognized by changes in functional title rather than promotion in rank." (Virginia Polytechnic Institute and State University, R1)

As Table 4-3 suggests, research institutions employ a greater proportion of nontenure-track faculty at the assistant professor, associate professor, and full professor ranks than any of the other Carnegie classifications. In contrast, Doctoral 1 institutions report no nontenure-track faculty within these traditionally tenure-related ranks.

Degree Requirements

The degree requirements for nontenure-track faculty, across all ranks and titles, tend to be vaguely stated in most policies.

♦ "[Senior lecturer] recognizes a lengthy and distinguished record of accomplishment as lecturer, here or elsewhere." (Northwestern University, R1)

♦ "Appointment or promotion to nontenure-eligible assistant professor will be recommended largely on evidence of promise, adequate training, depth of knowledge in a particular specialty, and capacity to undertake high quality teaching, research or service." (University of Arizona, R1)

Twenty-one of the 30 institutions with nontenure-track instructor positions do not require a terminal degree. Of the 15 institutions with nontenure-track assistant professor positions, three (Asbury College, B2; Langston University, B2; Elon College, M2) do not require a terminal degree, and the other 12 do not state specific degree requirements. Of the 16 institutions with nontenure-track associate professor positions, two institutions (Drew University, B1; Asbury College, B2) do not require a terminal degree, and two do (Langston University, B2 and Valparaiso University, M1). The rest do not state requirements. Finally, for nontenure-track full professor positions, three institutions (Langston University, B2; Elon College, M2; and Pacific University, M2) require a terminal degree. For instance,

◆ "Temporary Professor. Faculty appointed with this title hold an appropriate earned doctorate, professional degree, or appropriate advanced degree." (Langston University, B2)

◆ "[Term Appointment] Professor. The appointment for persons with the doctorate and at least six years experience as an associate professor." (Elon College, M2)

The remainder do not state requirements.

Time-in-Rank

Similar to degree requirements, policy language for time-in-rank requirements is frequently absent or ambiguous. Time-in-rank requirements are often closely linked with degree expectations. Fourteen of the institutions with nontenure-track instructors require no previous service in a lower or equivalent rank; the remaining 16 do not specify. Of the 15 policies noting nontenure-track assistant professor positions, Langston University (B2) is the only one that states no expected time-in-rank; the remaining 15 do not state requirements. For nontenure-track associate professor positions, only two of the 15 institutions state specific experience requirements:

◆ "[An] associate professor has a minimum of 36 semester credits completed in an approved graduate program beyond the master's degree and a minimum of eight years of full-time teaching experience at the college level." (Asbury College, B2)

◆ "Promotion to nontenure-eligible associate professorship is possible after a minimum of three years of service in rank." (University of Arizona, R1)

And finally, for full professors on the nontenure-track, one institution explicitly states time-in-rank standards:

"A faculty member with a completed terminal degree and with a minimum of twelve years of full-time teaching experience at the college level." (Asbury College, B2)

One possible explanation for the lack of specific time-in-rank requirements for nontenure-track appointments is that most institutions employ nontenure-track personnel to gain flexibility and enable response to emerging institutional or departmental needs. Nontenurable appointments provide greater latitude for institutions to meet emerging or special needs and employ practitioners and others with unique expertise. For instance, Northwestern University (R1) states that "members of the lecturer faculty hold renewable positions for specified terms, subject to institutional need and individual job performance, appointments are on-going." The policy also states that "some [nontenure-track faculty] meet continuing instructional needs—basic language instruction, for example, while others fill in for faculty on leave or teach specialized courses . . ." Other policies indicating a need-based motivation for nontenure-track employment read as follows:

♦ "Reappointments as [lecturer] are based on performance and a continuing need." (Lehigh University, R2)

♦ "[Lecturer] appointments are useful in meeting special needs of a discipline and in providing better service to students." (Valparaiso University, M1)

Roles and Responsibilities

Policies on the roles and responsibilities of full-time nontenure-track faculty reflect the institutional intent that these faculty serve special functions. For instance, four policies explicitly note that full-time nontenure-track faculty are not expected to maintain a balance in research, teaching, and service. Rather, one or two areas are explicitly noted as the primary focus.

♦ "Appointment or promotion to the level of nontenure-eligible associate professor will require evidence of an established and productive career in addition to adequate training, depth of knowledge in a particular specialty, and capacity to undertake high quality teaching, research, or service." (University of Arizona, R1)

♦ "Lecturers are untenured members of the faculty whose primary roles are instructional with no obligations of research or service." (Rice University, R2)

◆ "A person appointed to the special faculty rank of instructor in an academic department ordinarily assumes full responsibility for teaching undergraduate courses and generally has limited responsibility for other aspects of the standard faculty role, such as research or other scholarship, and service." (Virginia Polytechnic Institute and State University, R1)

◆ ". . . lecturers do not have responsibility for academic affairs beyond the classroom and the work of classroom-related committees; they are not expected to publish or conduct independent research as part of their university responsibilities." (Northwestern University, R1)

Other policies clearly delineate the contrast in roles between nontenure-track faculty and their tenure-eligible counterparts:

◆ "[Lecturer appointments] are intended to replace some appointments as adjuncts, and are not intended to substitute for the integrated role of teaching, scholarship and service provided by regular tenured and tenure-track faculty." (Lehigh University, R2)

◆ "Given the instructional focus of a lectureship, a full-time lecturer almost always teaches more courses than a tenure-line faculty member does." (Northwestern University, R1)

In–Residence Faculty Appointments

Another title in the nontenure-track ranks signifies individuals who contribute a unique form of scholarship to the institution. Nineteen institutions (11%) specifically note "in-residence" appointments (see Appendix 4-H) which allow for poets, artists, writers, and other professionals. American University (D1), for example, states that "in-residence faculty appointment allows for the flexibility where there is a desire to provide for the visit of a distinguished and prominent individual to American University."

For these nontenure-track employees, scholarship is often redefined, expectations and requirements are different, and supplementary roles are described:

♦ "Artists-in-residence are individuals who have attained notable public recognition for achievement in one of the performing or fine arts and are therefore qualified as full-time or part-time faculty members." (Saint Louis University, R2)

♦ "Individuals may be appointed in the non-professorial ranks [of artist-in-residence and composer-in-residence] . . . to academic positions that merit distinctive titles describing their special functions in the university . . . special appointments do not involve the same duties as professorial appointments." (Rice University, R2)

♦ "Writer-in-residence. This title is used for persons whose literary accomplishments qualify them for appointment to an academic department." (University of Mississippi, R2)

♦ "Distinguished artists, scholars, scientists, engineers, executives, statesmen and others may be granted appointments in-residence from time to time to enrich the life of the university community." (Santa Clara University, M1)

♦ "Professional-in-residence. This is an umbrella title for professionals, appointed to instructional positions with working titles, such as writer-in-residence, artist-in-residence, architect-in-residence, journalist-in-residence, etc." (University of New Orleans, D2)

Limitations on transfer to the tenure track are often explicitly stated:

♦ "Persons holding only [writer-in-residence] title are members of the support faculty and are not eligible for tenure or promotion." (University of Mississippi, R2)

♦ "Artists-in-residence are not eligible for tenure and may not apply for advancement or transfer to another type of faculty position." (Saint Louis University, R2)

Research 2 and Doctoral 1 institutions have the greatest proportion of policies for in-residence faculty. However, across Carnegie classifications, the policy language on requirements and responsibilities is similar.

Table 4-4   In-Residence Faculty

R1 n=20		R2 n=9		D1 n=10		D2 n=17		M1 n=47		M2 n=12		B1 n=24		B2 n=36		Total n=175	
#	%	#	%	#	%	#	%	#	%	#	%	#	%	#	%	#	%
1	5	3	33	4	40	2	12	4	9	1	8	0	0	4	11	19	11

Research and Clinical Faculty

Research 1, Research 2, and Doctoral 1 institutions use non-tenure-track research (see Table 4-5) and clinical positions (see Table 4-6) more frequently than institutions falling within any of the other Carnegie classifications. Many disciplines use research positions; however, clinical positions are often found in schools of law, medicine, or dentistry and other health-related or clinical programs. Policy provisions frequently make explicit the limited roles of research and clinical faculty. For an additional discussion of the roles of clinical faculty, see Gappa and Leslie (1997) and Gappa (1996).

◆ "Persons with [clinical] appointments conduct legal clinics for the school and give clinical instruction to its students. They may also teach nonclinical courses that are not part of the school's core curriculum." (Columbia University, R1)

◆ "[Research] modifier may be used in those instances where a person holding professional rank is engaged primarily in research. . . . [Clinical] modifier may be used in conjunction with those professional positions involved in teaching research, or extension functions in a hospital or other clinical environment." (Florida State University, R1)

◆ "The academic titles of research assistant professor, clinical assistant professor, research associate professor, clinical associate professor, research professor, or clinical professor may be granted to persons engaged full-time in research who are supported from external research funds or trust accounts." (North Carolina State University, R1)

◆ "Research faculty are those who have research as their principal assignment." (University of New Hampshire, D2)

◆ "A person engaged primarily in research or professional activities relevant to the work of the university." (American University, D1)

◆ "The clinical ranks are available only to appointees involved in providing clinical services and in teaching, but not in research." (University of Indiana, Bloomington, R1)

◆ "The [research] title is used for faculty members whose principal assignments are to conduct research." (University of Mississippi, R2)

For some institutions, such as the University of New Orleans (D2), policy language suggests that appointments to clinical and research faculty ranks are given to those not quite qualified for tenure-track positions:

> Any clinical specialist. This is a nontenure-track for full-time faculty in the clinical sciences who are effective in teaching and service programs and are essential for patient care, but whose research publications or scholarly activity does not warrant appointment or promotion to tenured positions. (University of New Orleans, D2)

Two institutions, Columbia University (R1) and Florida State University (R1), offer both tenure-track and nontenure-track options for faculty on full-time research appointments. As Florida State University notes in reference to research-related employment: "Appointment time may or may not be counted as tenure earning service. The university shall notify the appointee in writing of the tenure-earning status of the position at the time of appointment."

Of the 41 institutions with nontenurable full-time research faculty appointments, nine (22%) have research positions funded by outside sources only, while 12 (29%) institutions have research positions supported by internal or external funds. Of the 29 institutions with nontenurable full-time clinical faculty appointments, three support these positions with external funds only; one with internal funds only; and four have both internally funded and externally funded nontenure-track clinical positions.

Table 4-5   Nontenure-Track Research Faculty

R1 n=20		R2 n=9		D1 n=10		D2 n=17		M1 n=47		M2 n=12		B1 n=24		B2 n=36		Total n=175	
#	%	#	%	#	%	#	%	#	%	#	%	#	%	#	%	#	%
12	60	6	67	6	60	7	41	9	18	0	0	0	0	1	3	41	17

Table 4-6   Nontenure-Track Clinical Faculty

R1 n=20		R2 n=9		D1 n=10		D2 n=17		M1 n=47		M2 n=12		B1 n=24		B2 n=36		Total n=175	
#	%	#	%	#	%	#	%	#	%	#	%	#	%	#	%	#	%
10	45	5	56	4	40	3	18	5	11	2	17	0	0	0	0	29	16

Titles for research and clinical faculty typically follow standard ranks of assistant professor, associate professor, and full professor with the appropriate modifier (research or clinical) attached. At Northern Arizona University (D1), clinical professors are expected to have qualifications similar to their tenure-track colleagues.

> To be eligible for the rank of clinical professor, the faculty member must supply evidence of at least the following: 1) recognition of outstanding research contributions or scholarly or creative activity; and 2) an earned doctorate in the discipline of the faculty member or other terminal degree and/or certification or licensing in his/her field of competence . . .

At Northwestern University (R1) there are similar requirements for tenure-track and nontenure-track research faculty, yet nontenure-track faculty are excluded from some aspects of academic life including governance.

> Research faculty may not participate in governance of the university or of any academic unit, and are usually not assigned teaching responsibilities, although they may occasionally take part in classroom or seminar activities. In rare cases where a department wishes a research faculty member to teach a course, a separate part-time

teaching faculty appointment is required. The university views faculty-level research positions as appointments which recognize or enhance a scientific career. (Northwestern University, R1)

In contrast, other institutions grant voting privileges to research and clinical faculty.

◆ "Research faculty may attend faculty meetings and vote on all matters except those pertaining to tenure or exclusively to undergraduate affairs." (Rice University, R1)

◆ "Research faculty carry all faculty and campus privileges. Departments and colleges may extend to research appointees the right to vote in departmental meetings, serve on committees, and vote on curricular issues." (Montana State University, D2)

◆ "Individuals in the [nontenurable] clinical track will have voting rights in their respective departments and in the school . . ." (West Virginia University, R1)

Participation in Governance

Only 12 (7%) institutions extend voting privileges to nontenure-track faculty at the departmental, college, or university level (see Table 4-7).

◆ "Lecturers, who are not engaged in research, . . . are voting members of the faculty." (Connecticut College, B1)

◆ "Faculty-in-residence are not eligible for appointment with tenure or sabbatical leave, but are eligible for promotion, and may be allowed to vote for and be elected to the faculty and its committees." (University of New Hampshire, D2)

◆ "Nontenure-track faculty are not eligible for promotion or tenure, but do share . . . the general responsibilities, privileges, and benefits accorded regular faculty." (University of North Alabama, M1)

◆ " . . . voting rights may be extended by unit by-laws to include temporary faculty, honorary faculty, specialists, lecturers, research associates, assistant instructors, or adjunct faculty." (Michigan State University, R1)

Table 4-7   Policies Indicating Nontenure-Track Faculty Governance Voting Rights

R1 n=20		R2 n=9		D1 n=10		D2 n=17		M1 n=47		M2 n=12		B1 n=24		B2 n=36		Total n=175	
#	%	#	%	#	%	#	%	#	%	#	%	#	%	#	%	#	%
5	25	1	11	1	0	2	12	1	2	0	0	3	13	0	0	13	7

- " . . . individuals holding these appointments [as lecturers, demonstrators, or laboratory supervisors] shall have the privileges normally associated with the rank of instructor, including . . . voting membership in the general faculty." (North Carolina State University, R1)

Contract Length and Reappointment

The stated contract length for full-time nontenure-track appointments tends to range from nine months, or an academic year, to five years. The majority of initial appointments extend for no more than one to two years with a performance review determining opportunities for reappointment.

- "The basis for failure to reappoint . . . shall be the absence of one or more of continuing satisfactory performance of instructional and related faculty responsibilities, of continuing programmatic and/or staffing need within the unit, or of anticipated budgeted resources sufficient to support the position for the coming year." (Kent State University, R2)

- "Continuation of term appointments beyond the fifth year will be contingent upon successful completion of a fifth year review, and if successful, could result in a two-year term appointment." (Elon College, M2)

- "Annual reappointments to [nontenure-eligible] associate professor may be made an indefinite number of times, subject to satisfactory evaluation." (University of Arizona, R1)

Most institutions, such as the University of the Ozarks (B2) and the University of Southern Colorado (B2), indicate that contracts may be terminated by the institution or the individual at any time. Reasons for nonreappointment of faculty are broad, varied, and vague. When the institution terminates or fails to renew the appointment, written notification is required. Nineteen (11%) institutions provide termination notice three months in advance for faculty in their first year, six months for faculty in their second year, and twelve months for faculty in their third or higher year. Notification entails notice of nonrenewal, but does not require the institution to provide the faculty member with reasons. For instance,

◆ " . . . research faculty members have the expectation of continuing employment unless notified otherwise at the time of their appointment." (University of Mississippi, R2)

◆ " . . . nonreappointment of instructors may be for a number of reasons beyond non-meritorious service, such as modification of programmatic emphasis, enrollment trends, or simply the intention of seeking an appointee with superior qualifications." (Virginia Polytechnic Institute and State University, R1)

Although national data suggest that full-time nontenure-track faculty play a substantial role in colleges and universities, three institutions explicitly limit the proportion of nontenure-track faculty.

◆ "No more than 15% of all full-time teaching faculty appointments will be three-year rolling appointments." (Asbury College, B2)

◆ "No more than 20% of the total salaried faculty in any college (FTE) may hold such appointments [as clinical faculty] although individual colleges may set lower percentages." (University of Iowa, R1)

◆ "No more than ten appointments as lecturer may be extant in the university at one time." (Lehigh University, R2)

SUMMARY

It is certain that institutions will continue to weigh the benefits and costs, as well as the challenges and opportunities, associated with nontenured full-time faculty employment. While the use of nontenure-track appointments varies from campus to campus, nontenurable appointments are now a familiar and sizable part of the academic landscape.

Over 80% of the institutions in the FAPA archive provide some form of nontenure-track appointment opportunities; almost half permit full-time, long-term renewable positions. In many cases, nontenure-track faculty are assuming specialized roles on campuses as research faculty, clinical faculty, and in-residence faculty. For each of these appointment types, policy language often reflects different requirements and responsibilities for nontenure-track than for tenure-track faculty.

As institutions recognize the need to codify employment policies, they realize the inherent tension between providing specific terms and conditions and preserving the flexibility nontenure-track appointments provide. Consequently, policy language is frequently nebulous with regard to qualifications, roles, and the possibility of continued employment.

REFERENCES

American Association of University Professors. (1995). *Policy documents and reports* (8th ed.). Washington, DC: AAUP.

Chronister, J. L., Baldwin, R. G., & Bailey, T. (1992, Summer). Full-time nontenure-track faculty: Current status, condition and attitudes. *The Review of Higher Education, 15* (4), 383-400. Association for the Study of Higher Education.

Gappa, J. M. (1996). Off the tenure track: Six models for full-time, non-tenurable appointments. *New Pathways Working Papers Series*, No. 10. Washington, DC: American Association for Higher Education.

Gappa, J. M., & Leslie, D. W. (1997). Two faculties or one? The conundrum of part-timers in a bifurcated work force. *New Pathways Working Papers Series*, No. 6. Washington, DC: American Association for Higher Education.

Leatherman, C. (1999, April 9). Growth in positions off the tenure track is a trend that's here to stay, study finds. *The Chronicle of Higher Education*, A14-A16.

APPENDIX 4-A
Institutions with Full-Time Long-Term Nontenure-Track Positions

Research 1 Institutions
  1. Brown University
  2. Columbia University
  3. Emory University
  4. Florida State University
  5. Georgia Institute of Technology
  6. Michigan State University
  7. North Carolina State University
  8. Northwestern University
  9. University of Arizona
 10. University of California, Irvine
 11. University of Georgia
 12. University of Indiana, Bloomington
 13. University of Iowa
 14. University of Missouri, Columbia
 15. University of Nebraska, Lincoln
 16. University of Rochester
 17. Virginia Polytechnic Institute and State University
 18. West Virginia University

Research 2 Institutions
 19. George Washington University
 20. Kent State University
 21. Lehigh University
 22. Rice University
 23. Saint Louis University
 24. Southern Illinois University, Carbondale
 25. University of Mississippi
 26. University of Notre Dame

Doctoral 1 Institutions
 27. American University
 28. Marquette University
 29. Northern Arizona University
 30. Texas Woman's University
 31. United States International University
 32. University of Texas, Arlington
 33. University of Toledo

Doctoral 2 Institutions
 34. Clarkson University
 35. George Mason University
 36. Idaho State University
 37. Montana State University
 38. North Dakota State University

39. University of Central Florida
40. University of Detroit Mercy
41. University of New Hampshire
42. University of New Orleans
43. University of North Dakota
44. Wake Forest University

Master's 1 Institutions
45. Arkansas Tech University
46. Bowie State University
47. Butler University
48. College of Charleston
49. Creighton University
50. East Carolina University
51. Eastern Illinois University
52. Georgia College and State University
53. James Madison University
54. Millersville University of Pennsylvania
55. Northern Kentucky University
56. Pittsburg State University
57. Saginaw Valley State University
58. Saint Mary's University
59. Salve Regina University
60. Santa Clara University
61. Southeastern Louisiana University
62. Southeastern Oklahoma State University
63. Springfield College
64. University of Alaska
65. University of Colorado, Colorado Springs
66. University of Hartford
67. University of North Alabama
68. University of Northern Iowa
69. University of Southern Maine
70. University of Texas Pan American
71. University of Wisconsin, Superior
72. Valdosta State University
73. Valparaiso University
74. West Chester University of Pennsylvania
75. Whitworth College

Master's 2 Institutions
76. Elon College
77. Lincoln University of Pennsylvania
78. MidAmerica Nazarene University
79. Pacific University
80. Walsh University
81. Weber State University

Baccalaureate 1 Institutions
   82. Beloit College
   83. Connecticut College
   84. Davidson College
   85. Drew University
   86. Saint John's College
   87. Saint Olaf College
   88. Smith College

Baccalaureate 2 Institutions
   89. Asbury College
   90. Bethel College
   91. Carroll College
   92. Cedarville College
   93. Colby-Sawyer College
   94. Dillard University
   95. Langston University
   96. McMurry University
   97. Millikin University
   98. Saint Joseph's College
   99. Saint Vincent College
   100. University of Southern Colorado
   101. University of the Ozarks

APPENDIX 4-B

Institutions Appointing Nontenure-Track Faculty to the Instructor Level

Research 1 Institutions
   1. Brown University
   2. Georgia Institute of Technology
   3. Michigan State University
   4. University of Arizona
   5. Virginia Polytechnic Institute and State University

Research 2 Institutions
   6. Kent State University
   7. Saint Louis University
   8. Southern Illinois University, Carbondale
   9. University of Mississippi

Doctoral 1 Institutions
   10. Marquette University
   11. Northern Arizona University

Doctoral 2 Institutions
   12. Clarkson University
   13. George Mason University
   14. University of Central Florida

Master's 1 Institutions
15. Arkansas Tech University
16. College of Charleston
17. Georgia College and State University
18. James Madison University
19. Northern Kentucky University
20. Southeastern Louisiana University
21. Southeastern Oklahoma State University
22. Springfield College
23. University of Alaska
24. University of Hartford
25. University of North Alabama
26. Valparaiso University

Master's 2 Institutions
27. Elon College

Baccalaureate 1 Institutions
28. Saint Olaf College

Baccalaureate 2 Institutions
29. Langston University
30. University of the Ozarks

APPENDIX 4-C

Institutions Appointing Nontenure-Track Faculty to Assistant Professor

Research 1 Institutions
1. Georgia Institute of Technology
2. Michigan State University
3. University of Arizona

Research 2 Institutions
4. Kent State University
5. Saint Louis University

Doctoral 2 Institutions
6. George Mason University

Master's 1 Institutions
7. Georgia College and State University
8. University of Hartford
9. James Madison University
10. University of North Alabama
11. Valparaiso University

Master's 2 Institutions
12. Elon College

Baccalaureate 2 Institutions
13. Asbury College

14. Langston University
15. Saint Vincent College

APPENDIX 4-D

Institutions Appointing Nontenure-Track Faculty to Rank of Associate Professor

Research 1 Institutions
   1. Georgia Institute of Technology
   2. Michigan State University
   3. University of Arizona

Research 2 Institutions
   4. Kent State University
   5. Saint Louis University

Doctoral 2 Institutions
   6. George Mason University

Master's 1 Institutions
   7. Georgia College and State University
   8. James Madison University
   9. University of Hartford
   10. University of North Alabama
   11. Valparaiso University

Master's 2 Institutions
   12. Elon College

Baccalaureate 2 Institutions
   13. Asbury College
   14. Langston University
   15. Saint Vincent College

APPENDIX 4-E

Institutions Appointing Nontenure-Track Faculty to Rank of Full Professor

Research 1 Institutions
   1. Georgia Institute of Technology
   2. Michigan State University
   3. University of Arizona

Research 2 Institutions
   4. Kent State University
   5. Saint Louis University

Doctoral 2 Institutions
   6. George Mason University

Master's 1 Institutions
   7. Georgia College and State University
   8. James Madison University

9. University of Hartford
10. University of North Alabama
11. Valparaiso University

Master's 2 Institutions
12. Elon College

Baccalaureate 1 Institutions
13. Drew University

Baccalaureate 2 Institutions
14. Langston University
15. Saint Vincent College

APPENDIX 4-F
Institutions Appointing Nontenure-Track Research Faculty

Research 1 Institutions
1. Brown University
2. Columbia University
3. Emory University
4. Florida State University
5. Georgia Institute of Technology
6. North Carolina State University
7. Northwestern University
8. University of Georgia
9. University of California, Irvine
10. University of Indiana, Bloomington
11. Virginia Polytechnic Institute and State University
12. West Virginia University

Research 2 Institutions
13. George Washington University
14. Rice University
15. Saint Louis University
16. Southern Illinois University, Carbondale
17. University of Mississippi
18. University of Notre Dame

Doctoral 1 Institutions
19. American University
20. Marquette University
21. Northern Arizona University
22. Texas Woman's University
23. University of Toledo
24. United States International University

Doctoral 2 Institutions
25. Montana State University
26. University of Central Florida

27. University of Detroit Mercy
28. University of New Hampshire
29. University of New Orleans
30. George Mason University
31. Idaho State University

Master's 1 Institutions
32. Butler University
33. Creighton University
34. Georgia College and State University
35. Santa Clara University
36. University of Alaska
37. University of Southern Maine
38. University of Texas Pan American
39. Valdosta State University
40. Valparaiso University

Baccalaureate 2 Institutions
41. University of Southern Colorado

APPENDIX 4-G

Institutions Appointing Nontenure-Track Clinical Faculty

Research 1 Institutions
1. Brown University
2. Columbia University
3. Emory University
4. Florida State University
5. Michigan State University
6. North Carolina State University
7. University of California, Irvine
8. University of Indiana, Bloomington
9. University of Iowa
10. University of Rochester
11. West Virginia University

Research 2 Institutions
12. Rice University
13. Saint Louis University
14. Southern Illinois University, Carbondale
15. University of Mississippi

Doctoral 1 Institutions
16. Marquette University
17. Northern Arizona University
18. Texas Woman's University
19. University of Texas, Arlington

Doctoral 2 Institutions
20. George Mason University
21. University of Central Florida
22. University of New Orleans

Master's 1 Institutions
23. Butler University
24. East Carolina University
25. Salve Regina University
26. University of Alaska
27. University of Texas Pan American

Master's 2 Institutions
28. Pacific University
29. Walsh University

APPENDIX 4-H

Institutions with In-Residence Faculty Appointments

Research 1 Institutions
1. University of California, Irvine

Research 2 Institutions
2. Rice University
3. Saint Louis University
4. University of Mississippi

Doctoral 1 Institutions
5. American University
6. Texas Woman's University
7. United States International University
8. University of Toledo

Doctoral 2 Institutions
9. University of New Hampshire
10. University of New Orleans

Master's 1 Institutions
11. Saint Mary's University
12. Salve Regina University
13. Santa Clara University
14. Southeastern Louisiana University

Master's 2 Institutions
15. MidAmerica Nazarene University

Baccalaureate 2 Institutions
16. Bethel College
17. Colby-Sawyer College
18. Millikin University
19. Saint Joseph's College

APPENDIX 4-I

Institutions with Nontenure-Track Faculty Appointed as Lecturers

Research 1 Institutions
 1. Brown University
 2. Columbia University
 3. Northwestern University
 4. University of Arizona
 5. University of Missouri, Columbia
 6. Virginia Polytechnic Institute and State University

Research 2 Institutions
 7. Lehigh University
 8. Southern Illinois University, Carbondale
 9. University of Mississippi

Doctoral 1 Institutions
 10. Northern Arizona University
 11. Texas Woman's University

Doctoral 2 Institutions
 12. North Dakota State University
 13. University of Central Florida
 14. University of North Dakota

Master's 1 Institutions
 15. Bowie State University
 16. Pittsburg State University
 17. Saginaw Valley State University
 18. Salve Regina University
 19. Santa Clara University
 20. Southeastern Louisiana University
 21. Southeastern Oklahoma State University
 22. University of Alaska
 23. University of Southern Maine
 24. University of Texas Pan American
 25. Valparaiso University

Master's 2 Institutions
 26. Lincoln University of Pennsylvania
 27. MidAmerica Nazarene University
 28. Weber State University

Baccalaureate 1 Institutions
 29. Davidson College

Baccalaureate 2 Institutions
 30. Dillard University
 31. University of Southern Colorado

5

CLIMBING THE ACADEMIC LADDER: PROMOTION IN RANK

KerryAnn O'Meara

HIGHLIGHTS

Of the 196 Tenure-Granting Institutions with Academic Ranks

◆ 111 (57%) link institutional mission and priorities to promotion decisions.

◆ 163 (83%) explicitly describe the categories of teaching, research, and service for purposes of promotion.

◆ 86 (44%) outline specific criteria for assessing the quality of teaching, research, and service.

- 78 include criteria for evaluating teaching

- 73 include criteria for evaluating research/scholarship

- 53 include criteria for evaluating service

◆ 23 (12%) use nonstandard guidelines for documenting faculty work.

- 17 in the teaching category

- Six in the service category

- Four in the research category

◆ 65 (33%) evaluate faculty based on additional or different areas of faculty work (e.g., personal and religious, professional growth, advising and student-related, and administrative/university-wide contributions).

◆ 94 (48%) require that candidates for full professor must meet higher standards than candidates for assistant professor.

INTRODUCTION

This chapter summarizes and highlights promotion in rank policies at 196 tenure-granting institutions in the FAPA CD-ROM. Promotion is defined herein as advancement in rank to associate professor and to full professor. Promotion to tenure, on the other hand, is covered in Chapter 2. This chapter answers the following questions:

◆ What are the guidelines of the American Association for University Professors for promotion?

◆ To what extent do policies vary from this standard?

◆ On what is promotion based?

◆ What guidelines exist for assessing teaching, research, and service in promotion policies?

  ▪ How are teaching, research, and service defined? What are the components of each?

  ▪ What criteria are applied to assess the quality of teaching, research, and service?

  ▪ How do faculty document teaching, research, and service?

◆ To what extent is promotion based on categories of faculty work other than teaching, research, and service?

◆ Are criteria for evaluating candidates for associate professor different from those used for candidates for full professor?

ON WHAT IS PROMOTION BASED?

Promotion in rank is typically based on performance in the three primary areas of faculty work: teaching, research, and service, with an emphasis usually placed on either teaching or research. The emphasis on teaching or research is, in turn, based on institutional mission and/or institutional priorities. A very small number of institutions consider factors in addition to mission and priorities when making promotion decisions (e.g., financial conditions, market factors, enrollment patterns, demand for programs, departmental goals, diversity, percent of tenured faculty).

The AAUP "has addressed the question of faculty workloads and the appropriate balance between teaching and research" (1995, p. 129) and states that "[N]o single formula for an equitable faculty workload can be devised for all of American higher education" (1995, p. 125). While the AAUP does not provide a "formula" for faculty work, a section on "The Work of Faculty: Expectations, Priorities, and Rewards" states:

> Institutions should define their missions clearly and articulate appropriate and reasonable expectations against which faculty will be judged, rather than demanding all things from all their men and women. (AAUP, 1995, p. 132)

Institutional Mission

Institutional mission is a significant factor in determining which area of faculty work is emphasized in promotion decisions. Thirty (15%) of the FAPA institutions require that faculty advance the spirit of the institutional mission in order to be promoted (see Appendix 5-A). At nine institutions, faculty must be committed to, and exemplify, the religious values of the institution. For example, Taylor University (B2) states:

> As persons created in the image of God, admonished to live with a due sense of responsibility, and commissioned

to a life of service in our contemporary world, we at
Taylor University view a means through which we might
respond to the call and claims of Christ upon our lives.
Taylor is committed to the continuous process of providing an educational environment wherein faculty and students pursue academic excellence as an essential part of
one's personal spiritual development.

Asbury College (B2) is similarly direct:

Asbury College seeks to employ faculty who bear personal witness to the saving and sanctifying power of
Jesus Christ and who see teaching as an opportunity for
Christian service. A faculty member shall be exemplary
in Christian living so as to bring honor to Christ, the
Church, and the college; maintain high academic and
spiritual standards; conform to standards of campus life;
and develop spiritually through prayer, bible study and
regular church attendance. The faculty member must be
in continuing agreement with the College Statement of
Faith. Faculty members should be prepared to resign
when they no longer support the College Statement of
Faith and must refrain from propagating any theological
position other than the Wesleyan-Armenian confession
to which the college is committed.

Five institutions with religious missions require faculty to provide, as Valparaiso University (M1) does, a "narrative of how
the candidate's personal goals relate to the purpose and mission
of the university, including its Christian identity."

Springfield College (M1), while nonsecular, requires its faculty to demonstrate commitment to the Humanic's philosophy
as summarized in the following paragraph.

Humanics counsels us that people are holistic beings
(mind, body, and spirit); that enhancing the mind, body,
and spirit is a noble and collective responsibility; that
community is pursued by reaching out to one another
collaboratively; and that service requires the utmost
mutual respect and care.

Table 5-1   Promotion Policies That Emphasize Teaching or Research

Institutional Type	Institutions with a Policy Emphasis	Teaching Emphasis		Research Emphasis		Teaching and Research Equally Important	
		#	%	#	%	#	%
R1	9	4	44	3	33	2	22
R2	6	3	50	2	33	1	17
D1	2	0	0	1	50	1	50
D2	6	5	83	0	0	1	17
M1	32	29	91	0	0	3	9
M2	9	8	89	1	11	0	0
B1	3	3	100	0	0	0	0
B2	23	23	100	0	0	0	0
Total	90	75	83	7	8	8	9

The promotion criteria at 24 institutions address a faculty member's religious commitment and personal conduct. For example, Culver Stockton College (B2) requires "compatibility of personal and professional aims and interests of the college, loyalty to the institution, the highest professional ethics and appropriate decorum" as promotion criteria. Dana College (B2) includes "moral influence on campus and community at large" in its criteria for promotion. Marquette University (D1) requires that faculty demonstrate a "respectful attitude toward the religious beliefs of others."

These 24 institutions require: 1) compatibility between the interests of the college and the character of the faculty member, 2) overall loyalty to the institution, 3) professional esteem by colleagues, 4) commitment to the college as an academic community, and 5) responsible citizenship and participation in improving the welfare of the college.

Institutional Priorities

Almost half (90, 46%) of the FAPA institutions link promotion to institutional priorities by emphasizing either teaching or research in promotion criteria. Of these, 75 (83%) favor teaching, seven (8%) favor research, and eight (9%) value teaching and research equally for promotion in rank. See Table 5-1 and Appendix 5-B.

Baccalaureate and master's institutions are much more likely than research and doctoral institutions to prioritize faculty work in promotion policies (67 versus 23). Across all institutional types, the majority weight teaching as primary for promotion, including 12 doctoral and research institutions and 63 baccalaureate and master's institutions. It is interesting to note that seven Research 1 and 2 institutions place teaching above research for promotion. For example, the University of Iowa (R1) states that the "first step in promotion and tenure decision-making is an evaluation of teaching effectiveness. Only after affirmative judgment as to [teaching] effectiveness has been made can serious consideration be given to scholarship and professional service." The University of Rochester (R1) states that "two thresholds must be passed . . . the first of which is excellence in teaching. No matter how good the scholarly or artistic work, nobody belongs in the university unless he or she is a good teacher." Likewise, Saint Louis University (R2) states that "teaching should play a prominent role in tenure and promotion decisions. Academic excellence through research and scholarship is a second mechanism [for evaluation.]"

Making Priorities Known

Three approaches for prioritizing teaching or research in the promotion policy have been identified: 1) wording, 2) weighting or rank ordering, and 3) a sequential process. Each of these approaches is described below.

Wording. Fifty-eight of the 90 institutions (64%) make priorities known by using words such as "excellence in," "superior performance," or "expected" with teaching or research criterion for promotion in rank, while using "adequate," "effective," or "should be provided" with the other, lesser-emphasized category of work. For example, the University of California, Irvine (R1) prioritizes teaching over research and other categories of work by stating that "clearly demonstrated evidence of high quality teaching is an essential criterion [for promotion]," and the University of Massachusetts, Lowell (D2) states that "instructional effectiveness shall be considered indispensable for faculty appointment and advancement" for all ranks for promotion. The words "essential criterion" in the former example, and "indispensable" in the latter, are used with the teaching criterion for promotion in rank and not used with the criterion for research or other categories of work.

Likewise, Millersville University of Pennsylvania (M1) states that teaching effectiveness is the "most important" category for promotion. Southeastern Louisiana University (M1) prioritizes teaching by using "excellence," "distinction," and "adequacy" to describe expectations for teaching, professional activity, and service, respectively, for promotion to associate professor. Elon College (M2) gives "top priority" and Villanova University (M1) gives "priority" to teaching in all promotion decisions. Finally, the University of the Ozarks (B2) states that "of the criteria [for promotion] those concerning effective classroom teaching and institutional contributions shall dominate."

The University of Nebraska, Lincoln (R1) emphasizes research over teaching stating, "no special adjustments of norms for units or individuals shall alter the universities' fundamental criterion, that all faculty members must do scholarly or professional work that demonstrates creative achievement." Likewise, Brown University (R1) states that "mastery in scholarship is paramount." Weber State University (M2) prioritizes research as follows: "final determination of which items are of primary importance will be left to individual colleges with the exception that publication will be an item of primary importance in all colleges." The use of "fundamental," "paramount," and "primary importance" emphasizes the importance of research for faculty members of all ranks.

Weights and ranks. Thirteen of the 90 (14%) policies assign greater weights to emphasized categories of faculty work. For example, Union College (M2) places 25 to 30% more weight on teaching than on any other category. Arkansas Tech University (M1) has a weighting system where, for each category of work, candidates are given a five for extremely well-qualified performance, a four for well-qualified performance, a three for qualified performance, and a two to designate a deficiency. The policy states, "Deficiencies in either scholarly/creative activities or service may be counterbalanced by exceptional excellence in the other area. The criteria for teaching effectiveness may not be deficient . . ." Coker College (B2) weights teaching performance as 50% of its decision for promotion in rank and combines all other categories (professional growth, advising, administrative responsibility, external service, contribution to committee work, etc.) together for the other 50%, thereby demonstrating that teaching is their highest priority.

In a slightly different approach that effectively weights faculty work without actually assigning weights, eight institutions state that while adequate performance in one category could be compensated for, less than excellent performance, or merely satisfactory performance in teaching or research is not acceptable. West Virginia Wesleyan College (M2) states, "A pronounced weakness in teaching cannot be compensated for by strengths in other areas." Other examples include the University of Rochester's (R1): "No matter how good the scholarly or artistic work, nobody belongs in a university unless he or she is a good teacher." At Haverford College (B1), "The college does not award tenure and promotion to those who cannot teach a wide range of students effectively." The University of Mississippi's (R2) first hurdle is research: "Under no circumstances should a person be promoted to a higher rank without evidence of scholarly research or creative achievement."

Four (4%) policies list teaching as the first in a list of priorities. For example, the promotion policy at Virginia Intermont College (B2) states, "The basic criteria [for promotion] are listed in order of importance: teaching effectiveness, professional activities, and community service."

Sequential process. Seven institutions use a sequential approach to prioritizing teaching or research by requiring faculty to be effective teachers first and foremost. Only after teaching effectiveness has been established will the evaluation committee continue. At the University of Iowa (R1) and Southern Illinois University, Carbondale (R2), for example: "The first step in promotion is evaluation of teaching effectiveness. Only after an affirmative judgment has been made can serious consideration be given to the evaluation of scholarship and professional service."

Other Considerations

Ten policies (see Appendix 5-C) note that promotion committees must take into consideration financial and strategic planning issues such as changing enrollment patterns, percent of tenured faculty, fiscal constraints, preserving opportunities to remain flexible in appointments, goals of the department, program needs, and diversity. For example, Colby-Sawyer College (B2) states that promotion decisions are affected by the number of professors each department can have at each rank, documented program viability, institutional financial viability, and potential changes in the program. The Michigan State University (R1) promotion policy states that deans should consider departmental goals, the needs of the college, university, and program, the percentage of tenured faculty, fiscal constraints, and diversity when making promotion decisions.

In conclusion, just over half of FAPA institutions (111, 57%) follow AAUP guidelines that promotion criteria be linked with institutional mission. These colleges and universities represent every Carnegie classification; however, a greater percentage are baccalaureate and master's versus research and doctoral institutions (68% versus 32%). While one might expect that private institutions may be more likely to do so, linking the criteria for promotion and mission policy statements is no more common among private institutions than public ones (54% versus 46%, respectively, approximately the same as the representation of each type in the total sample).

DEFINING, ASSESSING, AND DOCUMENTING FACULTY WORK

Overview

In their statement titled *Fair Standards for Faculty Evaluation* (AAUP, 1995), the AAUP asserts that "criteria for reappointment, promotion, or tenure should have been made clear to the

Table 5-2   Institutions with Criteria for Assessing Teaching,
             Research, and Service

Institutional Type	Institutions with Criteria	Teaching Criteria	Research Criteria	Service Criteria
R1	10	7	8	4
R2	4	4	4	3
D1	5	5	5	4
D2	9	7	7	6
M1	27	27	24	20
M2	4	4	2	2
B1	4	3	3	2
B2	23	21	20	12
Total	86 (100%)	78 (90%)	73 (85%)	53 (61%)

candidate at the time of his/her appointment and reviewed with the appointee on a regular basis afterwards" (p. 169). One hundred sixty-three (83%) FAPA institutions define the categories of teaching, research, service, and "other."

In its *Statement on Teaching Evaluation*, the AAUP (1995) writes that, "as a first order of business," institutions should:

> declare their values and communicate them with sufficient clarity to enable colleges and departments to set forth specific expectations as to teaching, research, and service, and to make clear any other faculty obligations. (p. 133)

In the FAPA archive, 86 (44%) of the 196 institutions outline specific criteria for assessing performance in teaching, research, and service in the general faculty handbook (see Appendix 5-D). One should not assume that the remaining 110 institutions do not detail specific criteria for the assessment of faculty performance. It is likely that they do, but that they do so in the context of specific departments rather than in the general faculty handbook.

Of the 86 institutions that outline faculty performance criteria, 58 (67%) are baccalaureate and master's institutions. It is slightly more likely for baccalaureate and master's institutions to establish teaching criteria than research criteria, while doctoral and research institutions are equally likely to provide teaching and research criteria. Of the 86 institutions, 78 (90%) include criteria for evaluating teaching, 73 (85%) include criteria for evaluating research/scholarship, and 53 (61%) include criteria for assessing service. Table 5-2 outlines the breakdown of these criteria by type of institution.

Of the 196 tenure-granting institutions included in this study, 23 (12%) policies contain nonstandard documentation of teaching, service, research, and "other" categories (see Appendix 5-E). Nonstandard documentation language is found most often in the category of teaching (17 policies), followed by service (six policies), and research (four policies).

DEFINING, ASSESSING, AND DOCUMENTING TEACHING

Standard Practice

Teaching, as a category for promotion, is referred to in the policies as instruction, instructional performance, teaching and advising effectiveness, and effectiveness in the classroom. Fifty (31%) institutions define teaching activities as classroom performance, preparation, grading, and keeping office hours. The remaining institutions discuss teaching as a requirement for promotion but do not formally define it. Fully 174 (89%) policies include advising as part of teaching; the remaining 22 (11%) policies list advising as a separate category to be considered when faculty members apply for promotion.

Two institutions define teaching quite broadly; for example, "any activity undertaken by a faculty member that contributes to the efforts of Emory students to acquire intellectual skills, extend knowledge and understanding, or to develop attitudes and habits that foster continuing growth" (Emory University, R1) and "the broad area of student/faculty interaction for educational purposes" (Pittsburg State University, M1).

Nonstandard Practice

Of the 50 policies that detail what is included in the teaching category, 43 specify activities that are outside of the norm: curriculum development and the establishment of new, interdisciplinary, integrative, and team-taught courses (23, 53%); the development of new pedagogical techniques and pedagogical experimentation (12, 28%); the supervision of graduate and undergraduate research including the design of new lab experiments (10, 23%); attendance at workshops designed to improve teaching (7, 16%); writing about teaching, preparing innovative instructional materials, and learning aids (7, 16%); and the supervision of field trips, co-ops, internships, off-campus learning, clinical and field activities (4, 9%). Still less frequently cited are participation in study abroad (Agnes Scott College, B1), writing letters of recommendation (Saint Anselm College, B2), and maintenance of student library resources in their teaching categories (Elon College, M2).

Some institutions with graduate programs provide additional examples: developing postgraduate education programs and attracting graduate students (Georgia Technical University, R1), training and supervising teaching assistants (George Mason University, D2), mentoring graduate students (Northwestern University, R1), "stimulating the intellect of one's colleagues through disciplinary and interdisciplinary work" (Valparaiso University, M1), and grant-writing for instructional activities (Northern Kentucky University, M1).

Assessing Teaching

The AAUP provides relatively scant guidance on appropriate promotion criteria to evaluate faculty performance in research and service, but substantive recommendations on the evaluation of teaching. For example, in the "Statement on Teaching Evaluation" (AAUP, 1995):

> A judicious evaluation of a college professor as a teacher should include 1) an accurate factual description of what an individual does as a teacher, 2) various measures of the effectiveness of these efforts and 3) fair consideration of the relation between these efforts and the institution's and the department's expectations and support. (p. 134)

> Student learning, teaching performance, student perceptions, classroom visitation, self-evaluation, and outside

opinions should be a part of assessing the effectiveness of instruction. (pp. 134-135)

By far the most detailed and comprehensive criterion for evaluating faculty performance concerns the assessment of quality teaching. Seventy-eight (90%) institutions have promotion criteria to assess the quality of teaching. Of the 78 institutions with teaching criteria, 72 (92%) are teacher-focused, 65 (83%) are student-focused, and 33 (42%) are curriculum-focused.

Teacher-focused criteria. Seventy-two (92%) of the policies that provide examples of specific criteria that are used to assess teaching focus on skills and behaviors of the faculty member. Such criteria include the faculty member's knowledge of and expertise in their subject matter (44, 61%); presentation, communication, and organizational skills (41, 57%); conscientious preparation for all classes, and use of effective methodology and teaching techniques (29, 40%); ability to relate coursework to other fields and disciplines (17, 24%); willingness to evaluate their own learning situations and improve methods as a result of student input and continuous course evaluation (12, 17%); ability to communicate their own enthusiasm for their discipline and love of teaching (11, 15%); innovation, creativity, and experimentation in teaching (10, 14%); ability to establish and communicate course goals and requirements (7, 10%); and demonstration of personal and professional growth to students and faculty (6, 8%). In addition, Dickinson State University (B2) and Pacific University (M2) assess the degree to which faculty act as role models to students, and Montana State University (D2) evaluates the amount of recognition faculty receive for their teaching from peers and colleagues.

Student-focused criteria. Sixty-five (83%) institutions have teaching criteria that focus on the faculty member's ability to relate to students, inspire students, and increase student skills and understanding. Forty-five (69%) institutions evaluate faculty based on their ability to relate to students in and outside the classroom, including their respect for and rapport with students, concern for their academic progress, accessibility and flexibility in meeting student needs, and quality of academic advising. For example, Agnes Scott College (B1) requires that faculty "recognize the special needs of individual students and have a willingness and ability to meet them."

Thirty-three (51%) institutions evaluate faculty based on their ability to motivate, inspire curiosity, and stimulate the intellectual interests and enthusiasm of their students. For example, Georgia Institute of Technology (R1) wants to know: Does the faculty member inspire the students to do their best work? Marquette University (D1) states that teaching is evaluated on whether it "draws students to the power of invention and discovery," and the College of Charleston (M1) assesses whether teaching engenders in students "the intellectual curiosity to quest for knowledge."

Nine (14%) institutions assess the faculty member's ability to improve student skills including oral and written communication, problem solving, critical thinking, capability to reason, and analytical thinking skills. In addition to these skills, Saint Louis University (R2) requires that teaching contributes to the "growth and development of students to fulfill roles in society."

Seven institutions (11%) assess the ability of faculty members to engender student independence; four (6%) assess the faculty member's ability to expand students' content knowledge and contribute to their understanding of the subject matter; and four (6%) assess the faculty member's ability to teach students of different ages, and with varying capabilities and learning styles.

Still less frequent examples are whether faculty can stimulate advanced students to creative work and whether faculty have high standards for learning in their classrooms (University of California, Irvine, R1). Wiley College (B2) requires faculty to help all students to succeed in meeting course objectives.

Curriculum-focused criteria.   A third area of focus is curricular, found in 33 (42%) policies. Faculty are evaluated for their leadership in the development of new programs and courses (22, 66%); the preparation, scope, depth, and currency of course materials and learning aids (14, 42%); and whether course syllabi are well organized, well conceived, and well written (10, 30%). In addition, Santa Clara University (M1) assesses the quality and rigor of courses, Saint Norbert (B2) assesses the versatility of the faculty member's course offerings, and the Philadelphia College of Textiles and Science (M2) assesses the effective use of reference materials.

Documenting Teaching

One hundred seventy-nine (91%) FAPA policies instruct faculty members to use traditional means to document teaching including student evaluations, listing of courses, syllabi, peer evaluations, enrollment levels, number of students assigned to advise, hours assigned to advising, supervision of independent study courses, teaching awards and other forms of recognition, curriculum development materials, and development of textbooks.

Seventeen policies (9%) suggest or require unique documentation of teaching such as feedback beyond traditional end-of-course surveys. Santa Clara University (M1) requires faculty and/or their department chairs to collect evidence of student learning through representative samples of student papers, tests, and class projects. The College of Charleston (M1) collects feedback from 25 randomly selected recent graduates whom the faculty member taught. Brown University (R1) suggests that letters from students be included in the faculty member's teaching portfolio. North Carolina State University (R1) conducts student exit interviews and alumni surveys and includes information about each candidate from these sources. The University of California, Irvine (R1) solicits the opinions of graduates who have achieved notable professional success since leaving the university.

Other nonstandard methods for documenting teaching involve course development and pedagogy. For example, Tusculum College (M2) asks all faculty members to provide a description of the goals they have attempted to achieve in each course, methods employed to achieve these goals, and self-assessments of the extent to which they have been achieved. Duquesne University (D2) requests that faculty document the development of innovative pedagogical methods and materials and submit evidence of significant student learning as a result of their teaching. Southern Arkansas University (M2) includes tutorial work used in supporting instruction. Wiley College (B2) requires faculty annually to give evidence of a plan for advisory effectiveness. Southern Arkansas University (M2) reviews faculty members' written responses to student evaluations and to written comments. Georgia Institute of Technology (R1) documents faculty participation in programs, conferences, and workshops designed to improve teaching. MidAmerica Nazarene University (M2) suggests that faculty become participant-observers in their own teaching process by completing a self-report journal and videotaping their teaching throughout the semester. In addition, faculty publications on teaching and pedagogy are accepted as documentation of teaching.

DEFINING, ASSESSING, AND DOCUMENTING RESEARCH/SCHOLARSHIP

Defining Research/Scholarship

In the *Statement on Faculty Workload*, the AAUP (1995) warned that "lack of clarity or candor about what constitutes 'research responsibilities' can lead to excessive demands on the faculty" (p. 127).

Ernest Boyer's *Scholarship Reconsidered* (1990) has had a significant influence on the way in which higher education defines and evaluates faculty work, especially the category of research. Influenced by Boyer (1990), the AAUP is one of several national associations to advocate that colleges and universities expand their definition of research to include a broader consideration of scholarship. In *The Work of Faculty: Expectations, Priorities, and Rewards*, the AAUP (1995) makes the following recommendation:

> Research, generally understood to mean discovery and publication, should be related to a broader concept of scholarship that embraces the variety of intellectual activities and the totality of scholarly accomplishments.

Though discovery and publication are the core of scholarly endeavor, scholarship seen in its many forms offers a wider context within which to weigh individual contributions. (p. 131)

The AAUP supports a definition of research/scholarship that includes application, synthesis, and integration of knowledge, as well as new directions in pedagogy, and work in the creative and performing arts. Most colleges and universities in the archive reflect this way of thinking and label their "research" category as "scholarship." Other terms used to describe research/scholarship are research and publication, creativity and creative work or achievement, scholarly or artistic achievement, peer-reviewed publication, scholarly growth, academic achievement, knowledge of the discipline, contributions to advancement of knowledge, independent scholarship, achievement in the discipline or professional community, the scholarship of discovery, and continued learning in the discipline. The term "professional growth" is used as a synonym for the traditional category of research/scholarship at 26 (13%) institutions, meaning that institutions refer to categories of "teaching, professional growth, and service," and the definition of professional growth is identical to that of research/scholarship.

However, in 36 (18%) cases, "professional growth" is used to describe an additional category of faculty work. Policies refer to "teaching, research, service, and professional growth" where professional growth means involvement in activities which add to the intellectual development of the faculty member (e.g., attendance at workshops to improve teaching). In this way, professional growth is distinct from both research and service. This is outlined later in the chapter when criteria beyond teaching, research, and service are described.

Boyer's Scholarship

Boyer (1990) suggested that there were four expressions of scholarship: discovery, integration, application, and teaching. Several colleges and universities in the FAPA archive use Boyer's framework of multiple forms of scholarship to define faculty work. For example, West Virginia Wesleyan College (M2) states that "scholarship as defined at Wesleyan may take many forms including those described in the Carnegie Foundation's (1990) *Scholarship Reconsidered*. This 'scholarship expectation' is not intended to be code language for research and publication." While West Virginia Wesleyan College describes research/scholarship criteria as "continued learning," the activities listed in this category are consistent with Boyer's definition. Bethel College (B2) evaluates faculty based on a) scholarship that integrates faith and learning, b) research in one's discipline, c) applied research, d) integration research, and e) research on teaching. Similarly, Saint Joseph's College (B2) uses Boyer's four expressions of scholarship but then adds one additional area that is unique to Saint Joseph's, the "Scholarship of Core Lectures." This form of scholarship is "core lectures that provide professors with an opportunity to show the relevance of their discipline to the human search for meaning, communicate important insights from their field to nonspecialists, and make connections with other disciplines." The University of Louisville (R2) uses Boyer's four expressions of scholarship as its four categories of promotion criteria and notes that "unit policies may allow faculty to concentrate in one or two areas of scholarship for an extended period." Saint Norbert College (B2) includes the creation or discovery of new knowledge, the creation or discovery of new pedagogical techniques, the novel integration of preexisting ideas, and the application of theoretical knowledge to consequential problems. In addition, Saint Norbert looks at the process of scholarship as having three phases: self-development, productivity, and dissemination. Therefore, faculty are able to submit multiple forms of scholarship, in different phases of development, to meet their requirements for promotion in rank.

Of the 163 FAPA institutions that describe what is included in their teaching, research and/or service categories, 89 (55%) outline what constitutes research, including publications in or editing of academic journals, presses, and books; participation in professional associations; and papers delivered at conferences. However, 70 (79%) institutions have expanded research definitions to encompass Boyer's work. For example, additional areas of research found in FAPA policies include creative work (e.g., recitals, artistic creation, publicly demonstrated performance) (51, 73%); grant-writing, reviewing, directing (22, 31%); postdoctoral fellowships, academic awards, and honors (15, 21%); textbook publications and pedagogical publications (12, 17%); publication of research in nonacademic outlets including nonrefereed professional magazines aimed at segments of the general public and unpublished or scholarship in progress (11, 16%); incorporation of new disciplinary developments into courses or the development of experimental programs such as distance education (10, 14%); inventions, designs, innovations, and patents (9, 13%); innovative use of computers and the development of computer software (7, 10%); applied, theoretical or basic, and clinical research (5, 7%); initiation of new pedagogical methods (5, 7%); and keeping abreast in one's discipline including educational travel (4, 6%).

Fifteen institutions include what Boyer (1990) has called "the scholarship of application" within their research/scholarship section. Butler University (M1) provides a description of this kind of activity as "outreach to community that demonstrates professional expertise by communicating or applying knowledge in ways which benefit citizens outside the university." This form of scholarship is described as consulting with educational organizations, government and business agencies, and other nonacademic groups which contribute to the faculty member's professional development, enrich the discipline, and bring credit to the university. Agnes Scott College (B1) and Pittsburgh State University (M1) include collaborative work with students not necessarily leading to publication under their definitions of research/scholarship for promotion in rank.

Assessing Research/Scholarship

Seventy three (85%) institutions employ a wide spectrum of criterion to assess research, scholarship, and creative activity. Policies identify the following questions to assess the quality of faculty research/scholarship:

+ Is the faculty member's scholarship recognized and respected by peers and competent colleagues? (37, 51%)

+ Is the faculty member an active leader in professional activities? (32, 44%)

+ Does the faculty member's scholarship make a substantial contribution to the field? Is it significant? Is it of high quality? (26, 36%)

+ Does the faculty member have a broad, scholarly knowledge of his or her field? (15, 20%)

+ Is the scholarly work original and innovative? (9, 12%)

+ Is the scholarship broadly disseminated? (7, 9%)

+ Is the faculty member's research part of an ongoing program of study rather than an isolated project? (3, 4%)

+ Is the scholarship communicated effectively? (3, 4%)

+ Does the scholarship bring credit to the university? (2, 3%)

In the area of dissemination, California State University, Los Angeles (M1) looks not only at publication but also at computer designs, inventions, and other creative innovations, and assesses whether or not they have been adopted for professional use outside the faculty member's department. The University of North Alabama (M1) assesses effectiveness in planning for research and in the administration of research projects.

One criterion shared by four policies but not easily described is the "quality of the scholarly attitude." By the term "scholarly attitude," the University of North Alabama (M1) refers to the "capacity for independent thought, originality, contributions to knowledge, and creativity in approach to new problems." The University of Louisville (R2) describes this category as "contributing to human creativity," and Cleveland State University (D2) describes it as having a "working commitment to creative achievement." Finally, the Philadelphia College of Textiles and Science (M2) assesses whether the faculty member continues "to question, and investigate," as part of the appraisal of the scholarly attitude.

Documenting Research

Almost all (192, 98%) FAPA policies list traditional documentation for research, scholarship, and creative activity, including publications in scholarly journals and books, technical reports, grant applications, inventions, patents, presentation of papers at national conferences, and pieces of original artwork.

Four policies (2%) suggest nonstandard methods of documenting research and scholarship. For example, the University of Louisville (R2) includes works in progress and "those forms of activity which do not result in traditional documentary evidence" including oral and video presentations, interpretative work, creative art, and computer software. The University of Toledo (D1) requires documentation of contributions to the disciplines and the dissemination of scholarship through 1) the classroom, 2) among practitioners in the discipline, and 3) among a wider community. Finally, Tusculum College (M2) allows faculty to submit "descriptions of professional practice or of consulting which contributes to one's professional development and the enrichment of the discipline" as evidence of scholarship.

DEFINING, ASSESSING, AND DOCUMENTING SERVICE

Defining Service

Service is referred to in the FAPA policies as contributions to the general welfare of the university, public service, extension, outreach, university service, academically related service, professional service, contributions to the college, and administrative service. To some, service means university committee work; to others, it means involvement in community-based philanthropic activities. To avoid confusion over what is meant by the term "service," Lynton (1995) suggested that colleges and universities break the category of service into at least three components: disciplinary, university citizenship, and professional service.

In the FAPA archive, 87 (44%) institutions break the category of service into two or more components. The descriptions of service fall into the categories of service to students, university, disciplinary associations, the community without expertise, and the community with expertise. All 87 (100%) of the colleges and universities that break down the service category include university service. Service to the college/university means serving on or chairing committees, chairing departments, providing service to alumni and board of trustees, contributing to the intellectual life of the community, program development, student recruitment, and fundraising.

Thirty-eight (44%) institutions include service to students: nonacademic advising and counseling, participation in student events, sponsorship of student organizations, and the organization of activities that improve student life. Service to disciplinary associations, found in 26 (30%) policies, is holding leadership positions, reviewing conference proposals, and being a referee for granting agencies. Service to the community requiring no expertise is part of 38 (44%) policies. Leadership on nonprofit boards, civic associations, and churches are part of service to community requiring no expertise.

While 15 institutions include the scholarship of application, or professional service to the community involving academic expertise, under their scholarship category, 43 (49%) institutions list this same activity under service. Virginia Polytechnic Institute and State University (R1) describes this area of service as "entailing knowledgeable, professional applications and extensions of academic fields and specialties, grounded firmly in university purposes." The University of Arkansas (R2) notes that professional service is "intended to enhance the public understanding of the university or activities intended to develop the service function of the university." Professional service is further described as an activity that brings favorable attention to the faculty member and university; uses the faculty member's professional skills and training; can be funded or unfunded; contributes to the solution of problems faced by modern society; and enriches the life of the larger community served by the university. Descriptions of professional service and products of professional service include consulting and technical assistance, extension grants, extension publications, extension teaching, professional addresses to community groups, clinical activities, activities related to funding agencies, public policy and strategic studies, economic and community development, continuing education activities, field services, conferences, and seminars. The fact that 15 colleges and universities place professional service under the scholarship category and 43 place professional service under the service category may be reflective of the status of professional service as an emerging form of scholarship.

Assessing Service

Fifty-three (61%) policies contain criterion to assess service that fall into two categories: 1) community service, disciplinary service, and university citizenship; and 2) professional service. The primary criterion to assess the general category of service is the level of involvement. For example, Florida State University (R1) assesses service according to involvement, leadership, time, effort, and breadth. Santa Clara University (M1) assesses service by faculty dedication, initiative, and useful effort.

In addition to level of involvement, there are three other criteria identified by institutions to judge the quality of service: 1) whether the service effort brings favorable attention to the faculty member, department, university, and discipline; 2) whether it adds to the effective operation of the university; and 3) the extent or scope of the service. For example, Shepherd College (B1) assesses whether service adds to the positive image of the discipline, department, school, Shepherd College, and the state of West Virginia, and whether it contributes to the efficient administration of Shepherd College. West Virginia Wesleyan College (M2) evaluates the scope of the service by examining evidence of regular participation and active leadership in campus committees and community organizations.

Criteria used to assess professional service include qualified peer review, the use of academic and professional expertise, recognition in the professional field, the integration of the professional service with teaching and research, and the extent to which the programs are firmly grounded in the university's programs and the faculty member's role. For example, Virginia Polytechnic Institute and State University (R1) states that "it is important to show the professional quality of a candidate's achievements (in service) through qualified peer review." Elon College (M2) evaluates whether the service utilizes the faculty member's disciplinary expertise and experience. Pittsburg State University (M1) evaluates whether the service was performed "because of competencies relevant to the faculty member's role at the university."

Documenting Service

The typical documentation for service outlined in 190 (97%) FAPA policies includes lists of membership on university/departmental college meetings, participation in professional associations, professional service to community groups, testimony on professional matters, advising of student organizations, and service on boards. However, six (3%) FAPA institutions require deeper documentation.

Virginia Polytechnic Institute and State University (R1) suggests that faculty document their outreach through extension publications, applications for extension grants, contracts and awards, materials from seminars, programs, conferences organized or conducted, documentation of field services, strategic plans from economic and community development activities, and resource materials used in consultantships to public and private organizations. Montana State University (D2), University of Iowa (R1), and Saint Vincent College (B2) stress the importance of letters from peers and colleagues evaluating the quality of faculty service. Millikin University (B2) requires that each department list examples and/or provide case studies of faculty who have provided competent, excellent, and extraordinary service to the community. Faculty are asked to document how their work compares to these cases.

BEYOND THE "HOLY TRINITY"

To what extent is promotion based on categories of faculty work in addition to teaching, research, and service? Based, in part, on priorities established by institutional mission, 64 (33%) colleges (see Appendix 5-F) evaluate faculty on areas of faculty work beyond teaching, research, and service. These additional areas fall into four categories: personal and religious, professional growth, advising, and administrative/university-wide contributions. Sixty-nine percent of institutions with criteria for faculty work other than teaching, research, or service are baccalaureate and master's institutions; the rest are doctoral and research universities. The institutions which evaluate faculty based on personal and religious conduct and commitment were discussed previously.

Whereas the term "professional growth" is used as a synonym for the traditional category of research/scholarship at 26 institutions, in 36 other cases it is used to denote activities related primarily to the faculty member's professional development. In other words, 36 policies include the traditional categories of teaching, research/scholarship, and service, and, in addition, require "professional growth"—an area of faculty work that is distinct from the usual trinity. These 36 institutions require that faculty members participate in and make contributions to the activities of their professional associations, develop and maintain professional relationships, and contribute in a variety of ways to their disciplines. In-service study and attendance at professional meetings, as well as attendance at workshops and travel to improve teaching and scholarship, are included as professional growth. For example, Saint John's College (B1) requires candidates to develop a standing in their discipline/profession and show evidence that their "alertness and intellectual energy are respected outside the college."

Promotion policies also reflect that many faculty activities outside the classroom contribute to student learning. Whereas 174 policies state that advising is a part of teaching, 22 institutions evaluate faculty separately for advising effectiveness, accessibility to students, ability to counsel students in academic matters, engagement with students outside the classroom, special service to students, and any additional activities that enhance the teaching capabilities and proficiency of faculty.

In addition to teaching, research, and service, 15 polices specifically include administrative and institutional contributions.

This area of faculty work includes participation on faculty committees, administration of the department, other contributions to collegial governance, and overall development of the individual's program area. For example, Elon College (M2) includes a category that faculty should be "capable of undertaking institution-wide responsibilities which demonstrate understanding of the institutional mission."

QUALIFICATIONS FOR ASSOCIATE AND FULL PROFESSOR

The AAUP has no recommendations for the requisite qualifications for promotion from assistant to associate professor or from associate to full professor. Among FAPA institutions, 94 (48%) institutions describe higher hurdles for promotion to full professor. This does not mean that the remaining 102 (52%) institutions maintain the same general criteria for associate and full professor, it simply means that these 102 policies did not describe different standards in their policies and/or they provide autonomy for promotion committees and departments to make this distinction themselves.

Regardless of whether policies outline requisite qualifications for promotion to associate versus full professor, all policies imply that when faculty apply for promotion, they should show evidence that they have grown and achieved in all areas of evaluation since their last promotion. Also, all of the policies make statements that faculty are expected to have fulfilled the requirements for all ranks proceeding the rank for which they are applying.

Analysis reveals a total of four approaches used by institutions to differentiate between associate and full professors. While 65 institutions rely largely on a single approach to differentiate between associate and full professor, 29 use two or more approaches.

Higher Hurdles for Full Professors

Fifty-nine (63%) of the 94 institutions that describe higher hurdles for full professors use different "quality" adjectives to denote the levels of proficiency required for each rank. Adjectives such as "evidence of" versus "superior," or "competence in" versus "excellence," mark the different standards required for promotion to associate versus promotion to full professor for teaching, research, and service. For example, Le Moyne College (B2) requires associate professors to demonstrate "success in teaching" and full professors to demonstrate "superior teaching." Likewise, Hamilton College (B1) requires associate professors to document "teaching effectiveness" and full professors to document "eminence as a teacher." Cleveland State University (D2) requires that faculty be "fully competent teachers" for promotion to associate professor but have achieved "sustained excellence in teaching" for promotion to full professor.

The same approach is used to distinguish higher hurdles for full professors in the research/scholarship category. For example, while Walsh University (M2) requires associate professors to provide "evidence of research and publication," full professors must have "outstanding scholarship." Saint John's University (D1) requires associate professors to provide "evidence of scholarship" and full professors to achieve "distinctive achievement in scholarship." Similarly, Southern Illinois University, Carbondale (R2) requires faculty to provide a "record of peer-reviewed publication and or creative activity" for promotion to associate professor compared to "substantial peer reviewed publication . . ." for promotion to full professor.

Finally, the same approach is used for the service category. The University of North Alabama (M1) requires faculty candidates for associate professor to provide evidence of "effective service" and candidates for full professor to achieve "excellence in service." Southeastern Louisiana University (M1) requires candidates for associate professor to document "adequacy in service" and candidates for full professor to document "distinction in service." Emporia State University (M1) requires "involvement in university and professional service" for promotion to associate professor compared with "significant contributions to university and professional service" for promotion to full professor.

In a variation of this same approach, 15 institutions differentiate between the two ranks through an expectation for continuing growth or development at the associate level, and the fulfillment of that promise for full professors. For example, Montana State University (D2) notes that candidates for associate professor should have "a promise of excellence and potential for achievement in teaching, research, and service," while candidates for full professor should have "achieved a record of excellence in these three areas." San Jose State University (M1) requires that associate professors demonstrate "potential for leadership and promise of scholarly achievements" and that full professors show that this potential has been "realized and genuinely achieved."

One Category Versus All Categories

A second approach for distinguishing between the two ranks employed by ten of the 94 (11%) institutions is to state that candidates for promotion to associate professor must fulfill the qualifications in one category or another, while for full professor, candidates must satisfy the requirements for both or all categories. The University of Southern Colorado (B2) requires associate professors to document "significant accomplishment in teaching or scholarly activity," and full professors to document "significant accomplishment in both teaching and service and one other category." Taylor University (B2) requires candidates for associate professor to document service in two of the following areas: advising, faculty committees, administration of a department, or in the community, whereas candidates for full professor are required to document service in three of those areas.

Higher Numerical Values

Used by only two of the 94 institutions (2%), a third approach uses scores by requiring higher numerical values for promotion to the rank of full professor. For example, Arkansas Tech University (M1) requires a four or higher in teaching and a three or higher in other categories for associate professor, and a four in all categories or 5, 4, 3 or 5, 5, 3 in teaching, research, and service for full professor.

Extra Requirements

Finally, an approach used by 38 of the 94 (40%) institutions differentiates between associate and full professor by adding one or more extra criterion for promotion to full professor in the teaching, research, or service category. For example, Illinois Wesleyan University (B1) requires both associate and full professors to demonstrate "effective teaching" but, in addition, full professors must demonstrate "the ability to work with students at varying levels." Emporia State University (M1) requires that both associate and full professors demonstrate "excellence in teaching" and full professors must also demonstrate "leadership in creating an intellectual environment." Finally, the University of Mississippi (R2) requires both associate and full professors to achieve "quality teaching" but promotion to full professor requires an "extraordinary ability to stimulate in students a genuine desire for scholarly work."

The approach is used to differentiate between associate and full professors in the research/scholarship category at, for example, the University of Mississippi (R2) where promotion to associate professor requires establishing "a national reputation for scholarship" and "plans for future research." Full professors must demonstrate that they have fulfilled that promise and have "brought national recognition to the institution for their research." On top of this distinction, full professors are also required to have the "ability to direct the research of advanced students." Likewise, Manhattan College (M1) requires that associate professors demonstrate productivity "in some scholarly endeavor" and that full professors show evidence of "significant scholarly productivity." In addition to differentiating between the ranks in this way, the policy further stipulates that a full professor demonstrate "evidence that he/she has brought favorable notice to the college in the academic and professional world."

Regarding the service category, Central College (B1) requires associate professors to demonstrate "evidence of institutional service" and full professors to demonstrate "valuable institutional service." In addition, full professors must show "widespread recognition for distinctive performance" in the service category for promotion in rank.

Most often, the move from associate to full professor involves a move from adequate service to leadership in service, a move from significant scholarship to scholarship recognized by peers at the national level, and a move from effective teaching to teaching that reaches beyond the classroom to curriculum development, mentoring of other faculty, and pedagogical publications.

SUMMARY

Colleges and universities send an important message to faculty when they establish promotion criteria by communicating what the institution or department values and which faculty activities it rewards. The 196 promotion and tenure policies in the FAPA archive represent a broad continuum from standard practice to innovation in evaluation for promotion. One hundred twelve institutions have adopted the AAUP's suggestions to integrate institutional mission with promotion criteria. Ninety-one (81%) make explicit statements prioritizing teaching, research, or both, thereby integrating institutional mission through the weighting of promotion criteria.

One hundred sixty-three (83%) institutions define what is included in the categories of teaching, research, and service. Eighty-six (44%) institutions outline specific criteria for assessing the quality of teaching, research, and service. Twenty-four (12%) have innovative guidelines for documenting these and other categories. Sixty-five (33%) institutions evaluate faculty based on additional areas of faculty work, including personal and religious, professional growth, advising and student related, and administrative criteria. Finally, 94 (48%) institutions outline different criteria for promotion to associate and full professor.

Baccalaureate and master's institutions are slightly more likely (58% to 42%) to link mission and promotion criteria, outline criteria for evaluating teaching, research, and service (67% to 33%), and base promotion on categories in addition to teaching, research, and service (69% to 31%). As long as promotion remains a primary means by which institutions evaluate and reward faculty, promotion criteria will act as signs along the roadway, guiding faculty as they move through their careers. Signs cannot guarantee that no one will ever get lost, but they should help minimize the likelihood of wayward travel.

REFERENCES

American Association of University Professors. (1995). *Policy documents and reports* (8th ed.). Washington, DC: AAUP.

Boyer, E. L. (1990). *Scholarship reconsidered: Priorities of the professoriate.* Princeton, NJ: The Carnegie Foundation for the Advancement of Teaching.

Lynton, E. (1995). *Making the case for professional service.* Washington, DC: American Association for Higher Education.

APPENDIX 5-A

Faculty Must Advance the Spirit of the Institutional Mission for Promotion

Research 2 Institutions
1. Saint Louis University
2. University of Louisville
3. University of Notre Dame

Doctoral 1 Institutions
4. Marquette University

Doctoral 2 Institutions
5. George Mason University
6. Idaho State University
7. Wake Forest University

Master's 1 Institutions
8. Saint Mary's University
9. Santa Clara University
10. Springfield College
11. Valparaiso University

Master's 2 Institutions
12. MidAmerica Nazarene University
13. Tusculum College
14. Union College
15. West Virginia Wesleyan College

Baccalaureate 1 Institutions
16. Bethany College

Baccalaureate 2 Institutions
17. Asbury College (Religious mission)
18. Bethel College
19. Cedarville College (Religious mission)
20. Colby-Sawyer College
21. Culver-Stockton College
22. Dana College

23. Dillard University
24. Greensboro College
25. Le Moyne College
26. North Park College
27. Saint Francis College
28. Saint Vincent College
29. Taylor University
30. Wiley College

APPENDIX 5-B
Institutional Priorities Considered in Promotion Decisions

Research 1 Institutions
1. Brown University
2. Massachusetts Institute of Technology
3. Michigan State University
4. University of California, Irvine
5. University of Hawaii, Manoa
6. University of Iowa
7. University of Missouri, Columbia
8. University of Nebraska, Lincoln
9. University of Rochester

Research 2 Institutions
10. George Washington University
11. Rice University
12. Saint Louis University
13. Southern Illinois University, Carbondale
14. University of California, Santa Cruz
15. University of Mississippi

Doctoral 1 Institutions
16. Claremont Graduate University
17. Marquette University

Doctoral 2 Institutions
18. Indiana State University
19. Pace University
20. University of Detroit Mercy
21. University of Massachusetts, Lowell
22. University of New Hampshire
23. Wake Forest University

Master's 1 Institutions
24. Arkansas Tech University
25. Baldwin Wallace College
26. Bemidji State College
27. Bloomsburg University of Pennsylvania
28. California State University, Los Angeles

29. Chicago State University
30. College of Charleston
31. Eastern Illinois University
32. Fitchburg State College
33. Holy Names College
34. James Madison University
35. Manhattan College
36. Mankato State University
37. Millersville University of Pennsylvania
38. Northern Kentucky University
39. Norwich University
40. Saginaw Valley State University
41. Saint Mary's University
42. San Francisco State University
43. San Jose State University
44. Santa Clara University
45. Southeastern Louisiana University
46. Southeastern Oklahoma State University
47. Springfield College
48. University of Colorado, Colorado Springs
49. University of Hartford
50. University of Northern Iowa
51. University of Wisconsin, Superior
52. Valdosta State University
53. Valparaiso University
54. Villanova University
55. West Chester University of Pennsylvania

Master's 2 Institutions
56. Aquinas College
57. Elon College
58. MidAmerica Nazarene University
59. Philadelphia College of Textiles and Science
60. Southern Arkansas University
61. Tusculum College
62. Union College
63. Weber State University
64. West Virginia Wesleyan College

Baccalaureate 1 Institutions
65. Agnes Scott College
66. Hamilton College
67. Haverford College

Baccalaureate 2 Institutions
68. Albertson College of Idaho
69. Asbury College
70. Bethel College

71. Bloomfield College
72. Carroll College
73. Central State University
74. Coker College
75. Colby-Sawyer College
76. Dakota Wesleyan University
77. Dickinson State University
78. Greensboro College
79. Langston University
80. McMurry University
81. Millikin University
82. Mount Mercy College
83. Saint Anselm College
84. Saint Joseph's College
85. Saint Norbert College
86. Saint Vincent College
87. Shawnee State University
88. Taylor University
89. University of the Ozarks
90. Virginia Intermont College

APPENDIX 5-C

Strategic Planning Considerations for Promotion Decisions

Research 1 Institutions
  1. Florida State University
  2. Georgia Institute of Technology
  3. Michigan State University
  4. West Virginia University
  5. Virginia Polytechnic Institute and State University

Doctoral 2 Institutions
  6. Cleveland State University
  7. North Dakota State University
  8. University of North Dakota

Master's 1 Institutions
  9. University of Colorado, Colorado Springs

Baccalaureate 2 Institutions
  10. Colby-Sawyer College

APPENDIX 5-D

Institutions with Specific Criteria for Assessing Teaching, Research, and Service

Research 1 Institutions
  1. Columbia University
  2. Emory University

3. Florida State University
4. Georgia Institute of Technology
5. Johns Hopkins University
6. Northwestern University
7. University of California, Irvine
8. University of California, Santa Cruz
9. University of Iowa
10. Virginia Polytechnic Institute and State University

Research 2 Institutions

11. Auburn University
12. Saint Louis University
13. Southern Illinois University, Carbondale
14. University of Louisville

Doctoral 1 Institutions

15. American University
16. Illinois State University
17. Marquette University
18. United States International University
19. University of Toledo

Doctoral 2 Institutions

20. Clarkson University
21. Cleveland State University
22. Duquesne University
23. George Mason University
24. Indiana State University
25. Montana State University
26. University of Central Florida
27. University of Massachusetts, Lowell
28. Wake Forest University

Master's 1 Institutions

29. Bemidji State College
30. Bloomsburg University of Pennsylvania
31. Bowie State University
32. Butler University
33. California State University, Los Angeles
34. Chicago State University
35. College of Charleston
36. East Carolina University
37. Eastern Illinois University
38. James Madison University
39. Keene State College
40. Manhattan College
41. Mankato State University
42. Millersville University of Pennsylvania
43. Pittsburg State University

44. Saginaw Valley State University
45. Salve Regina University
46. San Francisco State University
47. San Jose State University
48. Santa Clara University
49. Southeastern Oklahoma State University
50. Saint Mary's University
51. University of Colorado, Colorado Springs
52. University of North Alabama
53. Valparaiso University
54. Villanova University
55. West Chester University of Pennsylvania

Master's 2 Institutions
56. Elon College
57. Pacific University
58. Philadelphia College of Textiles and Science
59. West Virginia Wesleyan College

Baccalaureate 1 Institutions
60. Agnes Scott College
61. Hamilton College
62. Haverford College
63. Shepherd College

Baccalaureate 2 Institutions
64. Asbury College
65. Bethel College
66. Cedarville College
67. Carroll College
68. Central State University
69. Colby-Sawyer College
70. Dakota Wesleyan University
71. Dickinson State University
72. Langston University
73. Greensboro College
74. Millikin University
75. Mount Mercy College
76. North Park College
77. Paine College
78. Saint Anselm College
79. Saint Francis College
80. Saint Joseph's College
81. Saint Norbert College
82. Saint Vincent College
83. Shawnee State University
84. Taylor University

85. Virginia Intermont College
86. Wiley College

APPENDIX 5-E

Nonstandard Documentation for Teaching, Research, Service, or Other Categories

Research 1 Institutions
  1. Brown University
  2. Emory University
  3. Florida State University
  4. Georgia Institute of Technology
  5. North Carolina State University
  6. University of California, Irvine
  7. University of Iowa
  8. Virginia Polytechnic Institute and State University

Research 2 Institutions
  9. University of California, Santa Cruz
  10. University of Louisville

Doctoral 1 Institutions
  11. University of Toledo

Doctoral 2 Institutions
  12. Duquesne University
  13. Indiana State University
  14. Montana State University
  15. University of Central Florida

Master's 1 Institutions
  16. College of Charleston
  17. Santa Clara University

Master's 2 Institutions
  18. MidAmerica Nazarene University
  19. Southern Arkansas University
  20. Tusculum College

Baccalaureate 2 Institutions
  21. Millikin University
  22. Saint Vincent College
  23. Wiley College

APPENDIX 5-F

Policies with "Other" Criteria for Promotion and Tenure

Research 1 Institutions
  1. Florida State University (Professional Growth)
  2. Massachusetts Institute of Technology (Administrative)

  3. North Carolina State University (Professional Growth, Administrative)
  4. University of California, Irvine (Professional Growth)
  5. University of Hawaii, Manoa (Advising/Student, Administrative)

Research 2 Institutions
  6. Auburn University (Administrative)
  7. George Washington University (Professional Growth)
  8. Saint Louis University (Personal/Religious, Advising/Student)
  9. University of California, Santa Cruz (Professional Growth)
  10. University of Louisville (Professional Growth)
  11. University of Notre Dame (Personal/Religious)

Doctoral 1 Institutions
  12. American University (Professional Growth, Advising/Student)
  13. Marquette University (Personal/Religious)
  14. Saint John's University, Jamaica, NY (Professional Growth)
  15. United States International University (Professional Growth, Advising/Student)

Doctoral 2 Institutions
  16. George Mason University (Personal/Religious)
  17. Idaho State University (Personal/Religious)
  18. Pace University (Advising/Student)
  19. University of Central Florida (Professional Growth)
  20. Wake Forest University (Personal/Religious)

Master's 1 Institutions
  21. Bemidji State College (Professional Growth, Advising/Student)
  22. California State University, Los Angeles (Professional Growth)
  23. Central Connecticut State University (Professional Growth)
  24. College of Saint Rose (Professional Growth, Administrative)
  25. Drake University (Professional Growth)
  26. Emporia State University (Professional Growth)
  27. Fitchburg State College (Professional Growth, Advising/Student)
  28. Georgia College and State University (Professional Growth)
  29. Hunter College, City University of New York (Professional Growth)
  30. Mankato State University (Professional Growth, Advising/Student)
  31. Saint Mary's University (Personal/Religious)
  32. San Jose State University (Professional Growth)
  33. Southeastern Oklahoma State University (Administrative)
  34. University of Southern Maine (Professional Growth, Advising/Student)
  35. University of Texas, El Paso (Advising/Student, Administrative)
  36. Valparaiso University (Personal/Religious, Professional Growth)

Master's 2 Institutions

37. Aquinas College (Advising/Student)
38. Elon College (Advising/Student, Administrative)
39. MidAmerica Nazarene College (Advising/Student)
40. Tusculum College (Personal/Religious)
41. Union College (Personal/Religious, Professional Growth, Advising/Student)
42. West Virginia Wesleyan College (Personal/Religious)

Baccalaureate 1 Institutions

43. Bethany College (Personal/Religious, Professional Growth, Administrative)

Baccalaureate 2 Institutions

44. Albertson College of Idaho (Professional Growth)
45. Asbury College (Personal/Religious, Professional Growth)
46. Bethel College (Personal/Religious)
47. Bridgewater College (Administrative)
48. Cedarville College (Personal/Religious)
49. Coker College (Professional Growth, Advising/Student, Administrative)
50. Colby-Sawyer College (Personal/Religious, Professional Growth, Advising/Student)
51. Culver-Stockton College (Personal/Religious)
52. Dana College (Personal/Religious, Professional Growth, Advising/Student, Administrative)
53. Dillard University (Personal/Religious, Professional Growth, Administrative)
54. Fairmont State College (Advising/Student)
55. Glenville State College (Professional Growth)
56. Greensboro College (Personal/Religious, Advising/Student)
57. Le Moyne College (Personal/Religious, Professional Growth)
58. North Park College (Personal/Religious)
59. Saint Francis College (Personal/Religious, Professional Growth, Administrative)
60. Saint Norbert College (Advising/Student)
61. Saint Vincent College and Seminary (Advising/Student)
62. Taylor University (Advising/Student)
63. University of the Ozarks (Professional Growth)
64. Wiley College (Personal/Religious, Professional Growth, Administrative)

6

AFTER THE BIG DECISION: POST-TENURE REVIEW ANALYZED

Cheryl Sternman Rule

HIGHLIGHTS

- 213 of 217 institutions (98%) in the Project on Faculty Appointments Archive provided policies on faculty evaluation.
- 192 of 213 policies (90%) are from institutions that grant tenure.
- 88 of 192 (46%) have post-tenure review.

Of the 88 Institutions with Post-Tenure Review

- 48 (55%) are public, and 40 (45%) are private.
- 78 (89%) conduct "cyclical reviews" of tenured faculty at intervals ranging from two to seven years.
- 37 (42%) conduct "triggered reviews"—triggered by poor performance or unsatisfactory annual or cyclical reviews, or at the request of an administrator or the faculty member under review.

- 27 (31%) conduct both cyclical and triggered reviews.

- 22 (25%) have purely developmental (formative) post-tenure reviews.

- 61 (69%) have post-tenure reviews that may result in administrative action (summative). Administrative action is defined as a reward, sanction, the creation of a faculty development plan, or the placing of an evaluation letter in the faculty member's personnel file.

- Five (6%) have hybrid post-tenure review policies, characterized by the institution as both "formative" and "summative."

- 38 (43%) may require the creation of a faculty development plan.

- 33 (38%) may impose sanctions in response to sustained unsatisfactory performance as documented in a post-tenure review.

- 12 (14%) may reward faculty for exceptional performance documented in a post-tenure review.

Table 6–1 The Sample

Carnegie Classification	213 Evaluation Policies	192 Tenure-Granting Institutions	88 Post-Tenure Review Policies	
			# of Post-Tenure Review Policies	% of Post-Tenure Review Policies
R1	18	18	8	44%
R2	16	16	6	38%
D1	9	9	5	56%
D2	17	17	7	41%
M1	59	56	30	54%
M2	13	13	6	46%
B1	26	25	8	32%
B2	55	38	18	47%

Key to Carnegie classification abbreviations: R1 = Research 1; R2 = Research 2; D1 = Doctoral 1; D2 = Doctoral 2; M1 = Master's 1; M2 = Master's 2; B1 = Baccalaureate 1; B2 = Baccalaureate 2 institutions.

Sample:

The Project on Faculty Appointments' 1998 Faculty Policy Archive (FAPA) CD-ROM contains policy provisions from the faculty handbooks of 217 randomly selected four-year colleges and universities stratified by Carnegie classification. Of these 217 institutions, 196 grant tenure. Of these 196, 192 (98%) provided sections on faculty evaluation for the CD-ROM. Of these 192, 88 (46%) have formal post-tenure review procedures. See Appendix 6-A.

INTRODUCTION

In the early 1980s, public demand for greater accountability from the academy led many states to consider mandating post-tenure review. In 1983, Committee A of the American Association of University Professors (AAUP) denounced post-tenure review as a threat to academic freedom and tenure. During the past two decades, controversy over both the necessity and propriety of such reviews has intensified on all fronts. The AAUP recently clarified and expanded its position; at the same time, the number of institutions adopting formal post-tenure review processes has continued to climb dramatically.

This chapter catalogs the post-tenure review policies of 88 four-year institutions and answers the following questions:

◆ How has the AAUP's position on post-tenure review evolved?

◆ How prevalent is post-tenure review in general, and how is it distributed across institutional type?

◆ How frequently and based upon what factors are such reviews conducted?

◆ What are the major categories of post-tenure review?

◆ What role, if any, do faculty development plans, sanctions, and rewards play in post-tenure review processes?

THE AAUP SPEAKS

The AAUP has never categorically endorsed the practice of post-tenure review. However, in the 15 years between 1983 and 1998, its position evolved significantly. In 1983, the association (1995) noted that post-tenure review "would incur unacceptable costs, not only in money and time but also in dampening of creativity and of collegial relationships, and would threaten academic freedom . . ." (p. 49). By 1998, the association expanded and clarified its original position, acknowledging the increased prevalence and broadening reach of post-tenure reviews. Preserving tenure and safeguarding academic freedom have remained the AAUP's primary concerns throughout the years, but the association now offers a set of standards "to assess the review process when it is being considered or implemented" by a growing number of institutions across the nation (*Post-Tenure Review: An AAUP Response*, 1998).

The following ten statements paraphrase the AAUP's "Minimum Standards for Good Practice if a Formal System of Post Tenure Review is Established," which appear in Part IV.B. of the 1998 *AAUP Response.*

♦ Academic freedom must be protected at all costs.

♦ Post-tenure review must not be a pretense for revisiting the tenure decision nor should the burden of proving "just cause" for dismissal shift from the administration to the faculty member under review.

♦ Faculty should play the primary role in developing and conducting post-tenure reviews, and the standard for appraisal should be the competent and conscientious discharge of one's duties.

♦ Post-tenure review should be developmental in nature, and institutional funds should be available to encourage faculty development and reward meritorious performance.

♦ Post-tenure review should be flexible based on discipline and career stage.

♦ Post-tenure review processes and outcomes should be kept confidential.

♦ A faculty development plan, if part of the review process, should be jointly designed by both the faculty member and the administration and should inspire a mutual commitment.

♦ Faculty members should be permitted to comment on and challenge the findings of their evaluations.

♦ In cases of severe and persistent underperformance, remedies should be mutually constructed and agreed upon; if they fail, faculty peers should be involved in any discussions of sanctions.

♦ The standard for dismissal should remain just cause, and the process must ensure ample procedural safeguards.

While we will not address these statements point by point, we will address several of the issues on which the association has taken a stand. In the course of this chapter, we will provide an indication of how closely institutional policies adhere to the AAUP's standard of developmental, peer-based post-tenure review.

PREVALENCE

A minimum of one-third of the institutions in each Carnegie classification have adopted a formal system of post-tenure review (see Table 6-1). In fact, more than half of all Doctoral 1 and Master's 1 institutions in the sample have such reviews. Post-tenure review is no longer an isolated phenomenon, nor is it confined to particular institutional types. Rather, it spans the spectrum from small, liberal arts colleges to large research universities in fairly equal proportions.

Given that post-tenure review was, at its inception, a response to the public call for greater accountability, one might expect the practice to be significantly more widespread among public colleges and universities than private ones. The two sec-

Table 6-2   Breakdown of Post-Tenure Review at Public and Private Institutions

I.	II.		III.		IV.		V.	
Carnegie Classification	Of 192 Institutions in Original Sample		% Private in Original Sample (n=192)		% Public of Those with PTR (n=88)		% Private of Those with PTR (n=88)	
	# Public	% Public	# Private	% Private	# Public	% Public	# Private	% Private
R1	14	78	4	22	8	100	0	0
R2	11	69	5	31	5	83	1	17
D1	5	56	4	44	4	80	1	20
D2	12	71	5	29	5	71	2	29
M1	37	66	19	34	23	77	7	23
M2	3	21	10	77	0	0	6	100
B1	2	8	23	92	0	0	8	100
B2	9	24	29	76	3	17	15	83
Total	*93/192 = 48%*		*99/192= 52%*		*48/88=55%*		*40/88=45%*	

tors are, in fact, more similar in this regard than one might surmise (see Table 6-2).

Looking at columns four and five in Table 6-2 (above), we see that at Research 1, Research 2, Doctoral 1, Doctoral 2, and Master's 1 institutions, post-tenure review is more prevalent at public than at private institutions. Yet at Master's 2, Baccalaureate 1, and Baccalaureate 2 institutions, the reverse holds true: Post-tenure review is more prevalent at private than at public institutions. Overall, the proportion of public institutions with post-tenure review is slightly greater than the proportion of private institutions with post-tenure review. Slightly more than half (55%) the total number of sample institutions with post-tenure review are public, and slightly fewer than half (45%) are private.

FREQUENCY

In addition to annual reviews, there are two other types of post-tenure review: those that occur on a fixed cycle (cyclical reviews) and those that are triggered by an event or an individual (triggered reviews). (These categories are informed, in large part, by Christine M. Licata and Joseph C. Morreale's working paper, *Post-Tenure Review: Policies, Practices, Precautions.* American Association for Higher Education, Washington, DC: 1997.)

Annual Reviews

Many institutions evaluate faculty each year, often for purposes of salary reviews. Such reviews may consist of a self-evaluation or a brief conversation with a department chair or dean. When such reviews occur routinely and across the board for all faculty, we have not considered them as meeting the definition of "post-tenure review." However, when tenured faculty also receive cyclical and/or triggered reviews, we have included them among the 88 institutions with post-tenure review.

Of these 88 institutions, 40 (45%) require that "faculty" or "all faculty" participate in some type of review each year (in addition to a more comprehensive cyclical or triggered review at another time). Annual reviews are generally based on materials the faculty members submit to their dean or department head. At the University of Alaska (M1), all faculty members produce annual "activity reports." At Culver-Stockton College (B2), tenured faculty members submit "an annual report . . . of the prior year's professional activities, scholarly achievements, pedagogical accomplishments, committee and college services, and services to the community." And at the College of Charleston (M1), "[e]ach faculty member shall present to his/her department chair a packet containing evidence that the criteria for teaching, research and development, and service have been met during the last calendar year."

Cyclical Reviews

We have categorized as cyclical any post-tenure evaluation that 1) occurs on a fixed cycle greater than one year, and 2) applies to all tenured faculty. The AAUP terms such evaluations "blanket" reviews because they do not target particular individuals and apply to all faculty regardless of prior performance (1998). Of the 88 FAPA institutions with post-tenure review, 78 (89%) conduct cyclical reviews.

Table 6-3   Cyclical Reviews

2 Years		3 Years		4 Years		5 Years		6 Years		7 Years	
#	%	#	%	#	%	#	%	#	%	#	%
1	1	10	13	6	8	28	35	7	9	3	4

In addition, 12 institutions (15%) review faculty at different intervals depending on rank. For example, Youngstown State University (M1) reviews tenured full professors every four years and all other tenured faculty every two years, and Rice University (R2) evaluates tenured associate professors every three years and tenured full professors every five years. Finally, 11 institutions (14%) preserve some flexibility in establishing their evaluation cycles by using the phrase "at least every [x] years." The peer review for tenured faculty at the University of Iowa (R1) takes place "at least once every five years." And at Dakota Wesleyan University (B2), tenured faculty members are evaluated "at least every three years," though they "may request to be evaluated on a more frequent basis." (See Appendix 6-C for a list of institutions with cyclical reviews.)

Triggered Reviews

Triggered or targeted reviews are those that occur not on a fixed cycle but on an as-needed basis. Suspected poor performance, an unsatisfactory prior review, or the request of a department chair or dean most commonly trigger these reviews. Such reviews, more often than not, supplement rather than supplant annual and/or cyclical evaluations.

Of the 88 institutions with post-tenure review, 37 (42%) employ triggered reviews. Of these 37, 21 trigger reviews due to poor performance, and 18 trigger reviews at the request of an administrator or a faculty member (two of the institutions fall into both categories).

Post-tenure review is triggered by an unsatisfactory prior review, for example, at Virginia Polytechnic Institute and State University, Valparaiso University, and Claremont Graduate University, among others. At Virginia Polytechnic Institute and State

University (R1), "[a] post-tenure review is mandatory whenever a faculty member with tenure or continued appointment receives two consecutive annual evaluations of unsatisfactory performance." At Valparaiso University (M1), a "further review" is triggered by "a determination of unsatisfactory performance" on annual evaluations. And at Claremont Graduate University (D1), where post-tenure review for full professors normally operates on a five-year cycle, more frequent (biennial) reviews are triggered by an unsatisfactory rating during the standard cyclical review.

At another group of institutions, post-tenure reviews are triggered not by a prior evaluation, but by a request from a faculty member, administrator, or department chair. At the University of Rhode Island (R2), where the typical review cycle for tenured faculty members is two to four years depending on rank:

> Upon request to the department chairperson by an individual faculty member, or upon the initiative of the department chairperson or dean, any faculty member shall be accorded a review during any year, whether or not such review falls within the department schedule.

Tenured faculty at Greensboro College (B2) are normally reviewed on a five-year cycle. Yet a "focused evaluation would be conducted at times when the faculty member is not scheduled for either a regular or a comprehensive evaluation" and "may be initiated by either the Vice President for Academic Affairs and Dean of the Faculty or the Academic Council, in consultation with the Division Chair." Finally, at Clarkson University (D2):

> . . . if a chair (or other academic administrator charged with conducting the annual conferences) feels that a tenured faculty member is consistently failing to fulfill the expectations associated with the faculty member's position, the chair may request that the president (or designee) convene a special review committee to assess the faculty member's performance.

The chair or other administrator at Clarkson "may not request a special review of a specific, individual faculty member more frequently than once every seven years." (See Appendix 6-D for a list of institutions with triggered reviews.)

In its 1998 response, the AAUP discusses the pros and cons of cyclical (or "blanket") and triggered (or "selective") reviews. The association notes that a cyclical review, which costs a great deal of time, money, and energy, nonetheless "reduces the stigma that may attach to faculty members" since all tenured faculty members must undergo such reviews on a regular basis. "Selective evaluation," on the other hand, "risks discriminatorily singling out of faculty members less well regarded for reasons that may or may not be related to professional performance." As noted above, several institutions make use of both evaluative structures, thus absorbing the pros and cons of each approach into a single, comprehensive post-tenure review system.

CATEGORIES

There are two main categories of post-tenure review: formative and summative. Our use of the terms formative and summative differs slightly from the definitions offered by both the AAUP and Licata and Morreale. For our purposes, a "formative" review is purely developmental and does not result in any administrative action. A "summative" review, by contrast, may have a developmental purpose, but may also result in administrative action. Administrative actions include rewards, sanctions, the creation of a faculty development plan, and/or placing the letter of evaluation in the faculty member's personnel file.

Of the 88 institutions with post-tenure review, 22 (25%) are clearly formative, 61 (69%) are clearly summative, and five (6%) are hybrids. (While our definition leaves little room for overlap, five institutions explicitly refer to their post-tenure review policies as both formative and summative.) The breakdown by Carnegie classification appears in Table 6-4. Within each classification, the percentage of summative post-tenure reviews far exceeds the percentage of formative post-tenure reviews.

Formative Reviews

Mount Mercy College and Pacific University are among those institutions with formative post-tenure review policies. At Mount Mercy College (B2), tenured faculty members submit materials to the vice president for academic affairs:

Table 6-4   Formative and Summative Post-Tenure Reviews

Carnegie Classification	Formative Review (n=22)		Summative Review (n=61)		Hybrid (n=5)	
	#	%	#	%	#	%
R1	1	13	7	88	0	0
R2	2	33	4	67	0	0
D1	0	0	5	100	0	0
D2	2	29	4	57	1	14
M1	10	33	19	63	1	3
M2	1	17	5	83	0	0
B1	1	13	6	75	1	13
B2	5	28	11	61	2	11

The review is completed with a conference of the faculty member, department chairperson (or division chairperson) and the vice president for academic affairs. The purpose of the conference is to provide feedback to the faculty member and discuss opportunities for future career development of the faculty member.

At Pacific University (M2), the post-tenure review consists of the following:

Every two years, the faculty personnel committee of the appropriate college or school should provide guidance in writing to tenured faculty regarding their record in meeting university expectations, and make suggestions as to how their performance and contributions to the university may be enhanced.

Formative reviews such as these have the clear purpose of guiding faculty members and assisting them in meeting their full potential. They do not mention, however, what should happen if a post-tenure review reveals deficiencies in production or performance.

Summative Reviews

In contrast, Georgia Institute of Technology, the University of Louisville, and California Lutheran University all conduct summative reviews of their tenured faculty. Such reviews have well defined consequences and can lead to rewards, sanctions, or other personnel or administrative actions. At Georgia Tech (R1), "where the review indicates outstanding performance," faculty members may receive "financial rewards and high development opportunities." Poor reviews at Georgia Tech require faculty members to design, with input from the chair and administrators, a development plan to correct deficiencies. Similarly, faculty members who fail to meet unit criteria at the University of Louisville (R2) shall also prepare "a development plan, including specific requirements to be met within a specified period." Disciplinary action may follow should the faculty member receive subsequent unsatisfactory evaluations. And at California Lutheran University (M1), unsatisfactory performance may lead to a further review and remedial activity, while exceptional performance may result in a letter of commendation, additional funds for development, or merit pay. In all three cases, as in the other 59 instances of summative reviews, consequences are clearly linked to the results of the review. (See Appendix 6-B for a list of institutions with formative and summative post-tenure review policies.)

FACULTY DEVELOPMENT PLANS

A total of 38 (43%) institutions use a faculty development plan as part of the post-tenure review process (see Appendix 6-E). At 13 (34%) of these institutions, the development plan serves not as a remedial tool to correct unsatisfactory performance, but rather as a goal-setting mechanism for all faculty members irrespective of performance. For faculty at Millikin University (B2), for example:

> At the end of each three-year growth plan, as part of the process of devising the next growth plan, each tenured and tenure-track faculty member will meet with his/her chair and dean to review the goals of the growth plan and the degree to which these goals were attained. This review carries special weight in tenure and promotion decisions, and, for tenured faculty, constitutes a thorough, periodic review.

At the other 25 institutions, a plan must be created in response to an unsatisfactory post-tenure review. Such plans generally incorporate one or more of the following components:

a set of goals for the coming year or review cycle, a list of remedies to correct unsatisfactory performance, and/or a timeline or
schedule of compliance. In many cases, these development
plans serve as the standard against which tenured faculty members are measured in subsequent reviews.

Among those institutions that use development plans to
help remedy poor performance are the University of Hawaii,
Manoa and Russell Sage College. At the University of Hawaii,
Manoa (R1), faculty members who do not meet "reasonable
expectations" confer with the department chair and dean in
order to create a professional development plan:

> Each plan must include: a) identification of deficiencies;
> b) objectives to address the deficiencies; c) specific activi-
> ties to implement the plan; d) timelines for meeting
> expectations; e) a process for annual progress review; f)
> source of funding (if required). (Procedures for Evalua-
> tion of Faculty at UH, Manoa, 1997, p. 3)

Similarly, if a post-tenure review at Russell Sage College (M1)

> . . . finds that the faculty member's performance is defi-
> cient in any of the areas of teaching and advising, schol-
> arship, or service, the vice president for academic affairs
> will meet with the faculty member for the purpose of
> designing a plan of action to remedy any deficiencies,
> with a timetable for the suggested improvements.

In both of these cases and in many others, the development plan
process, as well as the post-tenure review process in general,
includes a substantial degree of administrative presence, over-
sight, and involvement. Such planning processes generally
result from a process of "mutual negotiation" between administrators and faculty members, something the AAUP strongly recommends in its 1998 response (Part IVB, point #7).

Collaborative Development of Plans

In fact, of the 38 institutions with faculty development plans, 31
(82%) indicate that plans are designed jointly by the tenured faculty member and either an administrator or one or more mem-

bers of the review committee. Only at Austin College (B1) and Asbury College (B2) does the faculty member develop the plan on his or her own (and both of these plans are purely developmental; they are not designed to improve identifiably unsatisfactory performance). The policies of the remaining five (13%) institutions do not provide sufficient information to determine who is involved in the plans' design.

Time for Compliance

Of the 25 plans triggered by unsatisfactory performance, Colby-Sawyer College; Fitchburg State College; James Madison University; Texas Woman's University; the University of Arizona; the University of Colorado, Colorado Springs; the University of Louisville; and Valparaiso University specify firm timeframes within which faculty members must meet specified terms. At Colby-Sawyer College (B2), "the period of time for demonstrating improvement will last for one full academic year." Fitchburg State College (M1) requires annual evaluations for two years to address a plan's objectives and James Madison University (M1) gives faculty members two years to address performance issues. If these issues are not remedied, faculty must successfully complete an additional one-year remediation plan in order to avoid sanctions. At the University of Arizona (R1), "[i]n no case shall an improvement plan take more than three years to lead to satisfactory performance." And at Valparaiso University (M1), "[t]he affected faculty member will have a minimum of one (1) and a maximum of two (2) years in which these goals or outcomes could be accomplished."

In addition, nine institutions (Georgia Institute of Technology (R1); the University of Hawaii, Manoa (R1); the University of Nebraska, Lincoln (R1); Northern Arizona University (D1); Texas Woman's University (D1); Central Connecticut State University (M1); Russell Sage College (M1); Valdosta State University (M1); and Saint Joseph's College (B2)) require that all development plans include a "timetable" with a schedule of compliance during which a faculty member is expected to bring his or her performance up to par. Four institutions (North Carolina State University (R1), Middle Tennessee State University

(D2), California Lutheran University (M1), and Central College (B1)) continue to assess progress after one to three years to gauge general improvement (though not "compliance" with the plan per se). The policies of the final four institutions do not mention a timeline for compliance.

Funding

Of the 25 institutions that require compliance with a plan's terms and conditions, nine (36%) explicitly earmark funding or other resources for faculty members to meet their plans' conditions. At Colby-Sawyer College (B2), "support from the college will be provided." At Emporia State University (M1), the division chair may call for "provision for additional resources, where needed." At the Georgia Institute of Technology (R1), "[r]esources may be allocated to assist in faculty development." James Madison University (M1) "will provide funding for a focused program of activities designed to improve performance agreed upon by the department head and the faculty member." The University of Arizona (R1) "will make reasonable efforts to provide appropriate resources to facilitate the plan's implementation and success." The University of Nebraska, Lincoln (R1) provides "professional development support" and asks the unit administrator for the "resources" he or she "is willing and able to provide." Plans at Valparaiso University (M1) and the University of Hawaii, Manoa should identify the "source of funding" faculty members will need to meet their goals, and department heads at Valdosta State University (M1) identify "appropriate support for the approved plan."

In addition, funds may be available for general development activities at North Carolina State University (R1) and California Lutheran University (M1), but these funds are not necessarily tied to compliance with a development plan. At four institutions, the terms of the development plan are too vague to characterize, and the remaining nine institutions—Central College (B1); Central Connecticut State University (M1); Fitchburg State College (M1); Middle Tennessee State University (D2); Northern Arizona University (D1); Russell Sage College (M1); Saint Joseph's College (B2); Texas Woman's University (D1); the University of Colorado, Colorado Springs (M1); and the University of Louisville (R2)—make no mention of funding for development plan compliance.

At some of the institutions with development plans and at many without, a prolonged failure to improve performance comes with a price, namely, sanctions.

SANCTIONS

Of the 88 institutions with post-tenure review, 33 (38%) provide an explicit link to one or more sanctions (see Appendix 6-F). Such sanctions are generally triggered by prolonged, unremedied unsatisfactory performance. In most cases, sanctions are imposed only after a series of intermediary steps to improve performance has been thoroughly exhausted. The following list describes some of the sanctions imposed by various institutions in the FAPA sample: demotion in rank, denial of sabbatical privilege, ineligibility for promotion, loss of eligibility for travel funds, participation in career redirection program, placement in probationary position, reassignment of duties, reduction in salary, reprimand, revocation of tenure, salary freeze, suspension, and termination/dismissal. Nine institutions make oblique references to unspecified consequences such as "remedial action," "appropriate action," "adverse action," or "a resolution."

The University of Colorado, Colorado Springs (M1) considers a wide array of sanctions for faculty members who receive unsatisfactory post-tenure reviews. A faculty member who earns a rating of "below expectations" will first meet with:

> . . . members of the primary unit and/or the unit head to identify the causes of the unsatisfactory evaluation and to plan and implement a written Performance Improvement Agreement (PIA) to remedy their problems.

If the faculty member fails to meet the goals as agreed upon in the PIA, an "extensive review process shall be initiated." Such reviews occur only after a pattern of unsatisfactory performance, defined as "two evaluations of performance 'below expectations,'" has been established. Next, the parties create a faculty development plan:

> In cases where the development plan . . . has not produced the desired results, sanctions shall be imposed. Possible sanctions include: reassignment of duties; loss of eligibility for sabbaticals or for campus travel funds; salary freeze; salary reduction; demotion in rank; and revocation of tenure and dismissal.

At Claremont Graduate University (D1), a tenured full professor whose performance is deemed unsatisfactory in the course of a cyclical five-year review is then reviewed biennially:

> Following two or more consecutive unsatisfactory reviews by [the Appointments, Promotion, and Tenure committee], the dean may impose appropriate sanctions. Appropriate sanctions may include, but are not limited to, withholding salary increases, or denying sabbatical leave privilege.

Tenured faculty members at Idaho State University (D2) may find themselves out of work because of sustained poor performance. Cyclical reviews occur "at intervals not to exceed five years." At that time, if a faculty member's performance is questioned in writing by "(a) a majority of members of the department or unit, (b) the department chairperson or unit head, (c) the appropriate dean, (d) the vice president for academic affairs, or (e) the president," the faculty member may undergo a "full and complete review."

> If, following a full and complete review, a faculty member's performance is judged to have been unsatisfactory or less than adequate during the period under review, the faculty member may be recommended for dismissal or termination.

REWARDS

Twelve of the 88 institutions (14%) may reward tenured faculty when a post-tenure review reveals outstanding performance (see Appendix 6-G). Rewards may include letters of commendation, procurement of development funds, merit pay increases, increased sabbatical opportunities, or unspecified "rewards and recognition." At Montana State University (D2), the very "purpose of faculty review is to assess the quality of the faculty member's performance and reward performance that furthers the University's mission." At Valdosta State University (M1):

> Post-tenure review should help tenured faculty members improve their performance. One important means of achieving this objective is formally to recognize and adequately reward outstanding faculty accomplishments. The university will develop a reward structure that recognizes faculty excellence, supports distinguished faculty work, attracts and retains outstanding faculty, and enhances the academic reputation of VSU. Such a reward program should include, among other measures, the following:
>
> 1. Increased visibility for faculty achievements in teaching scholarship, and service
> 2. Substantial merit-pay increases that are in addition to those awarded through the annual evaluation process
> 3. Continuation, expansion, and support of course reassignment policy and an enhancement of the leave of absence program for the development of faculty scholarship, other creative professional activities, and teaching

North Carolina State University (R1) is similarly committed to "recognizing and rewarding exemplary faculty performance," as evidenced by post-tenure reviews. California Lutheran University (M1), Georgia Institute of Technology (R1), North Park College (B2), Northern Arizona University (D1), Santa Clara University (M1), and University of Louisville (R2) all consider awarding merit salary increases to reward outstanding tenured faculty performance. Overall, however, many more institutions make explicit their procedures for sanctioning underperforming tenured faculty than for rewarding those who excel.

SUMMARY

Controversy and suspicion often accompany institutions that modify traditional tenure policies. The proliferation of post-tenure review policies on campuses across the nation has proven no exception. It is important to keep in mind, however, the enormous variety of post-tenure review policies; post-tenure review on one campus may have little if anything in common with practices on another. The AAUP, which does not endorse the concept, accepts post-tenure reviews that are exclusively developmental and formative in purpose, well-funded, and faculty-initiated and implemented. Such versions of post-tenure review certainly do exist, but other institutions have adopted summative goals and the prospects of reprimands and sanctions. As with so many other aspects of American higher education, post-tenure review policies and practices reveal a wide array of locally determined variations on a basic theme: performance accountability for tenured faculty.

REFERENCES

American Association of University Professors. (1995). *Policy documents and reports* (8th ed.). Washington, DC: AAUP.

American Association of University Professors. (1998). *Post-Tenure Review: An AAUP Response.* [Online.] Washington, DC. Available: http://www.aaup.org/postten.htm.

Licata, C. M. & Morreale, J. C. (1997). Post-tenure review: *Policies, practices, precautions.* New Pathways Working Paper Series, no. 12. Washington, DC: American Association for Higher Education.

University of Hawaii, Manoa. (1997). *Procedures for evaluation of faculty at UH Manoa.* Manoa, HI: University of Hawaii, Board of Regents Bylaws and Policies.

APPENDIX 6-A
Breakdown of 217 Institutions in FAPA Archive

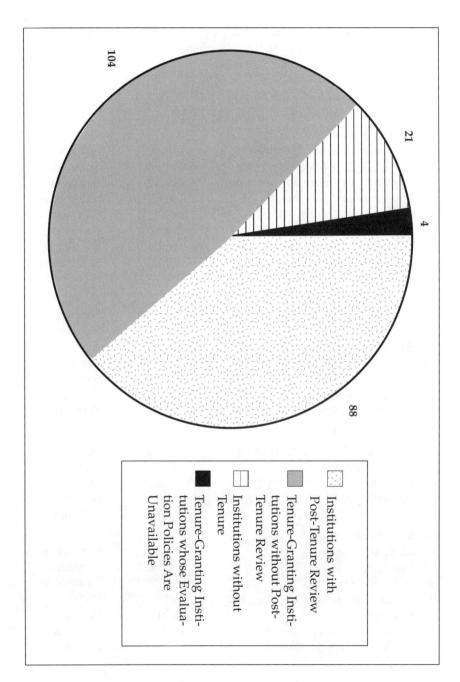

APPENDIX 6-B

List of Institutions That Review Tenured Faculty

(Institutions that review tenured faculty members annually as part of a faculty-wide evaluation process are only included on this list if a more formal system of post-tenure review—either cyclical or triggered—is also in place.)

Institution	Public or Private	Review Type
Research 1 Institutions		
1. Georgia Institute of Technology	Public	Summative
2. North Carolina State University	Public	Summative
3. University of Arizona	Public	Summative
4. University of California, Irvine	Public	Summative
5. University of Hawaii, Manoa	Public	Summative
6. University of Iowa	Public	Formative
7. University of Nebraska, Lincoln	Public	Summative
8. Virginia Polytechnic Institute and State University	Public	Summative
Research 2 Institutions		
9. Rice University	Private	Formative
10. University of California, Santa Cruz	Public	Summative
11. University of Delaware	Public	Summative
12. University of Idaho	Public	Summative
13. University of Louisville	Public	Summative
14. University of Rhode Island	Public	Formative
Doctoral 1 Institutions		
15. Claremont Graduate University	Private	Summative
16. Northern Arizona University	Public	Summative
17. Texas Woman's University	Public	Summative
18. University of Texas, Arlington	Public	Summative
19. University of Toledo	Public	Summative
Doctoral 2 Institutions		
20. Clarkson University	Private	Summative
21. Duquesne University	Private	Formative
22. Idaho State University	Public	Summative
23. Middle Tennessee State University	Public	Both
24. Montana State University	Public	Formative
25. North Dakota State University	Public	Summative
26. University of North Dakota,	Public	Summative
Master's 1 Institutions		
27. Bemidji State College	Public	Formative

28. Bloomsburg University of Pennsylvania	Public	Formative
29. California Lutheran University	Private	Summative
30. California State University, Los Angeles	Public	Summative
31. Central Connecticut State University	Public	Summative
32. College of Charleston	Public	Formative
33. Emporia State University	Public	Summative
34. Fitchburg State College	Public	Summative
35. Holy Names College	Private	Formative
36. James Madison University	Public	Summative
37. Keene State College	Public	Summative
38. Mankato State University	Public	Formative
39. Millersville University of Pennsylvania	Public	Formative
40. Russell Sage College	Private	Summative
41. Saint Mary's University	Private	Formative
42. San Francisco State University	Public	Summative
43. San Jose State University	Public	Both
44. Santa Clara University	Private	Summative
45. Southeastern Oklahoma State University	Public	Summative
46. University of Alaska	Public	Summative
47. University of Colorado, Colorado Springs	Public	Summative
48. University of Southern Maine	Public	Summative
49. University of Texas, El Paso	Public	Summative
50. University of Texas, Pan American	Public	Summative
51. University of Wisconsin, Superior	Public	Summative
52. Valdosta State University	Public	Summative
53. Valparaiso University	Private	Summative
54. West Chester University of Pennsylvania	Public	Formative
55. Whitworth College	Private	Formative
56. Youngstown State University	Public	Formative

Master's 2 Institutions

57. Aquinas College	Private	Summative
58. Drury College	Private	Summative
59. Elon College	Private	Summative
60. Pacific University	Private	Formative
61. Tusculum College	Private	Summative
62. West Virginia Wesleyan College	Private	Summative

Baccalaureate 1 Institutions

63. Agnes Scott College	Private	Summative

64. Austin College	Private	Both
65. Beloit College	Private	Summative
66. Central College	Private	Summative
67. Coe College	Private	Formative
68. Davidson College	Private	Summative
69. Haverford College	Private	Summative
70. Hendrix College	Private	Summative

Baccalaureate 2 Institutions

71. Albertson College of Idaho	Private	Summative
72. Asbury College	Private	Formative
73. Colby-Sawyer College	Private	Both
74. Culver-Stockton College	Private	Summative
75. Dakota Wesleyan University	Private	Summative
76. Dickinson State University	Public	Summative
77. Greensboro College	Private	Summative
78. Mayville State University	Public	Summative
79. Millikin University	Private	Summative
80. Mount Mercy College	Private	Formative
81. North Park College	Private	Formative
82. Saint Francis College	Private	Summative
83. Saint Joseph's College	Private	Summative
84. Saint Norbert College	Private	Formative
85. Taylor University	Private	Both
86. University of Southern Colorado	Public	Formative
87. Virginia Intermont College	Private	Summative
88. Wiley College	Private	Summative

APPENDIX 6-C

Institutions with Cyclical Post-Tenure Reviews

Every Two Years

| 1. Pacific University | Master's 2 | Private |

Every Three Years

2. College of Charleston	Master's 1	Public
3. Culver-Stockton College	Baccalaureate 2	Private
4. Dickinson State University	Baccalaureate 2	Public
5. Drury College (tenured full professors)	Master's 2	Private
6. Mayville State University	Baccalaureate 2	Public
7. Millikin University	Baccalaureate 2	Private
8. North Dakota State University	Doctoral 2	Public
9. Southeastern Oklahoma State University	Master's 1	Public
10. University of North Dakota	Doctoral 2	Public
11. Whitworth College	Master's 1	Private

Every Four Years

12. Coe College	Baccalaureate 1	Private
13. Cleveland State University	Doctoral 2	Public
14. Mount Mercy College	Baccalaureate 2	Private
15. North Park College	Baccalaureate 2	Private
16. University of Southern Maine	Master's 1	Public
17. Virginia Intermont College	Baccalaureate 2	Private

Every Five Years

18. Agnes Scott College	Baccalaureate 1	Private
19. Albertson College of Idaho	Baccalaureate 2	Private
20. Asbury College	Baccalaureate 2	Private
21. Austin College (every five to six years)	Baccalaureate 1	Private
22. Bloomsburg University of Pennsylvania	Master's 1	Public
23. California Lutheran University	Master's 1	Private
24. Central College	Baccalaureate 1	Private
25. Claremont Graduate University	Doctoral 1	Private
26. Elon College	Master's 2	Private
27. Georgia Institute of Technology	Research 1	Public
28. Hendrix College	Baccalaureate 1	Private
29. Holy Names College	Master's 1	Private
30. Millersville University of Pennsylvania	Master's 1	Public
31. Northern Arizona University (Dean's Level Audit)	Doctoral 1	Public
32. Russell Sage College	Master's 1	Private
33. Saint Francis College	Baccalaureate 2	Private
34. Saint Joseph's College	Baccalaureate 2	Private
35. Saint Norbert College	Baccalaureate 2	Private
36. San Francisco State University	Master's 1	Public
37. San Jose State University	Master's 1	Public
38. Tusculum College	Master's 2	Private
39. University of Arizona (Dean's Level Audit)	Research 1	Public
40. University of Louisville	Research 2	Public
41. University of Toledo	Doctoral 1	Public
42. University of Wisconsin, Superior	Master's 1	Public
43. Valdosta State University	Master's 1	Public
44. West Chester University of Pennsylvania	Master's 1	Public
45. Wiley College	Baccalaureate 2	Private

Every Six Years

46. Central Connecticut State University	Master's 1	Public
47. James Madison University (at the time of full program review)	Master's 1	Public

48. Texas Woman's University	Doctoral 1	Public
49. University of Texas, Arlington	Doctoral 1	Public
50. University of Texas, El Paso	Master's 1	Public
51. University of Texas, Pan American	Master's 1	Public
52. West Virginia Wesleyan College	Master's 2	Private

Every Seven Years

53. Aquinas College	Master's 2	Private
54. Davidson College	Baccalaureate 1	Private

    (the first post-tenure review is five years after tenure; subsequent reviews are every seven years)

55. Taylor University	Baccalaureate 2	Private

At Least Every [X] Years

56. Beloit College	Baccalaureate 1	Private

    (at least every six years)

57. California State University, Los Angeles	Master's 1	Public

    (reviews at intervals "no greater than five years")

58. Colby-Sawyer College	Baccalaureate 2	Private

    ("at least once every five years")

59. Dakota Wesleyan University	Baccalaureate 2	Private

    ("at least every three years")

60. Greensboro College	Baccalaureate 2	Private

    ("at least once every five years")

61. Idaho State University	Doctoral 2	Public

    ("at intervals not to exceed five years")

62. Saint Mary's University	Master's 1	Private

    ("at least once every six years")

63. University of Alaska	Master's 1	Public

    ("not less frequently than every three years")

64. University of Colorado, Colorado Springs	Master's 1	Public

    Colorado Springs ("at least once every five to seven years")

65. University of Hawaii, Manoa	Master's 1	Public

    ("at least once every five years")

66. University of Idaho	Research 2	Public

    ("at intervals not to exceed five years")

Duplicate Categories

67. Bemidji State College	Master's 1	Public

    (every four years for tenured faculty below the rank of professor; tenured full professors submit summaries every two years)

68. Keene State College	Master's 1	Public

    (every two years for tenured assistant and associate professors applying for promotion; every five years for all other tenured faculty)

69. Mankato State University   Master's 1   Public
    (every four years for tenured faculty below the rank of professor;
    tenured full professors submit summaries every two years)
70. North Carolina State University   Research 1   Public
    (no less than every three years for tenured associate professors; no
    less than every five years for professors)
71. Rice University   Research 2   Private
    (every five years for full professors)
72. Santa Clara University   Master's 1   Private
    (three years for tenured faculty, but tenured full professors have a
    five-year option)
73. University of California, Irvine   Research 1   Public
    (reviews may occur every two, three, or four years depending on
    rank and step)
74. University of California, Santa Cruz   Research 2   Public
    (reviews may occur every two, three, or four years depending on
    rank and step)
75. University of Delaware   Research 2   Public
    (tenured associate professors on a three to five-year cycle; tenured
    full professors on a five to seven-year cycle)
76. University of Iowa   Research 1   Public
    (tenured associate professors are reviewed by the dean and depart-
    mental executive officer and at least every seven years by depart-
    mental full professors; full professors are evaluated at least once
    every five years)
77. University of Rhode Island   Research 2   Public
    (every two years for assistant and associate professors; every four
    years for full professors)
78. Youngstown State University   Master's 1   Public
    (every three years for tenured faculty; every four years for
    tenured full professors)

APPENDIX 6-D
Institutions with Triggered Post-Tenure Reviews

(Reviews may be triggered by an unsatisfactory prior review or at the
request of a department chair, dean, other administrator, or the faculty
member.)

Research 1 Institutions
   1. University of Hawaii, Manoa   Public
   2. University of Nebraska, Lincoln   Public

3. Virginia Polytechnic Institute   Public
   and State University

Research 2 Institutions
4. Rice University   Private
5. University of Idaho   Public
6. University of Louisville   Public
7. University of Rhode Island   Public

Doctoral 1 Institutions
8. Claremont Graduate University   Private
9. University of Texas, Arlington   Public

Doctoral 2 Institutions
10. Clarkson University   Private
11. Duquesne University   Private
12. Idaho State University   Public
13. Middle Tennessee State University   Public
14. Montana State University   Public

Master's 1 Institutions
15. Bloomsburg University of Pennsylvania   Public
16. California Lutheran University   Private
17. Central Connecticut State University   Public
18. Emporia State University   Public
19. Fitchburg State College   Public
20. Keene State College   Public
21. Millersville University of Pennsylvania   Public
22. San Jose State University   Public
23. Southeastern Oklahoma State University   Public
24. University of Colorado, Colorado Springs   Public
25. University of Southern Maine   Public
26. University of Texas, El Paso   Public
27. University of Texas, Pan American   Public
28. Valparaiso University   Private
29. West Chester University of Pennsylvania   Public
30. Whitworth College   Private

Master's 2 Institutions
31. Tusculum College   Private

Baccalaureate 1 Institutions
32. Central College   Private
33. Haverford College   Private

Baccalaureate 2 Institutions
34. Albertson College of Idaho   Private
35. Greensboro College   Private

| 36. Taylor University | Private |
| 37. University of Southern Colorado | Public |

APPENDIX 6-E
Institutions That May Use Faculty Development
Plans as Part of the Post-Tenure Review Process

Research 1 Institutions

1. Georgia Institute of Technology	Public
2. North Carolina State University	Public
3. University of Arizona	Public
4. University of Hawaii, Manoa	Public
5. University of Nebraska, Lincoln	Public

Research 2 Institutions

| 6. University of Louisville | Public |

Doctoral 1 Institutions

| 7. Northern Arizona University | Public |
| 8. Texas Woman's University | Public |

Doctoral 2 Institutions

9. Middle Tennessee State University	Public
10. North Dakota State University	Public
11. University of North Dakota	Public

Master's 1 Institutions

12. Bemidji State College	Public
13. California Lutheran University	Private
14. Central Connecticut State University	Public
15. Emporia State University	Public
16. Fitchburg State College	Public
17. James Madison University	Public
18. Mankato State University	Public
19. Russell Sage College	Private
20. Santa Clara University	Private
21. University of Colorado, Colorado Springs	Public
22. Valdosta State University	Public
23. Valparaiso University	Private

Master's 2 Institutions

24. Drury College	Private
25. Elon College	Private
26. West Virginia Wesleyan College	Private

Baccalaureate 1 Institutions
| 27. Austin College | Private |
| 28. Central College | Private |

Baccalaureate 2 Institutions
29. Asbury College	Private
30. Colby-Sawyer College	Private
31. Culver-Stockton College	Private
32. Dickinson State University	Public
33. Greensboro College	Private
34. Mayville State University	Public
35. Millikin University	Private
36. Saint Joseph's College	Private
37. Taylor University	Private
38. Wiley College	Private

APPENDIX 6-F

Institutions That May Sanction Faculty for Sustained, Unremedied Unsatisfactory Performance on a Post-Tenure Review

Research 1 Institutions

1. Georgia Institute of Technology (public)
   Possible sanction(s): recommendation for termination/ dismissal
2. North Carolina State University (public)
   Possible sanction(s): "appropriate sanctions which may, in the most serious cases, include a recommendation for discharge"
3. University of Arizona (public)
   Possible sanction(s): recommendation for termination/dismissal (for failure to achieve the goals of the Development Plan)
4. University of Nebraska, Lincoln (public)
   Possible sanction(s): implementation of "those administrative processes defined by the Regent's By-Laws."
5. Virginia Polytechnic and State University (public)
   Possible sanction(s): demotion in rank, reduction in salary, revocation of tenure, suspension, recommendation for termination/ dismissal

Research 2 Institutions

6. University of Idaho (public)
   Possible sanction(s): recommendation for termination/ dismissal
7. University of Louisville (public)
   Possible sanction(s): "appropriate disciplinary action"

Doctoral 1 Institutions
  8. Claremont Graduate University (private)
      Possible sanction(s): denial of sabbatical privilege, withholding of salary increases, recommendation for termination/dismissal
  9. Northern Arizona University (public)
      Possible sanction(s): recommendation for termination/dismissal
  10. Texas Woman's University (public)
      Possible sanction(s): "appropriate disciplinary action which might include revocation of tenure and/or employment"
  11. University of Texas, Arlington (public)
      Possible sanction(s): "appropriate action, which may include remediation efforts or additional action under Board of Regents Rules"; recommendation for termination
  12. University of Toledo (public)
      Possible sanction(s): "adverse action"

Doctoral 2 Institutions
  13. Idaho State University (public)
      Possible sanction(s): recommendation for termination/dismissal
  14. North Dakota State University (public)
      Possible sanction(s): "appropriate remedial action" or initiation of dismissal for cause proceedings
  15. University of North Dakota (public)
      Possible sanction(s): "appropriate remedial action" or initiation of dismissal for cause proceedings

Master's 1 Institutions
  16. California Lutheran University (private)
      Possible sanction(s): recommendation for a salary freeze or readjustment, revocation of tenure, reassignment or initiation of dismissal for cause
  17. Central Connecticut State College (public)
      Possible sanction(s): potential invoking of policy section on "Reprimand, Suspension, and Termination"
  18. Emporia State University (public)
      Possible sanction(s): recommendation for dismissal
  19. Fitchburg State College (public)
      Possible sanction(s): "personnel action" as may be recommended by the department chair and/or president
  20. James Madison University (public)
      Possible sanction(s): reduction in salary, loss of tenure, termination
  21. Russell Sage College (private)
      Possible sanction(s): potential initiation of dismissal for cause proceedings

22. Southeastern Oklahoma State University (public)
    Possible sanction(s): dismissal
23. University of Colorado, Colorado Springs (public)
    Possible sanction(s): reassignment of duties, loss of eligibility for
    sabbaticals or for campus travel funds, salary freeze, salary reduc-
    tion, demotion in rank, revocation of tenure, dismissal
24. University of Texas, El Paso (public)
    Possible sanction(s): "appropriate action, which may include reme-
    diation efforts or additional action under Board of Regents Rules";
    recommendation for termination
25. University of Texas, Pan American (public)
    Possible sanction(s): "appropriate action, which may include reme-
    diation efforts or additional action under Board of Regents Rules";
    recommendation for termination
26. Valdosta State University (public)
    Possible sanction(s): potential initiation of sanctions or dismissal
    proceedings due to incompetent performance
27. Valparaiso University (private)
    Possible sanction(s): "a resolution," recommendation for termina-
    tion

Baccalaureate 2 Institutions
28. Albertson College of Idaho (private)
    Possible sanction(s): a tenure review (which may result in initia-
    tion of procedures for dismissal for cause)
29. Colby-Sawyer College (private)
    Possible sanction(s): participation in the College's Career Redirec-
    tion Program, termination of tenure and issuance of one-year con-
    tracts, termination of tenure after an additional year of service,
    suspension
30. Dickinson State University (public)
    Possible sanction(s): "appropriate remedial action" or initiation of
    dismissal for cause proceedings
31. Mayville State University (public)
    Possible sanction(s): "appropriate remedial action" or initiation of
    dismissal for cause proceedings
32. Taylor University (private)
    Possible sanction(s): placement in a probationary position
33. Wiley College (private)
    Possible sanction(s): freeze on salary and promotion,
    termination (after failing to show professional growth for seven
    years)

APPENDIX 6–G
Institutions That May Reward Faculty for Favorable or Outstanding Performance on a Post-Tenure Review

Research 1 Institutions

1. Georgia Institute of Technology (public)
   Possible reward: Institute will consider special merit pay increases and study and research leave opportunities.
2. North Carolina State University (public)
   Possible reward: University may recognize and reward exemplary faculty performance.
3. University of Arizona
   Possible reward: Faculty will be eligible for salary increases and other rewards which may exist or be established.

Research 2 Institutions

4. University of Louisville (public)
   Possible reward: Faculty may receive Performance Based Salary Increase awards as a supplementary salary increase.

Doctoral 1 Institutions

5. Northern Arizona University (public)
   Possible reward: Faculty may be eligible for merit pay increases.

Doctoral 2 Institutions

6. Montana State University (public)
   Possible reward: University may reward faculty performance that furthers its mission.

Master's 1 Institutions

7. California Lutheran University (private)
   Possible reward: Committee may recommend that the faculty member receive a letter of commendation, additional faculty development funds for scholarly activities, or a merit pay increase.
8. Santa Clara University (private)
   Possible reward: University may award merit raises depending on evaluation score.
9. University of Wisconsin, Superior (public)
   Possible reward: University will engage the "merit process and faculty review and development process to facilitate, enhance, and reward outstanding performance."
10. Valdosta State University (public)
    Possible reward: Faculty with three or more outstanding evaluations may be considered as candidates for reward and recognition. The University may also provide increased visibility for faculty achievements, substantial merit pay increases above and beyond

those awarded in the annual review process, "continuation, expansion, and support of course reassignment policy," and "an enhancement of the leave of absence program."

11. Valparaiso University (private)

Possible reward: University may provide resources for faculty who continue to do good work.

Baccalaureate 2 Institutions

12. North Park College (private)

Possible reward: Reviews provide a basis for merit increases for tenured faculty.

7

THE CONSEQUENCES OF MISBEHAVIOR: A CLOSER LOOK AT DISMISSAL FOR CAUSE AND LESSER SANCTIONS

Cheryl Sternman Rule

HIGHLIGHTS

Causes for Dismissal and/or Sanctions

◆ 192 (98%) of 196 tenure-granting institutions in the FAPA CD-ROM have policies on sanctions and/or dismissal for cause.

◆ 121 (63%) of 192 cite incompetence as adequate cause for dismissal or sanctions.

◆ 105 (55%) cite neglect of duty.

◆ 64 (33%) cite moral turpitude.

◆ 57 (30%) cite criminal behavior or conviction.

◆ 44 (23%) cite performance-related conduct.

◆ 43 (22%) cite misconduct.

◆ 36 (19%) cite misrepresentation and/or falsification of documents.

- ◆ 35 (18%) cite other forms of dishonesty.
- ◆ 27 (14%) cite unethical behavior.
- ◆ 25 (13%) cite violations of policy, and 14 (7%) cite violations of the rights of others.
- ◆ 22 (11%) cite personal conduct that impairs one's duties.

Types of Sanctions

- ◆ 52 (27%) institutions cite suspension as a possible sanction.
- ◆ 41 (21%) cite oral or written reprimands.
- ◆ 24 (13%) cite salary-related sanctions.
- ◆ 17 (9%) cite reassignment of duties.
- ◆ 15 (8%) cite demotion in rank.
- ◆ 14 (7%) cite removal of privileges, benefits, or perks.
- ◆ 13 (7%) cite warnings.

Sample:

The Project on Faculty Appointments' 1998 Faculty Policy Archive (FAPA) CD-ROM contains policy provisions from the

Table 7-1 The Sample

Carnegie Classification	217 Policy Provisions	196 Grant Tenure	192 Provided Information on Dismissal for Cause and/or Lesser Sanctions	
			#	%
R1	21	21	20	95%
R2	16	16	16	100%
D1	10	10	10	100%
D2	17	17	17	100%
M1	59	56	56	100%
M2	13	13	12	92%
B1	26	25	24	96%
B2	55	38	37	97%

Key to Carnegie classification abbreviations: R1 = Research 1; R2 = Research 2; D1 = Doctoral 1; D2 = Doctoral 2; M1 = Master's 1; M2 = Master's 2; B1 = Baccalaureate 1; B2 = Baccalaureate 2.

faculty handbooks of 217 randomly selected four-year colleges and universities stratified by Carnegie classification. Of these 217 institutions, 196 grant tenure. Of these 196, 192 (98%) provided information on dismissal for cause and/or lesser sanctions for inclusion on the CD-ROM.

INTRODUCTION

Just cause, a concept commonly applied in legal circles, appears just as widely in faculty handbooks. Unless an administration can prove "just" or "adequate" cause, faculty members, particularly those with tenure, can rarely be dismissed or sanctioned. But how is "cause" defined? And what exactly do the nebulous terms "just" and "adequate" mean in the context of faculty employment? Not surprisingly, institutional interpretations of cause vary enormously. Acceptable behavior at one institution may prove wholly unacceptable at another. Actions that merit a minor reprimand here may result in dismissal there. And all the while, institutions apply the broad rubric of "cause" when determining how to handle various misdeeds.

This chapter will answer the following questions:

◆ What is the position of the American Association of University Professors (AAUP) on cause for dismissal?

◆ What are the most commonly cited examples of cause, and what patterns exist across institutional type?

◆ What are some of the most unusual grounds for dismissal or sanction?

◆ What sanctions are most frequently mentioned? Least frequently mentioned?

PART ONE: GROUNDS FOR DISMISSAL AND SANCTIONS

The Position of the American Association of University Professors (AAUP)

While the AAUP provides a detailed 16-point discussion of dismissal procedures, it is remarkably succinct in its explanation of cause. According to the AAUP, "Termination of an appointment with continuous tenure, or of a probationary or special appointment before the end of the specified term, may be effected by the institution only for adequate cause" (1995, p. 23). Later, a section on dismissal procedures elaborates:

> Adequate cause for a dismissal will be related, directly and substantially, to the fitness of faculty members in their professional capacities as teachers or researchers. Dismissal will not be used to restrain faculty members in their exercise of academic freedom or other rights of American citizens. (AAUP, 1995, p. 26)

The AAUP neither provides examples of conduct that would meet its definition of "adequate cause" nor clarifies the term "fitness." Twenty-one (11%) of 192 FAPA dismissal policies either use the above language or simply state that faculty members may be dismissed only for "cause" (or "good," "just," or "adequate" cause) without elaboration. The other FAPA institutions go further and provide greater specificity in their grounds for dismissal, interpreting the concept of cause in a wide variety of ways.

Most Commonly Mentioned Grounds for Dismissal

In an analysis of 192 dismissal policies, the following causes for dismissal and sanctions appear (in decreasing order of frequency): incompetence, neglect of duty, moral turpitude, criminality, misconduct, performance-related causes, misrepresentation and falsification, dishonesty, ethical violations, violations of policy and others' rights, and personal conduct impairing duties. Each will be addressed below. (For practical reasons, this chapter intentionally does not address policies on sexual or racial harassment, drug abuse, or physical or mental incapacity. At some institutions, such issues fall under the definition of cause, and at others they are treated under entirely different sets of guidelines and procedures. Due to this lack of consistency and the difficulty in quantifying relevant institutional procedures, we have chosen to omit these issues from our analysis.)

Incompetence. By far the most commonly cited reason for dismissal among the 192 institutions in FAPA was incompetence, mentioned by 121 institutions (63%). Of these, 49 (40%) use the term incompetence with no qualification whatsoever. Thirty-five institutions (29%) refer to "professional incompetence." Two institutions (Claremont Graduate University (D1) and Clarkson University (D2)) employ the term "gross incompetence," and Texas Wesleyan University (M1) writes of "gross professional incompetence." Sixteen institutions (13%) cite "demonstrated incompetence." Other institutions qualify the term in various ways. Saint Louis University (R2) sanctions "incompetence in meeting faculty obligations." Russell Sage College (M1) and McMurray College (B2) cite "academic incompetence." And Culver-Stockton College (B2) includes "incompetence as a teacher" among several grounds for the termination of tenure.

Neglect of duty. Of the 192 FAPA institutions, 105 (55%) cite neglect of duty as adequate cause for dismissal. Some institutions describe neglect of duty with no mention of intention or degree. In fact, 24 (23%) institutions use the phrase with no qualification whatsoever. By contrast, 14 (13%) institutions define neglect of duty as "willful," "deliberate," and "intentional" or as a "refusal" or "unwillingness" to carry out one's duties.

For example, Cleveland State University (D2) defines neglect of duty as "substantial, willful, and persistent neglect, without justification or excuse, of an essential institutional duty, validly prescribed by the university." The University of Louisville (R2) sanctions "neglect of or refusal to perform one's duties." At Marquette University (D1), "Absolute cause shall include . . . an intentional failure or refusal to perform a substantial part of any assigned duties."

Other institutions require that neglect of duty persist over time. The words "continued," "habitual," "a pattern of," "persistent," or "repeated" precede the term "neglect of duty" at 23 (22%) of the 105 institutions. An additional 31 (30%) institutions qualify the term with adjectives such as "significant," "gross," "manifest," "grave," "serious," and "substantial." Still other institutions do not use the word neglect at all. Clarkson University (D2) and Agnes Scott College (B1) cite "dereliction of duty." Idaho State University (D2) refers to a "failure to perform . . . assigned or contractual duties." George Mason University (D2) employs the phrase "documented failure to carry out professional obligations or assigned responsibilities."

Moral turpitude. Sixty-four (33%) institutions may dismiss or sanction faculty members for moral turpitude or delinquency. Pittsburg State University (M1) and Mount Mercy College (B2), among others, accept the AAUP's definition.

> The concept of "moral turpitude" . . . applies to that kind of behavior which goes beyond simply warranting discharge and is so utterly blameworthy as to make it inappropriate to require the offering of a year's teaching or pay. The standard is not that the moral sensibilities of persons in the particular community have been affronted. The standard is behavior that would evoke condemnation by the academic community generally (AAUP, 1995, p. 7).

Eleven (17%) institutions refer specifically to the commission of or conviction for "a crime involving moral turpitude." Eleven (17%) institutions refer more generally to "immorality" or "immoral conduct." Several institutions offer these descriptions: "serious moral dereliction" (Middle Tennessee State University, D2); "moral delinquency of a grave order" (University of New Hampshire, D2); and "infraction of commonly accepted standards of morality" (Southeastern Louisiana University, M1). MidAmerica Nazarene University (M2) offers a vivid description, which reads:

> The faculty member has been determined to be guilty of immoral conduct as interpreted by the Church of the Nazarene including but not limited to adultery; fornication; homosexual practices; involvement in the preparation, use or dissemination of pornographic materials; and participation in the use or distribution of illegal drugs; . . .

Table 7-2 Most Common Causes for Dismissal by Carnegie Classification

	Overall Sample n=192		R1 n=20		R2 n=16		D1 n=10		D2 n=17		M1 n=56		M2 n=12		B1 n=24		B2 n=37	
	#	%	#	%	#	%	#	%	#	%	#	%	#	%	#	%	#	%
Incompetence	121	63	14	70	10	63	7	70	10	59	27	48	7	58	17	71	29	78
Neglect of duty	105	55	14	70	6	38	6	60	11	65	24	43	7	58	8	33	29	78
Moral turpitude	64	33	5	25	6	38	3	30	7	41	16	29	4	33	9	38	14	38

Only Culver-Stockton College (B2) qualifies the term moral turpitude to refer specifically to conduct that interferes with a faculty member's job performance, sanctioning "moral turpitude on the part of the teacher which threatens to render the teacher ineffective and which reflects discredit on the teacher and the college."

Tables 7-2 and 7-3 summarize the top three causes for dismissal across institutional type.

Criminality. Fifty-seven institutions (30%) consider criminal conduct to be adequate cause for dismissal or sanction. Of those 57, 43 institutions (75%) cite conviction as the standard. Of the 43 citing conviction, 19 (44%) further specify that the conviction must be for a felony, seven (16%) say the conviction must stem from a felony or from a crime involving moral turpitude, and one (2%) sets the standard at conviction for a crime of moral turpitude alone. Of the remaining 16 institutions mentioning conviction, nine (21%) indicate the crime must be related to the faculty member's "fitness to practice his or her profession"; three (7%) state the crime must be "serious"; and one each (a total of 9%)

Table 7-3 Most Common Causes for Dismissal by Public or Private Affiliation

	Total		Public		Private	
	#	%	#	%	#	%
Incompetence	121	63	51	42	70	58
Neglect of Duty	105	55	49	47	56	53
Moral Turpitude	64	33	33	52	31	48

sets the standard at "conviction of a crime" (Saint Vincent College, B2), "conviction of a crime indicating behavior incompatible with a faculty position" (Texas Wesleyan University, M1), "conviction of violating the criminal laws of any state or the United States" (College of Charleston, M1), and "conviction for a crime that would greatly affect the faculty member's discharge of university responsibilities or would greatly interfere with the mission of the University" (Saint Louis University, R2).

The remaining 14 (25%) of the 57 institutions citing criminal conduct do not specify conviction as the standard per se. Rather, they refer more generally to illegal conduct, violation of the law, and criminality as causes for dismissal or sanction. One institution, Virginia Polytechnic Institute and State University (R1), gives as one cause for dismissal the "inability to perform assigned duties satisfactorily because of incarceration."

Performance-related. While incompetence, discussed earlier, is a very specific type of performance-related ground for dismissal, an additional 44 (23%) FAPA institutions mention other types of performance-related causes: 1) those that relate to poor performance in general, and 2) those where poor performance is documented in a post-tenure review.

Poor performance in general. The faculty manual at the College of Saint Rose (M1) states, "Dismissal for adequate cause shall be related to persistent and/or severe deficiency in the performance of the faculty member in his or her professional capacity." At Youngstown State University (M1), "Just cause shall include, but is not limited to: a) Failure to correct serious, substantive, and persistent deficiencies in teaching, scholarship, or service; . . ." Dana College (B2) is, perhaps, the most succinct. There, adequate cause for dismissal includes "unsatisfactory performance of duties."

Poor post-tenure reviews. In the second category are institutions that sanction and/or dismiss tenured faculty for poor performance that has been substantiated through post-tenure review. (For a more complete discussion of post-tenure review and corresponding sanctions, see Chapter Six.) At Southeastern Oklahoma State University (M1), an unsatisfactory post-tenure review necessitates a second review within one year. "An unsatisfactory review at that time will be grounds for dismissal . . ." At the University of Arizona (R1), tenured faculty members must carry out a Performance Improvement Plan if their post-tenure review has proved unsatisfactory.

> Failure to demonstrate adequate progress relative to the benchmarks and performance goals of the Performance Improvement Plan shall lead to a recommendation for dismissal, . . .

And at Idaho State University (D2):

> If, following a full and complete [post-tenure] review, a faculty member's performance is judged to have been unsatisfactory or less than adequate during the period under review, the faculty member may be recommended for dismissal or termination.

As noted in Chapter Six, dismissal as a sanction for poor performance is a last resort. Faculty members are given a number of opportunities to improve their standing before being dismissed for performance-related reasons.

Misconduct. Misconduct can mean a number of different offenses. A total of 43 institutions (22%) cite some form of misconduct as adequate cause for dismissal or sanction. The University of Rochester (R1) offers the following definition of misconduct:

> "Misconduct" is defined as a known, intentional misrepresentation of data, of research procedures, or of data analysis; and plagiarism and other serious improprieties in proposing, conducting, or reporting the results of research. Federal regulations have also included within the definition of misconduct material failure to comply with federal requirements for the protection of researchers, human subjects, or the public; failure to ensure the welfare of laboratory animals; or failure to meet other material legal requirements governing research.

Other institutions, such as the University of Missouri, Columbia (R1), George Washington University (R2), Rice University (R2), and Southern Illinois University, Carbondale (R2), also refer to research-oriented or scientific misconduct in their definitions of cause. An additional 18 (9%) institutions refer specifically to "personal" misconduct as adequate cause. Sweet Briar College (B1), for example, cites "personal misconduct . . . which renders such member unfit for association with students."

Misrepresentation and falsification. Thirty-six (19%) of 192 FAPA institutions cite falsification or misrepresentation as part of their definitions of adequate cause. Of these 36, 32 (89%) refer explicitly to the falsification of documents used to secure one's position. The University of Arizona (R1), for example, cites "misrepresentation in securing an appointment, promotion, or tenure." George Mason University (D2) mentions "falsification of information relating to professional qualifications." And Western Montana College (B2) includes in its definition "fraud or willful misrepresentation of professional preparation, accomplishments, or experience in connection with initial hiring or in the submission of materials for evaluation for promotion, tenure, or salary adjustment purposes."

Four institutions (11%) do not specify that the misrepresentation need be related to the securing of one's position. The University of New Orleans (D2) refers to "representation of personal views as a statement of the position of the University or any of its agencies." Valdosta State University (M1) cites "false swearing with respect to official documents filed with the institution." "Substantial misrepresentation of facts requested by the university" qualifies as cause at Villanova University (M1). And Wiley College (B2) offers the generic "false information" as part of its definition of adequate cause.

Dishonesty. While the institutions referenced above cite misrepresentation or falsification of documents as cause for sanction or dismissal, 35 institutions cite dishonesty more generally. (Of these 35, 11 institutions cite both misrepresentation/falsification and dishonesty, creating some overlap.) The University of Arkansas (R2), Michigan State University (R1), and Middle Tennessee State University (D2) all cite "intellectual dishonesty" as adequate cause for dismissal. Massachusetts Institute of Technology (R1) and Langston University (B2) both consider "academic dishonesty" just cause. And Marquette University (D1) views "dishonorable" conduct as sufficient grounds. Most of the remaining institutions cite some combination of:

◆ Dishonesty in teaching and/or research (Brown University (R1), Georgia Institute of Technology (R1), University of Arizona (R1), Rice University (R2), Northern Arizona University (D1), Cleveland State University (D2), University of New Orleans (D2), North Dakota State University (D2), University of North Dakota (D2), Fitchburg State College (M1), Springfield College (M1), Saint Olaf College (B1), Albertson College (B2), Dickinson State College (B2), and Mayville State University (B2)).

◆ Dishonesty in the performance of professional duties or activities (West Virginia University (R1), Central College (B1), Shepherd College (B1), Fairmont State College (B2), and Glenville State College (B2)), and

◆ "Dishonesty, including, but not limited to, plagiarism, falsification of credentials or experience, or the misappropriation or misapplication of funds" (Hiram College (B1), Bethel College (B2), and Millikin University (B2)).

Only Cedarville College (B2), the University of Idaho (R2), the University of Notre Dame (R2), Idaho State University (D2), and Wofford College (B1) use the generic term "dishonesty" without qualification.

Ethical violations. Somewhat related to the concept of moral turpitude, ethical violations refer to behavior that is patently unacceptable in one's discipline or profession. Twenty-seven institutions (14%) cite some form of unethical conduct as adequate cause for dismissal. Twenty-one (78%) of these institutions specifically refer to unethical *professional* behavior as distinct from generally unethical conduct. Virginia Polytechnic Institute and State University (R1) and George Mason University (D2) cite "flagrant violation of professional ethics." Hiram College (B1), Bethel College (B2), Cedarville College (B2), and Millikin University (B2) cite "knowing or reckless" violations of professional ethics or the ethics of one's discipline. Dakota Wesleyan University (B2), California Lutheran University (M1), Saint Mary's University (B2), Colby-Sawyer College (B2), and Saint Vincent College (B2) all cite a "serious failure to follow the canons" and "professional ethics of one's discipline." Only five institutions (19%), Southern Illinois University, Carbondale (R2), Drew University (B1) Shepherd College (B1), Paine College (B2), and Wiley College (B2), refer to unethical behavior in general, without reference to professional ethics in particular.

Violations of policies and others' rights. Twenty-five institutions (13%) cite violations of institutional policy, and 14 (7%) cite violations of the rights of students and/or colleagues. The North Dakota State Board of Higher Education builds substantial protection for faculty members into its policy on dismissal for cause. Grounds for cause at the state institutions include:

> Significant or continued violations of board policy or institutional policy, provided that for violations of institutional policy, the faculty member must have been notified in advance in writing by the institution's chief executive that violation would constitute grounds for dismissal, or the institutional policy must have provided specifically for dismissal as a sanction.

Other institutions cast a wider net. Idaho State University (D2) sanctions "actions in violation of policies, directives, or orders of the regents." At Dana College (B2), grounds for dismissal include "violations of the rules of the institution." And at Dillard University (B2), "flagrant disregard for the policies and procedures of the university" is cause "for initiation of termination procedures."

Among the 14 institutions that sanction or dismiss faculty members for violating the rights of others is California Lutheran University (M1). There, adequate cause includes "deliberate and serious violation of the rights and freedom of fellow faculty members, administrators, or students." This language is typical of provisions found at Holy Names College (M1), Saint Mary's University (M1), Hiram College (B1), Colby-Sawyer College (B2), Saint Joseph's College (B2), Dakota Wesleyan University (B2), Langston University (B2), Saint Vincent College (B2), and the University of Southern Colorado (B2).

Personal conduct impairing duties.   In addition to the 43 institutions that cite misconduct, 22 (11%) mention personal conduct that impairs one's duties. Central College (B1) sanctions "personal conduct which significantly impairs the teacher's fulfillment of institutional responsibilities, usually related to the way such conduct may damage the teacher's credibility or effectiveness within the college community." The remaining institutions offer less elaboration, simply citing "conduct" or "personal conduct" impairing the individual's fulfillment of his or her responsibilities.

Less common grounds for dismissal or sanction

The grounds cited above as adequate cause are noteworthy because they appear with some degree of regularity throughout the various FAPA policies. Other grounds are worth mentioning precisely because they are infrequently cited and unusual in nature. In decreasing order of frequency, they include:

◆ Insubordination and/or refusal to cooperate (15x)

◆ Disrupting university operations (10x)

◆ Disregard for an institution's religious mission (8x)

◆ Inefficiency (6x)

◆ Irresponsibility (6x)

◆ Causing public scandal (6x)

◆ Using one's position as a faculty member to exploit others (5x)

◆ Conduct unbecoming a faculty member (3x)

◆ Contumacious conduct (Delta State University (M1), Wiley College (B2))

- Indifference (Wofford College (B1), Greensboro College (B2))
- Lack of scholarly objectivity (Ohio Wesleyan University (B1), Saint Norbert College (B2))
- Indolence (Middle Tennessee State University (D2))
- Breaking guidelines regarding divorce (Asbury College (B2))
- "Malicious and deliberate disloyalty to the College" (Culver-Stockton College (B2))

PART TWO: TYPES OF SANCTIONS

The AAUP on Sanctions

The American Association of University Professors' position on sanctions states:

Procedures for imposition of sanctions other than dismissal.

(a) If the administration believes that the conduct of a faculty member, although not constituting adequate cause for dismissal, is sufficiently grave to justify imposition of a severe sanction, such as suspension from service for a stated period, the administration may institute a proceeding to impose such a severe sanction . . .

(b) If the administration believes that the conduct of a faculty member justifies the imposition of a minor sanction, such as a reprimand, it will notify the faculty member of the basis of the proposed sanction and provide the faculty member with an opportunity to persuade the administration that the proposed sanction should not be imposed. A faculty member who believes that a major sanction has been incorrectly imposed . . ., or that a minor sanction has been unjustly imposed, may . . . petition the faculty grievance committee for such action as may be appropriate. (AAUP, 1995, p. 28)

Most Frequently Mentioned Sanctions

While the AAUP explicitly mentions only reprimand and suspension as examples of sanctions, the 192 FAPA institutions have adopted not only these, but a number of other penalties as well. This section deals with those sanctions that are most frequently *mentioned* by the 192 FAPA institutions for the offenses cited above. We have no indication, however, of which sanctions are most frequently *imposed*.

Tables 7-4 and 7-5 (below) present the frequency with which sanctions are mentioned, broken down by Carnegie classification and public/private affiliation.

Suspension.   Suspension occupies an unusual niche in the policies on dismissal and sanction. On the one hand, it is frequently

Table 7-4   Most Common Sanctions, by Carnegie Classificationn

	Overall Sample n=192		R1 n=20		R2 n=16		D1 n=10		D2 n=17		M1 n=56		M2 n=12		B1 n=24		B2 n=37	
	#	%	#	%	#	%	#	%	#	%	#	%	#	%	#	%	#	%
Suspension	52	27	5	25	2	13	1	10	2	12	19	34	6	50	5	21	12	32
Reprimand	41	21	3	15	2	13	2	20	4	24	16	29	2	17	4	17	8	22
Salary-related	24	13	2	10	0	0	2	20	4	24	7	13	0	0	3	13	6	17
Reassignment	17	9	2	10	1	6	0	0	3	18	3	5	1	8	2	8	5	14
Demotion	15	8	1	5	0	0	0	0	2	12	8	14	0	0	2	8	2	5
Removal of privileges	14	7	2	10	1	6	2	20	1	6	3	5	1	8	1	4	3	8
Warnings	13	7	1	5	0	0	0	0	0	0	3	5	3	25	0	4	5	14

Table 7-5   Most Common Sanctions, by Public or Private

	Total		Public		Private	
	#	%	#	%	#	%
Suspension	52	27	23	44%	29	56%
Reprimand	41	21	25	61%	16	39%
Salary-related	24	13	12	50%	12	50%
Reassignment	17	9	10	65%	7	35%
Demotion	15	8	10	67%	5	33%
Removal of privileges	14	7	4	29%	10	71%
Warnings	13	7	3	23%	10	77%

discussed as a procedural measure imposed during a dismissal hearing "if immediate harm to the faculty member or others is threatened by the faculty member's continuance" (AAUP, 1995, p. 12). On the other hand, many institutions consider suspension a sanction in and of itself. As this chapter does not discuss procedural issues, only the latter use of suspension is explored below.

Fifty-two institutions (27%) consider some form of suspension when imposing a disciplinary action. Of these 52, 30 (58%) specify whether the suspension should be paid or unpaid. Of these 30:

◆ 20 (67%) institutions indicate the suspension is "without pay." At Aquinas College (M2):

   If the administration believes that the conduct of a faculty member, although not constituting adequate cause for dismissal, is sufficiently grave to justify suspending the faculty member without pay for a stated period, the administration may institute a proceeding to impose such a suspension . . .

◆ Three (10%) institutions indicate that suspension "may" be without pay. At West Virginia Wesleyan College (M2), Saint Mary's University (M1), and Millikin University (B2):

   Such suspension may not last beyond a full year, but may entail the partial or total discontinuance of salaries and benefits, the suspension of promotion and salary increments and the temporary suspension or withdrawal of all faculty privileges.

◆ Two (7%) institutions consider the suspensions "with pay." At Dana College (B2), the president may immediately:

   . . . suspend a faculty member from teaching duties upon making a determination that a violation has occurred. Full pay and benefits shall be continued during the suspension period.

◆ And at five (17%) institutions, including Hiram College (B1), suspensions may be "with or without pay."

Of the 52 institutions that consider suspension as a sanction, eight (15%) specify a time frame within which this suspension must be complete. These time frames vary substantially. Michigan State University (R1) imposes suspensions both with or without pay, but those without pay "may not exceed six months." At Southern Illinois University, Carbondale (R2), a suspension without pay can last only "up to 30 calendar days." The limit at Bloomsburg University of Pennsylvania, Millersville University of Pennsylvania, and West Chester University of Pennsylvania (all M1, and all under the same Pennsylvania collective bargaining agreement) is 60 days. And at the University of Northern Iowa (M1), "suspension, without pay, [may not] exceed two years."

Reprimand. Considered by the AAUP to be "minor" sanctions, oral and written reprimands are mentioned by 41 (21%) institutions. Rice University (R2), Cleveland State University (D2), the University of North Dakota (D2), North Dakota State University (D2), Eastern Illinois University (M1), Dickinson State College (B2), and Mayville State University (B2) all speak of "letter[s] of reprimand." The University of Northern Iowa (M1) may issue a "letter of censure from the president, to be placed in the faculty member's permanent file." At Bemidji State University and Mankato State University (both M1), "Disciplinary action shall be progressive, beginning with oral reprimand, proceeding to written reprimand, then to suspension, and finally to dismissal." A reprimand is considered a "minor sanction" at 12 institutions, including Northwestern University (R1), American University (D1), and Delta State University (M1).

Salary-related sanctions. A total of 24 (13%) institutions consider sanctions that relate in some way to a faculty member's salary. These sanctions may take the form of salary cuts, denials of salary increases, completely withholding the faculty member's pay, or a combination of the three (yielding a total percentage greater than 100%).

Of these 24 institutions, 16 (67%) consider reducing a faculty member's salary. Santa Clara University (M1) considers a "temporary or indefinite reduction in salary." The University of New Orleans (D2) considers "a reduction in salary, not to exceed the prevailing promotional increment, for a period not to exceed one year." And Millikin University (B2) may simply impose a "pay cut" as a form of sanction.

Millikin University also considers the "withholding of scheduled promotions or pay raises," as do seven other institutions (33%). Michigan State University (R1) mentions "foregoing salary increase," Saint John's University (D1) considers "loss of any increment for a period up to but not exceeding one year," and California Lutheran University (M1) may impose the "suspension of regular or merit increases in salary." Both the University of Colorado, Colorado Springs (M1) and Wiley College (B2) consider a salary "freeze."

Finally, three institutions consider withholding a faculty member's salary completely. Both Mount Mercy College (B2) and Pittsburg State University (M1) mention denying "a year's teaching pay in whole or in part" in cases of moral turpitude. The University of Southern Maine (M1) mentions simply "withholding of pay" as one possible sanction.

Reassignment of duties. Of the 192 FAPA institutions, 17 (9%) mention reassigning a faculty member from his or her regularly assigned duties. After the University of Iowa (R1) has made a determination of "unfitness," it may make a change in the faculty member's "assigned duties." At the University of Colorado, Colorado Springs (M1), "in cases where the Development Plan has not produced the desired results," the administration considers a "reassignment of duties." Albertson College of Idaho (B2) may "transfer to another area" a faculty member as a form of sanction. Some institutions, such as California Lutheran University (M1), may reassign faculty members while other sanctions are being considered or are pending. In this case, the reassignment itself is not considered a sanction: "If reassignment is deemed necessary by the university while an ultimate determination of the faculty member's status is being made, the president of the university or his/her designee will present the reasons for such action . . ." (California Lutheran University).

Demotion in rank. Fifteen (8%) institutions permit demotion in rank as a sanction for misbehavior. North Carolina State University (R1) allows demotion in rank "only for incompetence, neglect of duty, or misconduct." Central College (B1) considers "revision of status or rank." At California State University, Los

Angeles, San Francisco State University, and San Jose State University (all M1), "Sanctions imposed in a disciplinary action shall be limited to dismissal, demotion, or suspension without pay." And the University of New Orleans (D2) considers "reduction in rank with loss of salary not to exceed the promotional increment." It continues: "This action in no way abrogates tenure."

Removal of privileges and/or perks. A total of 14 institutions (7%) list the removal of privileges or job perks as possible sanctions. Some institutions adjust a faculty member's benefits. Michigan State University (R1) refers to "foregoing benefit improvements." In cases of demonstrated irresponsibility or professional misconduct, Saint Olaf College (B1) imposes a "loss of prospective benefits." Massachusetts Institute of Technology (R1) cites "removal of privileges" and Millikin University and Saint Joseph's College (both B2) mention "withholding" faculty privileges. Other institutions offer greater specificity. At Saint John's University (D1), a faculty member may be deemed ineligible "for overtime teaching for a period up to but not exceeding one year." Rice University considers as a severe sanction the "removal as principal investigator from an already funded research project." And at the University of Colorado, Colorado Springs (M1), if a post-tenure review development plan "has not produced the desired results," then the institution may impose the "loss of eligibility for sabbaticals or for campus travel funds" among various other sanctions.

Warning. In the policy statements analyzed, 13 institutions (7%) mention warnings as either sanctions in and of themselves or as precursors to more serious sanctions. (We recognize the likelihood that additional FAPA institutions may warn their faculty members before imposing sanctions. Such warnings, however, may appear in procedural language or as part of a grievance process—one reason why the above percentage appears remarkably low.) At Aquinas College (M2):

> Verbal warning will be used in first offense instances, such as discourteous treatment of students, fellow employees, or the public; repetitive violations of parking regulations; unsatisfactory work performance; or

unexcused or excessive absences or tardiness.

As a precursor to more serious sanctions, warning is offered at Saint Vincent College (B2), Holy Names College (M1), Saint Joseph's College (B2), West Virginia Wesleyan College (M2), and others:

> In normal circumstances, dismissal for cause is preceded by a written admonition by the appropriate administrative officer describing the alleged problem and warning that the faculty member's contract status is in jeopardy. The warning must stipulate a period of time within which correction of the alleged problem is expected (West Virginia Wesleyan College (M2), Colby-Sawyer College (B2), and Saint Vincent College (B2)).

At Elon College (M2), disciplinary actions include "written warnings placed in an employee's personnel file," and at Western Montana College (B2), sanctions include the issuance of "warning letters."

Less Frequently Mentioned Sanctions

While suspension, reprimand, salary-related sanctions, reassignment of duties, demotion in rank, removal of perks or privileges, and warning are mentioned with some degree of regularity, several more unusual sanctions appear in institutional policies as well.

Eight institutions (4%) consider revocation of tenure. At Texas Woman's University (D1), "A faculty member may be subject to revocation of tenure or other appropriate disciplinary action if incompetency, neglect of duty, or other good cause is determined to be present." James Madison University (M1) and Santa Clara University (M1) both mention "loss of tenure" as a disciplinary sanction, while East Carolina University (M1) and Southeastern Oklahoma State University (M1) refer to "removal of tenure." It is unclear whether revocation of tenure is synonymous with dismissal, or whether faculty members so sanctioned may continue their employment in a nontenured status.

Eight institutions (4%) refer to probation. Among them is Northern Kentucky University (M1), which may place faculty members on probation for violations of professional ethics.

Five institutions (3%) may require restitution. The University of Northern Iowa (M1) imposes "monetary damages in reparation for whatever financial loss the university may have incurred as a result of the faculty member's misconduct." Saint Olaf College (B1) imposes "major fines" in cases of demonstrated irresponsibility or professional misconduct.

Among the least frequently mentioned sanctions are the following. Agnes Scott College (B1) may ask a faculty member to write "a letter of apology." At Villanova University (M1), a faculty member found guilty of misconduct in science will receive "special monitoring of future work." Hiram College (B1) may impose "restrictions on activities." And Central College (B1) considers "leaves of absence for retraining."

SUMMARY

After a thorough review of 192 policies on dismissal, a consensus on the operational meaning of just and adequate cause is as elusive as ever. A majority of institutions see certain behaviors—incompetent performance, neglect of duty, and moral turpitude among them—as clearly at variance with acceptable standards, but the list of unacceptable conduct runs far and wide, and few patterns emerge that lead to a conclusive definition of "cause." Institutional policy on the most appropriate sanctions for unacceptable behavior runs the gamut as well. The safest conclusion may well be that institutions adopt local variants of national standards in their interpretations of, and responses to, improper conduct among members of their faculty.

REFERENCE

American Association of University Professors. (1995). *Policy documents and reports* (8th ed.). Washington, DC: AAUP.

APPENDIX 7-A
Dismissal

#	Institution Name	Incompetence (total = 121)	Neglect of Duty (total = 105)	Moral Turpitude (total = 64)	Criminal Behavior (total = 57)	Performance-Related (total = 44)	Misconduct (total = 43)	Misrepresentation or Falsification (total = 36)	Dishonesty (total = 35)	Unethical Behavior (total = 27)	Violations of Policy and Others' Rights (total = 25)	Personal Conduct Impairing Duties (total = 22)
	R1											
1	Brown University	X	X						X			X
2	Columbia University	X	X				X					
3	Emory University	X	X	X								
4	Florida State University	X	X	X			X		X			
5	Georgia Institute of Technology	X	X						X			
6	Johns Hopkins University	X	X									
7	Massachusetts Institute of Technology	X	X		X	X	X		X		X	
8	Michigan State University	X	X	X	X		X	X	X		X	
9	North Carolina State University	X	X			X	X	X				
10	Northwestern University	X	X									
11	University of Arizona	X	X	X	X	X	X	X	X		X	X
12	University of California, Irvine		X	X		X						
13	University of Georgia											
14	University of Hawaii, Manoa				X							
15	University of Indiana, Bloomington	X					X					
16	University of Iowa	X										
17	University of Missouri, Columbia	X	X		X		X	X				
n/a	University of Nebraska, Lincoln					dismissal policy not available						
18	University of Rochester											
19	Virginia Polytechnic Institute and State University	X	X		X	X	X	X		X		
20	West Virginia University	X	X						X			X
	R2											
21	Auburn University											
22	George Washington University						X					
23	Kent State University											
24	Lehigh University											
25	Oklahoma State University	X	X	X					X			
26	Rice University	X	X				X	X				
27	Saint Louis University	X			X					X	X	
28	Southern Illinois University, Carbondale	X	X				X			X	X	
29	University of Arkansas, Main Campus	X	X	X					X			
30	University of California, Santa Cruz											
31	University of Delaware	X		X								
32	University of Idaho	X		X	X	X	X		X		X	
33	University of Louisville	X	X	X		X						
34	University of Mississippi						X					
35	University of Notre Dame	X	X		X				X			
36	University of Rhode Island	X		X								

APPENDIX 7-A, *continued*
Dismissal

	Institution Name	Incompetence (total = 121)	Neglect of Duty (total = 105)	Moral Turpitude (total = 64)	Criminal Behavior (total = 57)	Performance-Related (total = 44)	Misconduct (total = 43)	Misrepresentation or Falsification (total = 36)	Dishonesty (total = 35)	Unethical Behavior (total = 27)	Violations of Policy and Others' Rights (total = 25)	Personal Conduct Impairing Duties (total = 22)
	D1											
37	American University	X			X		X					
38	Claremont Graduate University	X				X						
39	Illinois State University											
40	Marquette University	X	X	X					X			
41	Northern Arizona University	X	X	X	X	X		X	X		X	X
42	Saint John's University, Jamaica, NY	X	X									
43	Texas Woman's University	X	X			X						
44	United States International University		X				X					
45	University of Texas, Arlington	X	X	X	X	X					X	
46	University of Toledo											
	D2											
47	Clarkson University	X	X									
48	Cleveland State University	X	X	X	X			X	X			
49	Duquesne University	X					X	X				X
50	George Mason University	X	X	X	X			X		X	X	X
51	Idaho State University		X		X				X		X	X
52	Indiana State University											
53	Middle Tennessee State University	X		X	X							
54	Montana State University		X	X				X	X			
55	North Dakota State University	X	X									
56	Pace University	X	X	X		X			X		X	X
57	University of Central Florida	X	X	X		X	X			X	X	
58	University of Detroit Mercy									X		
59	University of Massachusetts, Lowell	X	X	X	X			X				
60	University of New Hampshire	X	X									
61	University of New Orleans		X		X			X	X	X	X	
62	University of North Dakota	X	X	X	X	X		X	X		X	X
63	Wake Forest University											
	M1											
64	Arkansas Tech University											
65	Baldwin-Wallace College											
66	Bemidji State University											
67	Bloomsburg University of Pennsylvania											
68	Bowie State University											
69	Butler University	X										
70	California Lutheran University	X	X			X	X	X		X	X	X
71	California State University, Los Angeles					X		X				
72	Central Connecticut State University											
73	Chicago State University											
74	College of Charleston	X	X					X	X		X	
75	College of Saint Rose			X								
76	Creighton University	X	X	X	X	X	X	X				X

APPENDIX 7-A, *continued*
Dismissal

Institution Name	Incompetence (total = 121)	Neglect of Duty (total = 105)	Moral Turpitude (total = 64)	Criminal Behavior (total = 57)	Performance-Related (total = 44)	Misconduct (total = 43)	Misrepresentation or Falsification (total = 36)	Dishonesty (total = 35)	Unethical Behavior (total = 27)	Violations of Policy and Others' Rights (total = 25)	Personal Conduct Impairing Duties (total = 22)
77 Delta State University	X	X	X								X
78 Drake University	X	X									
79 East Carolina University	X					X				X	
80 Eastern Illinois University					X						
81 Emporia State University											
82 Fitchburg State College	X	X		X				X			
83 Georgia College and State University	X	X	X	X			X				
84 Holy Names College	X	X	X	X		X	X		X	X	
85 Hunter College, City University of NY	X	X									
86 James Madison University					X						
87 Keene State College											
88 Manhattan College	X		X				X				
89 Mankato State University											
90 Millersville University of Pennsylvania											
91 Northern Kentucky University	X	X	X						X		
92 Norwich University											
93 Pittsburg State University	X	X	X	X	X				X	X	
94 Russell Sage College	X	X	X								
95 Saginaw Valley State University	X	X		X		X	X		X	X	
96 Saint Mary's University											
97 Salve Regina University											
98 San Francisco State University											
99 San Jose State University											
100 Santa Clara University											
101 Southeastern Louisiana University	X	X	X	X	X					X	
102 Southeastern Oklahoma State University	X		X	X							
103 Springfield College	X	X	X	X			X	X			
104 Texas Wesleyan University	X	X	X	X					X		
105 University of Alaska	X	X	X	X	X						X
106 University of Colorado, Colorado Springs	X	X			X						
107 University of Hartford											
108 University of North Alabama	X			X						X	
109 University of Northern Iowa											
110 University of Southern Maine											
111 University of Texas, El Paso	X	X	X	X	X						
112 University of Texas, Pan American	X	X	X	X	X						
113 University of Wisconsin, Superior	X	X	X	X	X						
114 Valdosta State University	X	X	X	X	X		X				
115 Valparaiso University	X	X	X		X		X				
116 Villanova University						X					
117 West Chester University of Pennsylvania											
118 Whitworth College											
119 Youngstown State University		X		X	X						

APPENDIX 7-A, *continued*
Dismissal

Institution Name	Incompetence (total = 121)	Neglect of Duty (total = 105)	Moral Turpitude (total = 64)	Criminal Behavior (total = 57)	Performance-Related (total = 44)	Misconduct (total = 43)	Misrepresentation or Falsification (total = 36)	Dishonesty (total = 35)	Unethical Behavior (total = 27)	Violations of Policy and Others' Rights (total = 25)	Personal Conduct Impairing Duties (total = 22)
M2											
120 Aquinas College	X	X					X			X	
121 Drury College											
122 Elon College	X			X		X					
123 Lincoln University of Pennsylvania	X	X	X	X							
124 MidAmerica Nazarene University		X	X	X			X		X		
125 Pacific University	X	X			X	X					
126 Philadelphia College of Textiles/Science	X	X				X				X	
127 Southern Arkansas University	X	X	X								
n/a Tusculum College					dismissal policy not available						
128 Union College											
129 Walsh University		X	X								
130 Weber State University					X						
131 West Virginia Wesleyan College	X					X					
B1											
132 Agnes Scott College	X	X	X	X					X		
133 Austin College	X		X								
134 Beloit College	X										
135 Bethany College											
136 Birmingham–Southern College	X	X	X	X	X						X
137 Central College	X	X						X			X
138 Coe College											
139 Connecticut College											
140 Davidson College	X	X	X			X					
141 Drew University	X		X						X		
142 Hamilton College		X			X						
143 Haverford College	X				X	X					
144 Hendrix College											
145 Hiram College	X				X		X	X	X	X	
146 Illinois Wesleyan University	X		X						X		
147 Lake Forest College	X		X								
148 Ohio Wesleyan University		X				X					
149 Richard Stockton College of NJ, The					X						
n/a Saint John's College					dismissal policy not available						
150 Saint Olaf College	X	X						X			X
151 Shepherd College	X	X						X	X		X
152 Smith College	X										
153 Southwestern University	X		X			X					
154 Sweet Briar College	X		X			X					
155 Wofford College	X	X		X		X		X			
B2											
156 Albertson College of Idaho	X	X		X	X	X	X	X			X
157 Asbury College	X	X		X	X	X		X			X

APPENDIX 7-A, *continued*
Dismissal

	Institution Name	Causes for Dismissal										
		Incompetence (total = 121)	Neglect of Duty (total = 105)	Moral Turpitude (total = 64)	Criminal Behavior (total = 57)	Performance-Related (total = 44)	Misconduct (total = 43)	Misrepresentation or Falsification (total = 36)	Dishonesty (total = 35)	Unethical Behavior (total = 27)	Violations of Policy and Others' Rights (total = 25)	Personal Conduct Impairing Duties (total = 22)
158	Bethel College	X	X					X	X	X	X	
159	Bloomfield College						X					
160	Bridgewater College	X	X	X	X							
161	Carroll College	X	X	X	X							
162	Cedarville College	X	X	X				X				
n/a	Central State University				dismissal policy not available							
163	Coker College	X	X		X	X	X	X	X		X	
164	Colby-Sawyer College	X	X	X		X		X	X	X	X	
165	Culver-Stockton College	X	X		X		X	X		X	X	
166	Dakota Wesleyan University										X	
167	Dana College	X	X	X							X	X
168	Dickinson State University	X	X	X	X	X			X		X	
169	Dillard University	X	X	X	X	X			X		X	X
170	Fairmont State College	X	X						X			X
171	Glenville State College	X	X						X			
172	Greensboro College	X	X				X					
173	Langston University	X	X	X					X		X	
174	Le Moyne College	X	X									
175	Mayville State University	X	X			X			X		X	X
176	McMurry University	X	X		X			X				X
177	Millikin University	X	X		X				X	X	X	
178	Mount Mercy College	X	X	X				X				
179	North Park College	X	X									
180	Paine College	X	X	X	X					X		X
181	Saint Anselm College	X	X	X								
182	Saint Francis College	X	X									
183	Saint Joseph's College	X	X		X		X	X		X	X	
184	Saint Norbert College	X					X					
185	Saint Vincent	X	X	X	X		X	X		X	X	
186	Shawnee State University		X	X	X	X						
187	Taylor University					X						
188	University of the Ozarks	X	X	X	X			X			X	
189	University of Southern Colorado	X	X		X		X	X			X	
190	Virginia Intermont College	X	X	X	X	X	X	X			X	
191	Western Montana College		X	X	X			X				
192	Wiley College		X			X				X		

APPENDIX 7-B
Sanctions

	Institution Name	Suspension (total = 52)	Reprimand (total = 41)	Salary-Related Sanctions (total = 24)	Reassignment (total = 17)	Demotion (total = 15)	Removal of Privileges (total = 14)	Warning (total = 13)
	R1							
1	Brown University							
2	Columbia University	X						
3	Emory University							
4	Florida State University							
5	Georgia Institute of Technology							
6	Johns Hopkins University							
7	Massachusetts Institute of Technology	X	X	X			X	
8	Michigan State University	X	X	X			X	X
9	North Carolina State University				X	X		
10	Northwestern University	X	X					
11	University of Arizona							
12	University of California, Irvine							
13	University of Georgia							
14	University of Hawaii, Manoa	X						
15	University of Indiana, Bloomington							
16	University of Iowa				X			
17	University of Missouri, Columbia							
n/a	University of Nebraska, Lincoln				policy not available			
18	University of Rochester							
19	Virginia Polytechnic Institute and State University							
20	West Virginia University							
	R2							
21	Auburn University							
22	George Washington University							
23	Kent State University							
24	Lehigh University							
25	Oklahoma State University							
26	Rice University	X	X		X		X	
27	Saint Louis University							
28	Southern Illinois University, Carbondale	X	X					
29	University of Arkansas							
30	University of California, Santa Cruz							
31	University of Delaware							
32	University of Idaho							
33	University of Louisville							
34	University of Mississippi							
35	University of Notre Dame							
36	University of Rhode Island							

APPENDIX 7–B, *continued*
Sanctions

	Institution Name	Types of Sanctions						
		Suspension (total = 52)	Reprimand (total = 41)	Salary-Related Sanctions (total = 24)	Reassignment (total = 17)	Demotion (total = 15)	Removal of Privileges (total = 14)	Warning (total = 13)
	D1							
37	American University	X	X					
38	Claremont Graduate University			X			X	
39	Illinois State University							
40	Marquette University							
41	Northern Arizona University							
42	Saint John's University, Jamaica, NY			X			X	
43	Texas Woman's University							
44	United States International University							
45	University of Texas, Arlington							
46	University of Toledo		X					
	D2							
47	Clarkson University							
48	Cleveland State University	X	X	X		X		
49	Duquesne University							
50	George Mason University							
51	Idaho State University							
52	Indiana State University							
53	Middle Tennessee State University							
54	Montana State University							
55	North Dakota State University		X	X	X			
56	Pace University							
57	University of Central Florida							
58	University of Detroit Mercy							
59	University of Massachusetts, Lowell							
60	University of New Hampshire							
61	University of New Orleans	X	X	X	X	X	X	
62	University of North Dakota	X	X	X	X			
63	Wake Forest University							
	M1							
64	Arkansas Tech University							
65	Baldwin-Wallace College							
66	Bemidji State University	X	X					
67	Bloomsburg University of Pennsylvania	X						
68	Bowie State University							
69	Butler University							
70	California Lutheran University	X	X	X	X			
71	California State University, Los Angeles	X	X			X		
72	Central Connecticut State University	X	X					
73	Chicago State University							
74	College of Charleston	X	X					
75	College of Saint Rose		X					
76	Creighton University			X	X			

APPENDIX 7-B, *continued*
Sanctions

#	Institution Name	Suspension (total = 52)	Reprimand (total = 41)	Salary-Related Sanctions (total = 24)	Reassignment (total = 17)	Demotion (total = 15)	Removal of Privileges (total = 14)	Warning (total = 13)
77	Delta State University		X					
78	Drake University							
79	East Carolina University	X	X			X		
80	Eastern Illinois University	X	X					
81	Emporia State University							
82	Fitchburg State College							
83	Georgia College and State University							
84	Holy Names College							X
85	Hunter College, City University of NY							
86	James Madison University			X				
87	Keene State College							
88	Manhattan College							
89	Mankato State University	X	X					
90	Millersville University of Pennsylvania	X						
91	Northern Kentucky University		X					X
92	Norwich University							
93	Pittsburg State University			X				
94	Russell Sage College							
95	Saginaw Valley State University	X						X
96	Saint Mary's University	X					X	
97	Salve Regina University							
98	San Francisco State University	X	X			X		
99	San Jose State University	X	X			X		
100	Santa Clara University	X	X	X				
101	Southeastern Louisiana University						X	
102	Southeastern Oklahoma State University	X						
103	Springfield College							
104	Texas Wesleyan University							
105	University of Alaska							
106	University of Colorado, Colorado Springs			X	X	X	X	
107	University of Hartford							
108	University of North Alabama							
109	University of Northern Iowa	X	X					
110	University of Southern Maine		X	X		X	X	
111	University of Texas, El Paso							
112	University of Texas, Pan American							
113	University of Wisconsin, Superior							
114	Valdosta State University							
115	Valparaiso University							
116	Villanova University	X	X	X		X		
117	West Chester University of Pennsylvania	X						
118	Whitworth College							
119	Youngstown State University							

APPENDIX 7-B, *continued*
Sanctions

Types of Sanctions

	Institution Name	Suspension (total = 52)	Reprimand (total = 41)	Salary-Related Sanctions (total = 24)	Reassignment (total = 17)	Demotion (total = 15)	Removal of Privileges (total = 14)	Warning (total = 13)
	M2							
120	Aquinas College	X						X
121	Drury College	X	X					
122	Elon College	X						X
123	Lincoln University of Pennsylvania							
124	MidAmerica Nazarene University							
125	Pacific University							
126	Philadelphia College of Textiles/Science	X						
127	Southern Arkansas University							
n/a	Tusculum College				policy not available			
128	Union College							
129	Walsh University							
130	Weber State University	X	X		X			
131	West Virginia Wesleyan College	X					X	X
	B1							
132	Agnes Scott College					X		
133	Austin College							
134	Beloit College							
135	Bethany College							
136	Birmingham–Southern College							
137	Central College			X	X	X		
138	Coe College		X		X			
139	Connecticut College							
140	Davidson College							
141	Drew University	X	X					
142	Hamilton College							
143	Haverford College	X	X					
144	Hendrix College							
145	Hiram College	X						
146	Illinois Wesleyan University							
147	Lake Forest College							
148	Ohio Wesleyan University	X	X					
149	Richard Stockton College of NJ, The			X				
n/a	Saint John's College				policy not available			
150	Saint Olaf College	X		X			X	
151	Shepherd College							
152	Smith College							
153	Southwestern University							
154	Sweet Briar College							
155	Wofford College							
	B2							
156	Albertson College of Idaho	X			—			
157	Asbury College		X		X			

APPENDIX 7–B, *continued*
Sanctions

	Institution Name	Suspension (total = 52)	Reprimand (total = 41)	Salary-Related Sanctions (total = 24)	Reassignment (total = 17)	Demotion (total = 15)	Removal of Privileges (total = 14)	Warning (total = 13)
158	Bethel College							
159	Bloomfield College							
160	Bridgewater College							
161	Carroll College							
162	Cedarville College							
n/a	Central State University				policy not available			
163	Coker College							
164	Colby-Sawyer College	X		X			X	X
165	Culver-Stockton College							
166	Dakota Wesleyan University							
167	Dana College	X						
168	Dickinson State University		X	X	X			
169	Dillard University							
170	Fairmont State College							
171	Glenville State College							
172	Greensboro College							
173	Langston University							
174	Le Moyne College							
175	Mayville State University		X	X	X			
176	McMurry University							
177	Millikin University	X	X	X	X	X	X	X
178	Mount Mercy College		X	X				
179	North Park College	X	X					
180	Paine College							
181	Saint Anselm College	X	X					
182	Saint Francis College							
183	Saint Joseph's College	X					X	X
184	Saint Norbert College	X	X					
185	Saint Vincent College	X						X
186	Shawnee State University	X				X		
187	Taylor University							
188	University of the Ozarks	X						
189	University of Southern Colorado							
190	Virginia Intermont College							
191	Western Montana College	X	X		X			
192	Wiley College			X				X

8

EXTRAORDINARY CIRCUMSTANCES: DISMISSAL OF TENURED FACULTY FOR FINANCIAL EXIGENCY AND PROGRAM DISCONTINUANCE

Lara K. Couturier

HIGHLIGHTS

Of the 196 Institutions with Tenure Systems

- 178 (91%) provided policies on faculty employment security in the event of institutional financial distress, referred to herein as *financial exigency.*

- 159 (81%) provided policies on faculty employment security in the event of program changes, reduction, curtailment, or elimination, referred to herein as *program discontinuance.*

Of the 178 Financial Exigency Policies

- 100% allow the institution to terminate tenured faculty members in the event of financial exigency.

◆ 21 (12%) state that faculty members can be terminated because of financial exigency, but do not include specific policy provisions.

◆ 14 (8%) explicitly refer to the policies and guidelines of the American Association of University Professors (AAUP) by citing or mentioning the AAUP by name.

◆ 71 (40%) use some or all of the AAUP's language on financial exigency found in the *Recommended Institutional Regulations on Academic Freedom and Tenure* (AAUP, 1995, pp. 23-25), but neither cite nor mention the AAUP by name.

Of the 159 Program Discontinuance Policies

◆ 156 (98%) allow the institution to terminate tenured faculty members in the event of program discontinuance. Three institutions specifically state that tenured faculty will not be terminated in the event of program discontinuance not mandated by financial exigency.

◆ Ten (6%) state that faculty members can be terminated because of program discontinuance, but do not include specific policy provisions.

◆ Ten (6%) explicitly refer to the policies and guidelines of the American Association of University Professors (AAUP) by citing or mentioning the AAUP by name.

◆ 61 (38%) use some or all of the AAUP's language on program discontinuance found in the *Recommended Institutional Regulations on Academic Freedom and Tenure* (AAUP, 1995, p. 25), but neither cite nor mention the AAUP by name.

ACADEMIC TENURE AND TERMINATION OF FACULTY MEMBERS

The American Association of University Professors (AAUP) attributes two primary purposes to academic tenure: "1) freedom of teaching and research and of extramural activities, and 2) a sufficient degree of economic security to make the profession attractive to men and women of ability" (1995, p. 3).

While tenure provides faculty members with continuous employment until retirement, and protects them from arbitrary dismissal, the AAUP's *Recommended Institutional Regulations on Academic Freedom and Tenure* (1995, pp. 21-30) does not preclude termination of tenured faculty due to "Financial Exigency" or "Discontinuance of Program or Department Not Mandated by Financial Exigency." The AAUP's *1940 Statement of Principles on Academic Freedom and Tenure* allows for termination due to financial exigency under "extraordinary circumstances":

> After the expiration of a probationary period, teachers or investigators should have permanent or continuous tenure, and their service should be terminated only for adequate cause, except in the case of retirement for age, or under extraordinary circumstances because of financial exigencies. (1995, p. 4)

The AAUP's 1957 version of the *Recommended Institutional Regulations* later codified the language on program discontinuance:

> Termination of an appointment with continuous tenure, or of a probationary or special appointment before the end of the specified term, may occur as a result of *bona fide* formal discontinuance of a program or department of instruction. (1995, p. 25)

Educational and Academic Freedom Considerations

While the AAUP's policies on financial exigency and program discontinuance recognize that institutions may need to adopt extreme measures during times of crisis, the association also makes clear that educational, not financial, considerations must be paramount:

> The financial conditions that bear on such decisions should not be allowed to obscure the fact that instruction

and research constitute the essential reason for the existence of the university. (1995, p. 193)

The decision to discontinue formally a program or department of instruction will be based essentially upon educational considerations. (1995, p. 25)

Balancing educational considerations, the financial viability of an institution, and academic freedom presents a formidable challenge in policy and in practice. Policy provisions that allow the curtailment of tenure rights must not intrude upon academic freedom, a concern reflected in the policies of the University of Delaware (R2) and Columbia University (R1). The University of Delaware's (R2) policy relating to the "curtailment of academic programs . . . because of the 'extraordinary financial circumstance'" notes: "It is important that the curtailment be bona fide in relation to the financial emergency, not a subterfuge to dismiss controversial individuals or programs." Similarly, Columbia University's (R1) policy entitled "Termination Due to the Discontinuation of a Unit of Instruction" states:

The appointment of a tenured member of the faculty may be terminated when serious financial needs force the university to discontinue his or her unit of instruction, provided that the unit is large enough to exclude the possibility that its closing is aimed at specific individuals.

On the other hand, those tasked with fiduciary or management responsibility of an institution may find that the inflexibility imposed by tenure impedes financial equilibrium and program balance. Indeed, critics of tenure argue that an institution's inability to terminate tenured faculty restricts its ability to react and adapt to market fluctuations.

This chapter examines policies governing financial exigency and program discontinuance, and highlights how institutions attempt to protect academic freedom and educational missions, and at the same time retain the flexibility to respond to financial troubles and program changes. The chapter answers the following questions:

- How is financial exigency defined?
- How is program discontinuance defined?
- To what extent are the AAUP's *Recommended Institutional Regulations on Academic Freedom and Tenure* reflected in financial exigency and program discontinuance policies?
- Which faculty may be released under these policies?
- To what degree are faculty involved in financial exigency and program discontinuance processes?
- What are the provisions for faculty members affected by these policies?

Sample:

The Project on Faculty Appointments' 1998 Faculty Appointment Policy Archive (FAPA) CD-ROM contains policy provisions from the faculty handbooks of 217 randomly selected four-year colleges and universities stratified by Carnegie classification. Of these 217 institutions, 196 grant tenure to faculty members and thus are covered in this study.

FINANCIAL EXIGENCY

The Terminology

Of the 196 tenure-granting institutions covered in this chapter, 178 (91%) sent the Project on Faculty Appointments policies on the termination of tenured or probationary faculty due to financial distress (see Table 8-1). This number includes all institutions that discuss whether faculty members may be released due to some form of financial distress, regardless of the length or detail of the policy. The material sent by 18 institutions did not include such a policy. One should not infer, however, that these institutions lack such a policy, as the relevant clause may be part of a document other than the faculty handbook submitted to the project.

Of those 178 policies, 138 (78%) use the term "financial exigency" (see Table 8-2). The other terms used by Coker College (B2) and Wofford College (B1) are indicative of the ranging degree of financial distress necessary before institutions may terminate tenured faculty members. While Coker College (B2)

Table 8-1   The Sample

Carnegie Classification	196 Institutions with Tenure	178 Policies on Financial Exigency	
		# with Policies on Financial Exigency	% with Policies on Financial Exigency
R1	21	17	81%
R2	16	15	94%
D1	10	9	90%
D2	17	15	88%
M1	56	54	96%
M2	13	12	92%
B1	25	23	92%
B2	38	33	87%

Key to Carnegie classification abbreviations: R1 = Research 1; R2 = Research 2; D1 = Doctoral 1; D2 = Doctoral 2; M1 = Master's 1; M2 = Master's 2; B1 = Baccalaureate 1; B2 = Baccalaureate 2 institutions.

Table 8-2   Policies Using the Term "Financial Exigency"

R1 n=17		R2 n=15		D1 n=9		D2 n=15		M1 n=54		M2 n=12		B1 n=23		B2 n=33		Total n=178	
#	%	#	%	#	%	#	%	#	%	#	%	#	%	#	%	#	%
13	76	10	67	8	89	14	93	37	69	9	75	21	91	26	79	138	78

requires "extraordinary financial emergencies," Wofford College (B1) references the need to "preserve the financial soundness of the college." At Springfield College (M1), "A faculty member may be laid-off in response to a financial exigency, [or] financial difficulties not qualifying as a financial exigency," a phrase not further defined. All of these policies are included as financial exigency policies for the purpose of analysis. The analyses that follow are based on a sample size of 178.

Financial Exigency Defined

The AAUP defines a bona fide financial exigency as "an imminent financial crisis that threatens the survival of the institution as a whole and which cannot be alleviated by less drastic means" than the "termination of an appointment with continuous tenure, or of a probationary or special appointment before the end of the specified term" (1995, p. 23). Only 15 (8%) of the policies actually incorporate this definition; other institutions have developed local definitions (23%) or do not include any definition at all (69%). Thirty-three percent of both the Research 2 and the Doctoral 1 institutions crafted their own definitions, compared to only 13% of the Baccalaureate 1 institutions.

From narrow to broad.   Definitions of financial exigency range from precise and detailed to broad and open to interpretation. Bloomfield College (B2), which actually declared financial exigency in the mid-1970s (Cook, 1974), has adopted an unusually lengthy and detailed definition. Bloomfield College's definition is the only one in the sample to include specific numbers:

> The following set of circumstances, in any combination, may be indicative of [financial exigency]:
> a.   When total liabilities exceed total assets;
> b.   When current liabilities exceed current assets and the college is unable to secure additional funding;
> c.   When the college is unable to meet its financial obligations on long-term liabilities or covenants required of those obligations;
> d.   When there has been substantial drop in day enrollment for each of two consecutive years;
> e.   When the college has operated at an actual deficit of $200,000 or more for three or more consecutive fiscal years (a deficit exists when total incurred expenses exceed total actual revenues);
> f.   When the college has operated at an actual deficit of $500,000 or more during the previous fiscal year. (1997, p. 26)

MidAmerica Nazarene University's (M2) definition is more detailed than the AAUP's, but the definition does not include specific figures:

> Financial exigency is an urgent need to reorder the nature and magnitude of financial obligations in such a way as to restore or preserve the financial ability of the institution. The financial ability of the university is the capability of providing from current and accrued income

the funds necessary to meet operational expenses including current debt payment and sound reserves without invading or depleting capital.

The University of Delaware's (R2) *Handbook for Faculty* exemplifies the elasticity of financial exigency and the difficulty of defining the precise point where the university can terminate tenured faculty:

An "extraordinary financial circumstance" is difficult to define, but in general it must represent more than a temporary operating or liquidity problem. Though not requiring bankruptcy to be declared, such a condition is one where survival of the institution as a whole is at issue, and in the absence of other feasible remedies, the well-being and future of the university require that drastic actions be taken.

In stark contrast to these lengthy definitions that describe urgent circumstances, the collective bargaining agreement governing the University of Central Florida (D2) and Florida State University (R1) allows "layoff . . . as a result of adverse financial circumstances" without further definition. Policies like Bowie State University's (M1) leave plenty of room for interpretation: "The president may terminate any appointment because of . . . lack of appropriations or other funds with which to support the appointment."

A further divergence from the AAUP's definition of financial exigency is whether or not the financial exigency must threaten "the survival of the institution as a whole" (AAUP, 1995, p. 23). Contrary to AAUP policy, Creighton University (M1), an institution at which the decision to close programs for financial reasons in the 1970s was upheld in court (Spiro, 1980), asserts that "Financial exigency for termination is a condition of such demonstrably bona fide financial distress of the university or one of its schools or colleges that the survival of the university or one of its schools or colleges is threatened."

The Board of Regents for the University System of Georgia (1999), which governs Georgia College and State University

(M1), Georgia Institute of Technology (R1), and the University of Georgia (R1) contends:

> Financial exigency occurs when circumstances cause a shortfall in projected revenues for general operations as compared with projected expenditures over the same period and such shortfall would have a material adverse effect on the operation of either an institution or an academic or other unit of an institution or the system generally.

The policy further defines "unit" to mean "any identifiable component of the system at any level of its organization which has an annual budget for the operation of such component."

From these examples it is clear that the financial exigency policies in the sample are varied, and while the AAUP's policies and regulations have been an influential model, not all institutions adhere to that single standard. A detailed discussion of objective, operational definitions of financial exigency can be found in Kent John Chabotar and James P. Honan's (1996) working paper, "New Yardsticks to Measure Financial Distress." See Appendix 8-F for their suggested definition of financial exigency at a college or university.

Exhausting the Alternatives

Sixty-one (34%) of the institutions stipulate that alternatives must be explored before faculty layoffs for reasons of financial exigency are enacted. Drake University (M1) defines financial exigency as the point at which it becomes necessary to terminate tenured faculty members: "a critical financial condition of the university as a whole, such that a failure to dismiss tenured faculty members would threaten the welfare of the university." The underlying assumption is that all other alternatives have been exhausted, including the termination of nontenured faculty. According to the Kansas Board of Regents, governing Emporia State University (M1) and Pittsburg State University (M1), a financial exigency exists only after "the elimination of nontenured positions and operating expenditures to such point that

further reductions . . . would seriously distort the academic programs." However, the policy continues, "It is not a requirement
of financial exigency that all nontenured positions throughout
the university be first eliminated."

The collective bargaining agreement governing the University of Toledo (D1) suggests a number of alternatives,
including:

> income generation . . . reduction of support staff and
> administrative personnel and services; encouragement
> of voluntary early faculty retirement, leaves of absence,
> and resignations through financial inducements includ-
> ing "buyout" plans; reduction in internal funds allocated
> to research and equipment; reduction in the number of
> graduate assistants; replacement of part-time, visiting,
> retiring, superannuate, resigning and nontenured faculty
> with existing tenured faculty members where qualified
> to teach . . . (1998)

The University of Arkansas (R2) states that:

> Alternatives to termination of personnel shall be consid-
> ered such as early retirement, transfer, voluntary salary
> reduction, leave of absence without pay, as well as
> normal attrition of personnel, and reductions or post-
> ponements in benefits. Within a given department, any
> faculty member with tenure must be retained over a
> person who does not have tenure.

In an interesting combination of the two issues addressed in
this chapter, Fairmont State College (B2) must conduct an evaluation of programs, and subsequently discontinue or reduce programs to lower expenditures, before terminating faculty for
financial reasons. Similarly, the *Rules and Regulations of the Board
of Regents* of the University of Texas System, which apply to the
University of Texas, Arlington (D1), the University of Texas, El
Paso (M1), and the University of Texas, Pan American (M1), state
that a committee shall recommend "which academic positions

and/or academic programs should be eliminated as a result of the financial exigency," based upon a review that:

> Will include, but not be limited to, an examination of the course offerings, degree programs, supporting degree programs, teaching specialties, and semester credit hour production.

When Tenured Faculty Are Terminated

The AAUP's *Recommended Institutional Regulations on Academic Freedom and Tenure* (1995, pp. 21-30) contains a section on the "Termination of Appointments by the Institution." Paraphrased below are guidelines for institutions to follow when faced with financial exigency:

- A financial exigency must be "demonstrably bona fide" (p. 23).
- Faculty should have a participatory role in declaring that a financial exigency exists, identifying alternatives to termination, defining in which academic programs terminations will occur, choosing the criteria for termination, and determining which appointments should be terminated.
- Faculty members who have received notice of termination should have the right to a hearing by a faculty committee.
- Tenured faculty will not be terminated before untenured faculty, and new appointments will not be made at the same time as others are terminated, "except in extraordinary circumstances where a serious distortion of the academic program would otherwise result" (pp. 24-25).
- The institution will "make every effort to place" faculty in other positions before terminating their appointments (p. 25).
- If a faculty member is terminated, he/she will receive appropriate notice or severance pay.
- If a terminated faculty member's position is to be filled within three years of the termination, the faculty member will be given right of first refusal on the position.

Adherence to AAUP Policy

In addition to the 14 (8%) institutions that actually cite the AAUP by name in their policies, another 71 (40%) use AAUP language in their financial exigency policies without citing the association. Lake Forest College (B1) accepts the AAUP policy as its guideline:

> For provisions and procedures governing termination for cause [including financial exigency], the college will use as guidelines the 1976 Recommended Institutional Regulations on Academic Freedom and Tenure printed in the summer, 1976, *AAUP Bulletin*, pp. 186-187.

Provisions and Protections

Even in cases where institutions do not use the specific language of the AAUP, financial exigency policies typically cover many of the key provisions recommended by the AAUP (see Table 8-3).

Faculty role. Consistent with the AAUP's policy, 92 (52%) institutions attribute a role to the faculty at some point in the process of declaring a financial exigency and terminating tenured faculty. When analyzed by Carnegie classification, a wide discrepancy emerges. Master's 2 institutions are at one

Table 8-3 Breakdown of Key AAUP Provisions Included in Financial Exigency Policies

Carnegie Classification	Faculty Role Specified (Roles Vary)		Preference for Retaining Tenured Faculty		Placement in Another Suitable Position		Notice and/or Severance Pay		Reinstatement	
	#	%	#	%	#	%	#	%	#	%
R1	12	71	4	24	4	24	12	71	7	17
R2	8	53	7	47	12	80	11	73	11	73
D1	7	78	7	78	7	78	7	78	8	89
D2	8	53	7	47	11	73	12	80	10	67
M1	27	50	28	52	36	67	44	81	41	76
M2	3	25	3	25	6	50	10	83	5	42
B1	11	48	5	22	8	35	12	52	12	52
B2	16	48	11	33	18	55	23	70	22	67
Total	92	52	72	40	102	57	131	74	116	65

end of the spectrum, with only 25% defining the role of the faculty, and the Doctoral 1 institutions are at the other end with 78%. Definitions of faculty involvement also vary significantly. Mount Mercy College (B2) declares that decisions about the termination of tenured faculty because of an extraordinary financial emergency "may not be made without appropriate faculty involvement throughout the decision-making process." And at George Mason University (D2), "the faculty will participate with others in the decision-making process."

Coe College's (B1) policy is more specific, stipulating that "The faculty as a whole shall be kept continuously informed of factors likely to affect termination," that budget recommendations will be presented "to the faculty as a whole for discussion and comment," and that terminated faculty members will have the right to a hearing of their case before a "Faculty Review Committee." Similarly, in the case of "financial stress" at Auburn University (R2), "the Board supports the principles that":

> 1) faculty members be apprised of the extent and seriousness of the financial problem with appropriate documentation; and 2) that faculty members as well as administrators should be involved in formulating any plans which would result in discontinuation of either programs or personnel.

Colby-Sawyer College (B2) both attributes a role to the faculty and limits their role:

> The faculty shall be represented in administrative processes relating to program reorganization, or the curtailment or termination of instructional programs due to financial exigency through the Faculty Standing Committee. Faculty shall not, however, necessarily be represented in individual personnel decisions; the president and the board of trustees shall have final authority in all matters related to financial exigency.

Retaining tenured faculty. The AAUP specifically states that "The appointment of a faculty member with tenure will not be terminated in favor of retaining a faculty member without tenure, except in extraordinary circumstances where a serious distortion of the academic program would otherwise result" (1995, p. 25). Forty percent of the policies include a similar stated preference for retaining tenured faculty over nontenured. Again there is disparity among Carnegie classifications, with only 22% of Baccalaureate 1 and 24% of Research 1 institutions including this provision, compared to 78% of Doctoral 1 institutions. Oklahoma State University (R2) reasons that:

> In most cases, a tenured faculty member will have given numerous years of productive and faithful service to the university. Giving preferred status to tenured faculty during a state of financial exigency, therefore, is not merely providing protection of an individual's rights under academic tenure, it is practicing humaneness and responsible action within the university by those charged with its administration.

The collective bargaining agreement for Cleveland State University (D2) specifically states that tenured faculty members can replace nontenured faculty members rather than face termination. The University of Toledo's (D1) UT-AAUP collective bargaining agreement asserts that "Any tenured member scheduled for layoff who is qualified to teach in a different department or college can 'bump' untenured faculty in said department or college." In contrast, the University of Idaho (R2) and Idaho State University (D2) place the emphasis on programmatic needs: "Those employees who are deemed to be of key importance to the specific program will be retained in preference to other employees, whatever their status." Kent State University's (R2) collective bargaining agreement stipulates that faculty members outside the bargaining unit shall be released before faculty in the bargaining unit, provided the bargaining unit members are qualified to perform the necessary services.

In addition to policy provisions with a stated preference to retain tenured faculty, policy provisions may include differential timing and privileges based upon rank and tenure status. For example, the University of the Ozarks (B2) specifies:

For regular faculty on nontenured appointments, appointments may be cancelled with 30 days notice in cases of bona fide financial exigency. Tenured faculty shall be given 12 months notice in such cases.

The collective bargaining agreement governing the University of Toledo (D1) allows faculty members to be terminated due to financial emergency "notice, or salary in lieu thereof, in accordance with the following schedule":

- At least three (3) months if the final decision is reached by March 1 . . . of the first year of probationary service, if the member is untenured;

- At least six (6) months, if the decision is reached by December 15 of the second year . . . of probationary service, if the member is untenured;

- At least one year, if the decision is reached after eighteen (18) months of probationary service, if the member is untenured;

- Completion of the current academic year plus one (1) year, if the member is tenured . . . (1998)

Identifying faculty for termination. Identifying faculty members to be released upon declaration of a financial exigency is a complex process involving a number of considerations. The collective bargaining agreement governing Florida State University (R1) and the University of Central Florida (D2) describes the following "Layoff Considerations": tenure, affirmative action, and "length of continuous university service . . . performance evaluation by students, peers, and supervisors . . . academic training, professional reputation, teaching effectiveness, research record or quality of the creative activity . . . and service to the profession, community, and public."

As mentioned earlier, Idaho State University's (D2) policy on "staff reduction criteria" focuses on programmatic needs first, but it also lists other criteria:

In making any staff reduction recommendation to the board, the president must utilize as the first criterion the preservation of the quality and effectiveness of the programs of the university. Those employees who are deemed to be of key importance to the specific program will be retained in preference to other employees, whatever their status. . . . Other criteria that must be considered include, but are not limited to, tenure, rank, time in rank, length of service, field of specialization, maintenance of necessary programs or services, maintenance of affirmative action programs, and quality of service and work.

Displaced faculty: Another "suitable" position. Just over half (102, 57%) of the policies state that the institution will attempt to place the faculty member in a different position in the institution in lieu of termination. The biggest variance between Carnegie classifications is found within the research institutions, with 80% of Research 2 institutions including this provision, and only 24% of Research 1 institutions including it. Representative provisions include Weber State University (M2): "Faculty members should be given special consideration in filling any existing vacancies for which they are professionally qualified," and Saint Mary's University (M1): "a serious and documented institutional effort will be made to assist [ranked] faculty members to find employment either at Saint Mary's College or elsewhere."

Thirty-five (20%) of the policies state that the institution's obligation extends to helping the displaced faculty member find work outside of the institution. While none of the Research 2 or Master's 2 institutions include this provision at all, 19 (35%) of the Master's 1 institutions do. It is interesting that while the Research 2 institutions have the largest percentage of institutions including the "placement in another suitable position" provision, none of the Research 2 policies discuss expanding that effort outside of the institution. The University of Colorado (M1) provides "counseling regarding employment opportunities outside of the university." At both Saint Joseph's College (B2) and Colby-Sawyer College (B2), the institution assists tenured faculty in finding employment internally, as well as "in industry, government, or in other educational institutions." The University of Southern Colorado (B2) has an especially extensive policy:

In the event of scheduled terminations of tenure contract faculty, the university shall, in the period between notification and the effective date, assist faculty members to prepare for assignment to other degree or program areas where vacancies exist or are anticipated. Assistance may include, but need not be limited to, awarding of a development or enhancement leave or participation in other faculty development programs; provision of outplacement seminars dealing with employment search strategies, career changes, and the like; use of university resources, as approved by the provost, in the employment search; and other appropriate services offered through the office of the provost for a period of six months from the effective date of termination.

Notice and/or severance pay.   Terms of notice and/or severance pay are found in 131 (74%) of the policies. At Baldwin-Wallace College (M1), "the faculty member concerned shall be given not less than a 12-month notice in writing commencing with the end of the current academic year." Baldwin-Wallace also stipulates that "In lieu of a 12-month written notice, a faculty member shall receive one year's salary." Clarkson University (D2) provides tenured faculty members with "their salaries for not less than one year from the date the board of trustees confirmed their termination whether or not they are continued in their duties at the institution."

Because a state of financial exigency might require drastic action, notice and severance provisions sometimes include a waiver. For example, the collective bargaining agreement for Chicago State University (M1) and Eastern Illinois University (M1) states, "Notice requirements shall not apply in cases of extreme and immediate financial exigency." West Virginia Wesleyan College's (M2) policy says, "In extreme situations, where timely notice cannot be given, financial compensation proportionate to the lateness of the notice will be awarded in lieu of full notice."

Right to reinstatement.   One hundred and sixteen (65%) of the policies address the right to reinstatement of a terminated faculty member. Common elements of these policies include:

- The type of position that must be offered to a faculty member
- Whether the policy applies to tenured or nontenured faculty
- The length of the reinstatement period
- The terms and conditions for rehire

For example, Fairmont State College's (B2) policy applies to both tenured and probationary faculty who are "qualified" for an open position:

> If within two years following the terminated employment of a tenured or probationary faculty member due to financial exigency a position(s) for which the faculty member is qualified becomes vacant, the president will offer the position to the affected faculty by certified mail, return receipt requested.

The University of the Ozarks' (B2) policy does not specify if it applies to tenured or nontenured faculty but restricts reappointment to the position held by the faculty member before release: "the released faculty member's position will not be filled by a replacement within a period of two years, unless the released faculty member has been offered reappointment and at least six weeks time within which to accept or decline."

Marquette University (D1) asserts:

> For a period of three years following termination, any tenured faculty member who is terminated because of financial exigency will be given the first opportunity for the position from which he or she was separated in the event that that position is reinstated. To the extent to which it is reasonable to do so, this same consideration will be extended to nontenured faculty who have been separated from the faculty because of financial exigency.

In contrast, the University of Idaho's (R2) provisions for tenured faculty specify:

- ◆ The position concerned may not be filled by replacement within a period of three years from the effective date of the layoff unless the faculty member has been offered a return to employment in that position and has not accepted the offer within 30 calendar days after the offer is extended.

- ◆ If an offer of reinstatement is not accepted, the employee's name may be deleted from the reinstatement list and, if so deleted, the board has no further obligation to the employee.

- ◆ An employee who is laid off may continue to contribute toward and receive the benefits of any UI insurance program if the laws, rules, regulations, policies, and procedures governing the administration of such insurance program so permit.

- ◆ A tenured faculty member who has been laid off and who accepts reemployment at UI will resume tenure and the rank held at the time of layoff, be paid a salary commensurate with the rank and length of previous service, be credited with any sick leave accrued as of the date of layoff, and be credited with any annual leave accrued as of the date of layoff for which payment has not been made.

The above provisions are the same for nontenured faculty members in permanent positions at the University of Idaho, except the period during which the position cannot be filled by a replacement is reduced to only one year, and the faculty member does not resume tenure.

The terms and conditions for reinstatement under the University of Hawaii's (R1) collective bargaining agreement prescribe that a faculty member who had previously gained tenure could be subjected to probation if offered a different position:

A retrenched tenured faculty member reappointed to a position other than the one from which the faculty member was retrenched may be granted immediate tenure. If the faculty member is not granted immediate

tenure, then the faculty member shall serve a probationary period of not more than two (2) years.

Retraining. The AAUP suggests that an institution should
offer to retrain a faculty member facing termination due to program discontinuance, but does not explicitly suggest retraining
in cases of financial exigency. In contrast, 32 (18%) of the policies
on financial exigency mention retraining for faculty members in
order to qualify them for a different type of work. These policies
vary significantly in scope. The collective bargaining agreement
for the University of Massachusetts, Lowell (D2) states, "The
chancellor may in his discretion and upon request of the
retrenched unit member, authorize retention of such member
where, with limited retraining, he would be able to perform in a
vacant position." Drake University (M1) goes a step further:
"For purposes of retraining, a dismissed faculty member may
pursue without charge a degree program or other approved
program of study at Drake University for which he/she enrolls
within one year following dismissal."

West Virginia Wesleyan College (M2) diverges from this ten-
dency with the following statement: "Tenured faculty members
will be informed of other staff openings and given a reasonable
opportunity to readapt within a division or elsewhere within
the college, but the college is not required to retrain faculty."

PROGRAM DISCONTINUANCE

The Terminology

Of the 196 tenure-granting institutions covered in this study, 159
(81%) provided the Project on Faculty Appointments with policies relating to the reduction of tenured and probationary faculty members due to the broad category of changes in educational programs (see Table 8-4). This number includes all
institutions that discuss whether faculty members may be
released due to a change in educational program, regardless of
the length or detail of the policy. The material sent by 37 (19%)
institutions did not include such a policy. One should not infer,

however, that these institutions lack such a policy, as the relevant clause may be part of a document other than the faculty handbook submitted to the project.

Eighty-one (51%) of those policies refer to program "discontinuance" or "discontinuation" (see Table 8-5). Similar to the diverse terms and definitions used for financial exigency, policies discuss termination in case of program changes, curtailment, modification, consolidation, reorganization, reduction, abandonment and even curricular exigency. In fact, 101 (64%) policies referred to termination of faculty members because of changes in an educational program in addition to, or rather than, program discontinuance.

Saint John's University (Jamaica, NY) (D1), for example, refers to a diverse set of program changes:

> The administration and/or the faculty may initiate action to abolish academic programs, eliminate an academic department and/or reduce the size of the faculty in an academic department due to loss of, or imminent reasonable expectation of the loss of, state registration or on the basis of bona fide need. . . . Bona fide need shall include departmental financial exigency, loss of necessary accreditation or denial of an application for necessary accreditation by a recognized accrediting agency or seriously deficient programs as determined by outside evaluation.

Agnes Scott College (B1) allows dismissals for curricular exigency, or "the elimination of a major structural element of the curriculum, based essentially on educational considerations." Saint Louis University (R2) defines academic reorganization as "the reduction or discontinuance of a program, department, college or school that may result in the termination of faculty members, following one or more program reviews . . . and based upon educational considerations other than financial exigency."

For analysis purposes, all related terms are herein referred to as program discontinuance policies. The analyses that follow are based on a sample size of 159.

Table 8-4 The Sample

Carnegie Classification	196 Institutions	159 Policies on Program Discontinuance	
		# with Policies on Program Discontinuance	% with Policies on Program Discontinuance
R1	21	17	81%
R2	16	15	94%
D1	10	6	60%
D2	17	13	76%
M1	56	49	88%
M2	13	11	85%
B1	25	18	72%
B2	38	30	79%

Key to Carnegie classification abbreviations: R1 = Research 1; R2 = Research 2; D1 = Doctoral 1; D2 = Doctoral 2; M1 = Master's 1; M2 = Master's 2; B1 = Baccalaureate 1; B2 = Baccalaureate 2 institutions.

Table 8-5 Policies Using the Terms "Program Discontinuance" or "Program Discontinuation"

R1 n=17		R2 n=15		D1 n=6		D2 n=13		M1 n=49		M2 n=11		B1 n=18		B2 n=30		Total n=159	
#	%	#	%	#	%	#	%	#	%	#	%	#	%	#	%	#	%
7	41	7	47	0	0	8	62	22	45	7	64	11	61	19	63	81	51

Education Versus Finance

The AAUP's *Recommended Institutional Regulations on Academic Freedom and Tenure* stipulates that program discontinuance decisions should be "based essentially upon educational considerations" (1995, p. 25). Fifty-five (35%) institutions in the sample adhere to the spirit of this statement, providing reasons for program discontinuance such as programmatic review, educational considerations, mission-related considerations, or other nonfinancial reasons (see Table 8-6). The classification with the largest percentage of institutions asserting only nonfinancial reasons for program discontinuance is Baccalaureate 2 (50%).

The AAUP refers institutions back to the recommended regulations on financial exigency "when discontinuance of a program or department is mandated by financial exigency of the institution" (1995, p. 25). Twenty-eight (18%) of the policies in the sample mention both educational and financial reasons in their policies on program discontinuance, while six policies are based on discontinuance for financial reasons only.

The University of Missouri, Columbia (R1) first quotes the AAUP's recommendation that the decision should be "based essentially on educational considerations," but later in the paragraph expands the policy to say, "Financial considerations may play a role in the decision to discontinue a program, since occasionally the University may have to reduce the range of programs offered in order to maintain acceptable educational quality."

In contrast, Columbia University's (R1) policy is based solely on discontinuance for "serious financial needs," and includes a reappointment provision that mimics the language from the AAUP's policy on financial exigency. These examples illustrate how thin the line can be between financial exigency and program discontinuance. If a program discontinuance policy is based solely on financial considerations, should it be classified as a program discontinuance policy or a financial exigency policy? For the purposes of this chapter, such policies were classified as program discontinuance based on financial considerations.

Table 8-6   Program Discontinuance Policies Based on Educational/
Programmatic/Mission-Related Considerations

R1 n=17		R2 n=15		D1 n=6		D2 n=13		M1 n=49		M2 n=11		B1 n=18		B2 n=30		Total n=159	
#	%	#	%	#	%	#	%	#	%	#	%	#	%	#	%	#	%
7	41	5	33	2	33	2	15	15	31	4	36	5	28	15	50	55	35

The Purposes of Program Discontinuance

Policy provisions at West Virginia University (R1) and Central Connecticut State University (M1) explain why program discontinuance policies benefit the institution:

All University System institutions, especially those which are tax supported, exist to serve the higher educational needs of one or more identifiable potential student populations in the State . . . Just as the educational needs of these potential student populations evolve with the passage of time, so too should the program arrays which purport to address these needs. (West Virginia University, R1)

This article [Programmatic Adjustment and Redeployment of Resources] is not an extension of Article 17 [Retrenchment]; rather its objective is to bring about the kind of prior study and change necessary to meet educational objectives without reaching the point of dislocation and hard feelings resulting from a declaration of financial exigency in the academic community. (Central Connecticut State University, M1)

The University System of Georgia (1999) gives authority to the Board of Regents to "modify programs offered by the system generally or at various institutions of the system. Such modification may be a part of a change of institutional mission and may result in discontinuation of programs or reduction in size thereof."

These policies combine educational, financial, and mission-related considerations. West Virginia University's (R1) policy stresses meeting the "educational needs" of the state's students in relation to the expectations of taxpayers. In comparison, Central Connecticut State University (M1) sees program discontinuance as a way to avoid a future financial exigency.

WHEN TENURED FACULTY ARE TERMINATED

The AAUP's *Recommended Institutional Regulations on Academic Freedom and Tenure* lists "Discontinuance of Program or Department Not Mandated by Financial Exigency" as an adequate cause for "termination of an appointment with continuous tenure, or of a probationary or special appointment before the end of the specified term" (1995, p. 25). The AAUP's procedures for program discontinuance are summarized as follows:

◆ The formal discontinuance of a program must be "bona fide" (p. 25).

◆ Discontinuance of a program will be for "educational considerations" (p. 25).

◆ Faculty will determine the need for program discontinuance.

◆ The institution will "make every effort" to place faculty in other positions before terminating their appointments. This effort may extend to supporting training for a faculty member that would qualify the faculty member for a new position (p. 25).

◆ A terminated faculty member will receive appropriate severance pay.

◆ Faculty members who have received notice of termination shall have the right to appeal their cases to a faculty committee.

Adherence to AAUP Policy

Sixty-one (38%) of the institutions use AAUP language in their program discontinuance policies without mentioning the AAUP by name, while ten others explicitly cite the AAUP. Of the 61 policies with AAUP language, 11 use language appearing in the AAUP's policy on financial exigency without using any language from the AAUP's policy on program discontinuance.

Provisions and Protections

Program discontinuance policies typically include a number of provisions that are the same as, or similar to, those found in the program discontinuance section of the AAUP's *Recommended Institutional Regulations* (see Table 8-7).

No termination of tenured faculty. Butler University's (M1) policy on "Discontinuance of program or department not mandated by financial exigency" is not uncommon in its statement that "Except in the most extraordinary circumstances, all tenured faculty members and those on continuous appointment will retain their positions." While it is clear that the termination of tenured and continuing faculty will be rare, the policy does allow termination if necessary. Only three of the institutions specifically state that faculty members will not be terminated for

Table 8-7   Breakdown of Key AAUP Provisions Included in Program
Discontinuance Policies

Carnegie Classification	Faculty Role Specified (Roles Vary)		Place in Other Suitable Position		Support for Retraining		Notice and/or Severance Pay	
	#	%	#	%	#	%	#	%
R1	13	76	12	71	6	35	12	71
R2	8	53	12	80	4	27	14	93
D1	3	50	5	83	1	17	5	83
D2	8	62	11	85	5	38	11	85
M1	25	51	37	76	15	31	41	84
M2	3	27	7	64	4	36	9	82
B1	10	56	10	56	3	17	12	67
B2	16	53	23	77	7	23	24	80
Total	86	54	117	74	45	28	128	81

reasons of program discontinuance or change not mandated by financial exigency, and all three are Research 1 institutions: University of Indiana, University of Iowa, and the Massachusetts Institute of Technology. According to the Massachusetts Institute of Technology's (R1) policy:

> The tenure of faculty members does not constrain the Institute from reorganizing or closing a department or other academic unit. However, tenure may not be terminated because of such a reorganization or closing unless the termination is necessitated by a financial exigency that affects the Institute as a whole.

The policies of these institutions are even stricter than the AAUP's recommended regulations. The AAUP does allow the termination of faculty because of program discontinuance for reasons other than financial exigency.

The faculty role. Eighty-six (54%) policies consider the level of faculty participation in the program discontinuance process. Similar to the findings for financial exigency, the Master's 2 classification has the lowest percentage of institutions citing a role for faculty (27%). Carroll College's (B2) policy language follows closely the AAUP guidelines: "The decision to discontinue formally a program or department of instruction will be based essentially upon educational considerations, as determined primarily by the faculty assembly as a whole or an appropriate committee thereof and approved by the college's board of trustees."

Northwestern University's (R1) policy addresses the interests of students and faculty alike: "While the final decision rests with the administration and the board of trustees, the administration recognizes the legitimate interests of faculty and students who may be affected by the discontinuation of a program."

Glenville State College (B2) explicitly draws the administration into the process: "Institutional policy for accommodating major reduction in or discontinuance of an existing program shall be developed through a collaborative assessment by representatives of administration and faculty."

Displaced faculty: Another "suitable" position. The AAUP *Recommended Institutional Regulations* on program discontinuance require that "the institution will make every effort to place the faculty member concerned in another suitable position" (1995, p. 25). Found in nearly three-fourths of the policies, this is one of the most common provisions in the sample. Michigan State University's (R1) policy emphasizes the benefits that may accrue to a department that receives a transferred tenured faculty member:

> Administrators in the potential receiving units shall urge their faculty to consider especially carefully the broader social good that derives from having tenure in the university in cases in which reassignment results from dissolution or curtailment of a department or school.

Virginia Polytechnic Institute and State University (R1) suggests helping faculty members find work elsewhere: "Where placement in another position is not possible, the university will provide appropriate and reasonable career transition assistance such as clerical support, communications, office space, and outplacement services."

The University of Colorado's (M1) policy closely parallels the AAUP, stating "every reasonable effort will be made to find another suitable position for the faculty member within the university." The policy then defines "'reasonable efforts' to find another 'suitable' position":

> A review of all academic and research programs of, and all faculty, administrative, and staff positions in, the university where the faculty member might, if transferred, be reasonably able to use his or her professional training and skills, (with or without further retraining), and in which his or her contributions could reasonably be expected to be of value to the university.

The *Rules and Regulations of the Board of Regents* of the University of Texas System acknowledges that reallocation of one faculty member might result in the displacement of another tenured faculty: "If retention of a tenured faculty member results in displacement of a tenured faculty member in another area, the displaced faculty member is entitled to [the termination procedures outlined]."

Support for retraining. Forty-five (28%) policies stipulate that the institution should provide opportunities to retrain faculty members for other "suitable positions." For example, Northern Kentucky University's (M1) policy asserts, "The university shall offer reassignment or paid leave for retraining to tenured faculty affected by the program reduction or termination, and shall make every reasonable effort in the case of untenured faculty." Norwich University (M1) "may consider on an individual basis such special arrangements as early retirement, retraining . . ." Retraining at Saint Norbert College (B2) hinges on the faculty member's service:

> If placement in another position can be accomplished by a reasonable period of training, financial and other support for such training will be offered. The extent of such an offering, however, shall be equitably adjusted to the faculty member's length of past and potential service.

Notice and/or severance pay. The most common provision, found in 81% of all of the program discontinuance policies and

93% of the Research 2 policies, describes terms of notice and/or severance pay for terminated faculty members. Notice and severance pay are linked in Agnes Scott College's (B1) policy:

> Faculty members affected shall receive at least one year's notice from the date of their notification by the president. Severance pay may be equitably adjusted to the length of past and potential service to the college but will not be less than one year's salary.

It is interesting to note that the notice requirements for program discontinuance not based on financial exigency can be longer than the requirements for financial exigency. At Virginia Polytechnic Institute and State University (R1), notice for tenured faculty who have been terminated because of "restructuring" is "not less than three years," whereas for financial exigency the university provides a minimum of one year of notice "whenever possible." Cedarville College (B2) provides written notice to "full-time or part-time ranked faculty" as follows:

- In the case of a termination because of financial exigency, not less than ninety (90) calendar days prior to the effective date
- In the case of a termination because of reorganization, elimination, or curtailment of academic programs of the college, not less than 270 calendar days prior to the effective date

Beyond the AAUP. Fifty-one (32%) of the program discontinuance policies in the sample include a statement on tenure preference, and 98 (62%) of the policies include a clause on reinstatement rights. The AAUP's regulations for program discontinuance do not explicitly state a preference for retaining tenured faculty or discuss procedures for reinstatement. However, the AAUP's regulations on financial exigency do include such statements. Apparently, these institutions have applied the financial exigency requirements to program discontinuance, making their policies more stringent and extensive than the AAUP's regulations. James Madison University's (M1) policy includes the following clauses:

◆ The college may not renew a discontinued program or department for five years without offering renewed positions first to displaced faculty members.

◆ The appointment of a tenured faculty member will not be terminated in favor of retaining a faculty member without tenure in the same department.

Virginia Polytechnic Institute and State University (R1) specifies similar protections:

◆ Within programs identified for restructuring or discontinuance, tenured faculty must not ordinarily be terminated before untenured faculty.

◆ In all cases of termination of appointment because of program reduction or discontinuance, the position of a faculty member with tenure or continued appointment will not be filled by a replacement within a period of three years following separation unless the released faculty member has been offered reinstatement and a reasonable time in which to accept or decline.

SUMMARY

It is evident that the AAUP's recommended regulations serve as the prevalent guideline to most institutions in the sample. However, institutions sometimes omit parts of the AAUP's policy, sometimes add to the AAUP's recommendations, and sometimes borrow from other AAUP policies. Financial exigency and program discontinuance, while treated separately by the AAUP, are often melded together in one policy, with the same regulations for each circumstance.

As further evidence that these two policies are often viewed in the same light, we note that the three most common policy provisions are the same for each policy. The three policy provisions that were included most often in the financial exigency policies are 1) notice and/or severance pay (74%), 2) reinstatement terms (65%), and 3) placement in another suitable position (57%). The three policy provisions that were included most often in the program discontinuance policies are 1) notice and/or severance pay (81%), 2) placement in another suitable position (74%), and 3) reinstatement terms (62%).

The majority of the institutions in the sample crafted financial exigency and program discontinuance policies, along the lines recommended by the AAUP. The policies remain respectful of tenure, academic freedom, and the educational mission of the institution, as evidenced by the faculty's central role in the process, protections for tenured faculty members, and the need for program discontinuance policies to be based upon educational considerations.

REFERENCES

American Association of University Professors. (1995). *Policy documents and reports.* Washington, DC: AAUP.

Bloomfield College. (1997). *Agreement between Bloomfield College and Bloomfield College chapter of the American Association of University Professors.* Bloomfield, NJ: Bloomfield College.

Bowie State University. (1997). *Policy on appointment, rank, and tenure of faculty.* Adelphi, MD: Bowie State University.

Chabotar, K. J., & Honan, J. P. (1996). *New yardsticks to measure financial distress.* New Pathways Working Paper Series, no. 4. Washington, DC: American Association for Higher Education.

Columbia University. (1987). *The faculty handbook.* New York, NY: Columbia University.

Cook, J. (1974, April 30). Information bank abstracts. *The New York Times,* p. 87.

James Madison University. (1994). *Faculty handbook, 1994-1995.* Harrisonburg, VA: James Madison University.

Oklahoma State University. (1999, September 17). Appendix D: Policy statement to govern appointments, tenure, promotion, and related matters of the faculty of Oklahoma State University. Section D: Financial exigency policies and procedures. *Online faculty handbook* [On-line]. Available: www2. okstate.edu/acad/fachanind.htm.

Spiro, G. (1980, Summer). Facing reductions in force in higher education. *Journal of the College & University Personnel Association, 31*(2), 18-24.

State University System of Florida. (1996). *Collective bargaining agreement between Board of Regents State University System of Florida and United Faculty of Florida.* Tallahasee, FL: State University System of Florida.

University of Colorado. (1988). *Faculty handbook.* Boulder, CO: University of Colorado.

University of Delaware. (1999). *Handbook for faculty* [On-line]. Available: www.udel.edu/provost/fachb/.

University of Toledo. (1998). *UT-AAUP contract* [On-line]. Available: www.utoledo.edu/POLICIES-PROCEDURES-AND-CONTRACTS/UT-AAUP-CONTRACT

University System of Georgia. (1999). *Policy manual of the Board of Regents* [On-line]. Available: www.usg.edu/admin/humex/policy/sec800.html.

APPENDIX 8-A

Financial Exigency Policies Citing the AAUP

Research 1 Institutions
   1. Northwestern University
   2. University of Indiana, Bloomington

Doctoral 1 Institutions
   3. Illinois State University

Doctoral 2 Institutions
   4. Duquesne University

Master's 1 Institutions
   5. College of Saint Rose
   6. Drake University
   7. James Madison University
   8. Springfield College
   9. University of Hartford

10. Valparaiso University

Baccalaureate 1 Institutions
11. Agnes Scott College
12. Coe College
13. Lake Forest College

Baccalaureate 2 Institutions
14. Virginia Intermont College

APPENDIX 8-B
Program Discontinuance Policies Citing the AAUP

Research 1 Institutions
1. Northwestern University
2. Virginia Polytechnic Institute and State University

Master's 1 Institutions
3. Drake University
4. James Madison University
5. Springfield College
6. University of Colorado, Colorado Springs
7. Valparaiso University

Baccalaureate 1 Institutions
8. Agnes Scott College
9. Lake Forest College

Baccalaureate 2 Institutions
10. Virginia Intermont College

APPENDIX 8-C
Financial Exigency Policies Including a Stated
Preference for Retention of Tenured Faculty Members

Research 1 Institutions
1. Florida State University
2. University of Hawaii, Manoa
3. University of Missouri, Columbia
4. Virginia Polytechnic Institute and State University

Research 2 Institutions
5. Auburn University
6. Kent State University
7. Oklahoma State University
8. Saint Louis University
9. University of Arkansas
10. University of Delaware
11. University of Rhode Island

Doctoral 1 Institutions
12. American University
13. Illinois State University
14. Marquette University
15. Saint John's University, Jamaica, NY
16. United States International University
17. University of Texas, Arlington
18. University of Toledo

Doctoral 2 Institutions
19. Cleveland State University
20. George Mason University
21. Montana State University
22. University of Central Florida
23. University of Detroit, Mercy
24. University of Massachusetts, Lowell
25. University of New Hampshire

Master's 1 Institutions
26. Bemidji State College
27. Butler University
28. California State University, Los Angeles
29. Central Connecticut State University
30. Chicago State University
31. College of Saint Rose
32. Creighton University
33. Drake University
34. East Carolina University
35. Eastern Illinois University
36. Emporia State University
37. James Madison University
38. Mankato State University
39. Northern Kentucky University
40. Pittsburg State University
41. Saint Mary's University
42. San Francisco State University
43. San Jose State University
44. Santa Clara University
45. Southeastern Louisiana University
46. Springfield College
47. University of Alaska
48. University of Colorado, Colorado Springs
49. University of Northern Iowa
50. University of Southern Maine
51. University of Texas, El Paso
52. University of Texas, Pan American

53. Youngstown State University

Master's 2 Institutions
54. Pacific University
55. Weber State University
56. West Virginia Wesleyan College

Baccalaureate 1 Institutions
57. Coe College
58. Connecticut College
59. Drew University
60. Hamilton College
61. Lake Forest College

Baccalaureate 2 Institutions
62. Albertson College of Idaho
63. Bloomfield College
64. Carroll College
65. Colby-Sawyer College
66. Dakota Wesleyan University
67. Fairmont State College
68. Saint Joseph's College
69. Saint Norbert College
70. University of Southern Colorado
71. Virginia Intermont College
72. Western Montana College

APPENDIX 8-D

Program Discontinuance Policies Including a
Stated Preference for Retention of Tenured Faculty Members

Research 1 Institutions
  1. Florida State University
  2. University of Hawaii, Manoa
  3. Virginia Polytechnic Institute and State University

Research 2 Institutions
  4. Kent State University
  5. Saint Louis University
  6. University of Arkansas
  7. University of Rhode Island

Doctoral 1 Institutions
  8. Saint John's University, Jamaica, NY
  9. United States International University

Doctoral 2 Institutions
  10. Cleveland State University
  11. George Mason University

12. Montana State University
13. University of Central Florida
14. University of Detroit Mercy
15. University of Massachusetts, Lowell
16. University of New Hampshire

Master's 1 Institutions
17. Bemidji State College
18. Butler University
19. California State University, Los Angeles
20. Central Connecticut State University
21. Chicago State University
22. College of Saint Rose
23. East Carolina University
24. Eastern Illinois University
25. Emporia State University
26. James Madison University
27. Mankato State University
28. Northern Kentucky University
29. Saint Mary's University
30. San Francisco State University
31. San Jose State University
32. Springfield College
33. University of Alaska
34. University of Colorado, Colorado Springs
35. University of Southern Maine

Master's 2 Institutions
36. MidAmerica Nazarene University
37. Pacific University
38. Weber State University

Baccalaureate 1 Institutions
39. Coe College
40. Connecticut College
41. Hiram College

Baccalaureate 2 Institutions
42. Albertson College of Idaho
43. Bloomfield College
44. Colby-Sawyer College
45. Fairmont State College
46. Langston University
47. Saint Joseph's College
48. Saint Norbert College
49. University of Southern Colorado
50. Virginia Intermont College
51. Western Montana College

APPENDIX 8-E

Program Discontinuance Policies Based on Nonfinancial
Considerations Only (e.g., Educational, Programmatic)

Research 1 Institutions
1. North Carolina State University
2. University of Arizona
3. University of California, Irvine
4. University of Hawaii, Manoa
5. University of Iowa
6. Virginia Polytechnic Institute and State University
7. West Virginia University

Research 2 Institutions
8. Oklahoma State University
9. Saint Louis University
10. Southern Illinois University, Carbondale
11. University of California, Santa Cruz
12. University of Louisville

Doctoral 1 Institutions
13. Illinois State University
14. University of Texas, Arlington

Doctoral 2 Institutions
15. George Mason University
16. University of New Hampshire

Master's 1 Institutions
17. Arkansas Tech University
18. California State University, Los Angeles
19. Central Connecticut State University
20. Creighton University
21. Drake University
22. James Madison University
23. Northern Kentucky University
24. San Francisco State University
25. San Jose State University
26. Santa Clara University
27. Springfield College
28. University of Alaska
29. University of Colorado, Colorado Springs
30. University of Texas, El Paso
31. University of Texas, Pan American

Master's 2 Institutions
32. Drury College
33. Pacific University
34. Philadelphia College of Textiles and Science

35. West Virginia Wesleyan College

Baccalaureate 1 Institutions
36. Agnes Scott College
37. Drew University
38. Lake Forest College
39. Saint Olaf College
40. Shepherd College

Baccalaureate 2 Institutions
41. Albertson College of Idaho
42. Bethel College
43. Carroll College
44. Cedarville College
45. Central State University
46. Colby-Sawyer College
47. Dakota Wesleyan University
48. Dickinson State University
49. Fairmont State College
50. Glenville State College
51. Greensboro College
52. Mayville State University
53. Mount Mercy College
54. North Park College
55. Virginia Intermont College

APPENDIX 8-F

According to Chabotar and Honan (1996), a financial exigency "statement that attempts to incorporate suitable yardsticks might stipulate" (p. 29):

> Financial exigency at XYZ University shall be defined as the existence of two or more of the following conditions: 1) a downgrade of the institution's bond rating to the minimum investment grade of *Baa or BBB* or below in a given year; 2) an operating budget deficit equivalent to 3 percent or more and that is greater than last year's; 3) three or more years of decline in FTE enrollment; and 4) real decline in the market value of the endowment, adjusted for inflation, for three or more years. (p. 29)

9

STANDARD DEVIATIONS: FACULTY APPOINTMENT POLICIES AT INSTITUTIONS WITHOUT TENURE

William T. Mallon

HIGHLIGHTS

◆ 21 (10%) of the 217 randomly selected four-year colleges and universities in the Faculty Appointment Policy Archive do not offer academic tenure.

Of the 21 Contract Institutions

◆ 20 (95%) include statements on academic freedom.

- Six (29%) quote verbatim the academic freedom section of the AAUP's 1940 *Statement of Principles on Academic Freedom and Tenure*.

◆ 15 (71%) offer multiyear contracts of lengths varying from three to ten years, and three colleges offer only one-year contracts.

◆ 17 (81%) contain notice-of-nonrenewal policies.

   ▪ Five of 17 policies (29%) conform to AAUP guidelines.

◆ 13 (62%) have no provisions for faculty involvement in the evaluation process.

◆ Seven (33%) annually evaluate all faculty.

◆ 17 (81%) offer rank and promotion.

   ▪ 14 colleges have committee structures for promotion review.

   ▪ Three colleges offer promotion but have no committee structure.

   ▪ Only two of 17 institutions with rank require a doctorate or terminal degree for appointment or promotion to assistant professor.

   ▪ Seven of the 17 require a doctorate or terminal degree for promotion to associate professor.

◆ 20 (95%) include statements about dismissal for cause.

   ▪ 12 (60%) conform to AAUP guidelines on dismissal procedures.

◆ Eight (38%) explicitly mention the role of faculty in financial exigency/program discontinuation processes.

   ▪ Three colleges do not have such policies.

   ▪ Ten colleges do not include faculty in the process of financial exigency and program discontinuation.

INTRODUCTION

With the tremendous rise in part-time and nontenure-track faculty, traditional tenured and tenure-track faculty positions in American higher education have declined dramatically. Part-time positions have increased 100% from 1970 to 1995 (National Center for Education Statistics, 1998). In the same period, the proportion of nontenure-track, full-time faculty climbed from 19% to 28%, while the proportion of tenure-track faculty fell from 29% to 20% (Leatherman, 1999). According to one source, "perhaps as few as 38-40% of all faculty appointments made in recent years are 'traditional' in the sense of being full-time and either tenured or tenurable" (Schuster, 1998).

At a campus or system level, however, tenure still predominates. The vast majority of four-year college campuses continue to offer tenure. The most recent statistics indicate that 100% of public doctorate-granting institutions and public four-year colleges offer tenure (although sampling error and nonresponse may have affected the percentages), and only 88 of 573 private four-year liberal arts colleges do not award tenure (National Center for Education Statistics, 1996). If institutions with tenure are the norm in higher education, then colleges without tenure—contract colleges—are the deviations.

This chapter examines the policy provisions at institutions without tenure and answers the following questions:

◆ What are faculty appointment policies at these contract institutions?

◆ What variations from standard policy exist at these colleges?

◆ What are the differences in policy among this group of institutions?

This chapter investigates the areas of academic freedom, nature of appointments, evaluation, promotion, rank, dismissal for cause, and financial exigency/program discontinuation.

Sample:

The sample for this analysis comes from the Project on Faculty Appointments' 1998 Faculty Appointment Policy Archive (FAPA) CD-ROM. Of the 217 randomly selected four-year colleges and universities in FAPA, 21 (10%) do not offer tenure. The FAPA contract colleges included in the analysis are quite similar to one another in size and scope: 18 of the 21 are classified as Baccalaureate 2 institutions, and all 21 are privately controlled (see Table 9-1). Additionally, 11 of the 21 (52%) contract colleges have a religious affiliation or an explicit religious mission.

Table 9-1   Contract Institutions Included in FAPA

College	Institutional Control	Institutional Mission	Carnegie Classification
Allen University	Private		Baccalaureate 2
Brenau University	Private		Master's 1
College of the Atlantic	Private		Baccalaureate 1
College of the Ozarks	Private	Christian	Baccalaureate 2
Endicott College	Private		Baccalaureate 2
Florida Southern College	Private	Christian	Baccalaureate 2
King College	Private	Christian	Baccalaureate 2
Lesley College	Private		Master's 1
Liberty University	Private	Christian	Master's 1
Lourdes College	Private	Catholic	Baccalaureate 2
Northwest Christian College	Private	Christian	Baccalaureate 2
Olivet College	Private		Baccalaureate 2
Pacific Union College	Private	Christian	Baccalaureate 2
Prescott College	Private		Baccalaureate 2
Rust College	Private		Baccalaureate 2
Shimer College	Private		Baccalaureate 2
Simpson College	Private	Christian	Baccalaureate 2
Trinity College of Vermont	Private	Catholic	Baccalaureate 2
Warren Wilson College	Private		Baccalaureate 2
Wayland Baptist University	Private	Christian	Baccalaureate 2
Western Baptist College	Private	Christian	Baccalaureate 2

ACADEMIC FREEDOM

Of the contract colleges in FAPA, all but one (Shimer College, B2) contain statements on academic freedom. If nothing else, this high percentage indicates that faculty and administrators at contract colleges acknowledge the importance of academic freedom; how these institutions define it is another matter.

The American Association of University Professors (AAUP) 1940 *Statement of Principles on Academic Freedom and Tenure* sets the standard in the academy (AAUP, 1995, pp. 3-10). Six of the contract institutions quote verbatim the first section of the 1940 *Statement* on Academic Freedom, and another eight use their own language to cover the same three areas of freedom in 1) research and publication, 2) discussion of one's subject in the classroom, and 3) speaking and writing as citizens. Therefore, 14 of 21 contract institutions (67%) include standard provisions in their academic freedom policy statements.

Three institutions that cover all three areas of academic freedom add caveats related to their unique religious missions. For
example, Liberty University (M1) "subscribes" to the 1940 *Statement*, but cautions its faculty that "not all areas of research might
be compatible with the purposes of Liberty University." Northwest Christian College (B2) provides for the freedom to pursue
and publish research and to write and speak as a citizen "provided that such activities do not . . . conflict with the purpose
and objectives of the college." Wayland Baptist University (B2)
notes:

> The constitutionally protected rights of faculty members,
> as citizens, to freedom of expression on matters of public
> concern must be balanced with the interest of the univer-
> sity and the Baptist General Convention of Texas. . . . [A
> faculty member's statements] are not protected free
> speech if they either substantially impede the faculty
> member's performance of daily duties or materially and
> substantially interfere with the regular operation of the
> university, or if they are part of a continuing pattern of
> expression of such nature as to destroy the harmony and
> morale of his or her division.

Five of the 21 (24%) contract institutions include statements
on academic freedom but omit one or more of the three traditional areas of protection. Two of these colleges (Olivet College
(B2) and Rust College (B2)) do not explicitly mention freedom in
research and publication, though they guarantee freedom in
teaching. It is possible that faculty at these colleges, primarily
teaching institutions, do not undertake research. Three colleges
(Lesley College (M1), Allen University (B2), and College of the
Ozarks (B2)) do not encompass freedom of extramural speech.
Lesley College includes a statement about faculty members'
responsibility to "indicate when they are speaking as official representatives of the college," but omits the freedom from institutional censorship or discipline when they speak otherwise. Allen
University "upholds" the AAUP "philosophy" on academic freedom, but makes no mention of the freedom to speak and write as
citizens. College of the Ozarks (B2) specifically prohibits faculty

members from making "statements which are detrimental to the mission and/or operation of the college."

College of the Ozarks' restriction on criticism of the college stands in stark contrast to the policy of College of the Atlantic (B1). The latter affirms that "all faculty and staff members are protected in the right to speak outside the classroom, *including criticism of practices at the college*, provided that they are qualified in doing so either by training or professional involvement in the present situation" (emphasis added).

All 19 policies, whether or not they cover the standard areas of the AAUP's 1940 *Statement*, are more protective of faculty rights than the academic freedom statement of Western Baptist College (B2). It offers a highly circumscribed freedom to faculty in teaching, research, and extramural speech:

> Faculty members are expected to discuss their subjects fully and fairly, regardless of political, social, economic, or doctrinal bias and should support their teaching with valid evidence. However, no instructor may advocate views at variance with the doctrinal statement and standards of the college. . . . Faculty members need to be careful in signing public statements or documents and should realize there is always the tacit representation of the college in whatever they say, write, attend, or sign. Before signing such items, they may wish to confer with the vice president for academics or the president. Faculty members should not engage in public criticism of their colleagues, the administration, or the college.

While Western Baptist's statement of academic freedom is comparatively restrictive, it serves a college with an unambiguous religious mission, where professors perform a "teaching ministry" to serve God and abide by the college's statement of faith.

NATURE OF APPOINTMENTS

The most distinguishing characteristic of colleges with term contracts is the defined period of employment. The appointment procedures at 19 contract colleges are included in FAPA

Table 9-2   Nature of Appointments

College	Length of Probationary Period	Longest Contract Offered	Compliance with AAUP notice of renewal
Allen University	Not applicable	1 year	No
Brenau University	5 years	5 years	Yes
College of the Atlantic	5 years	5 years	No
College of the Ozarks	6 years	6 years	No
Endicott College	Unknown	Unknown	Unknown
Florida Southern College	Not applicable	1 year	Yes
King College	10 years	5 years	No
Lesley College	Unknown	10 years	Yes
Liberty University	Not applicable	1 year	No
Lourdes College	3 years	3 years	No
Northwest Christian College	3 years	Unknown	No
Olivet College	5 years	5 years	Yes
Pacific Union College	7 years	Continuous	No
Prescott College	2 years	3 years	Unknown
Rust College	8 years	5 years	No
Shimer College	3 years	Continuous	No
Simpson College	Unknown	Unknown	Unknown
Trinity College of Vermont	5 years	5 years	Yes
Warren Wilson College	7 years	7 years	Unknown
Wayland Baptist University	1 year	3 years	No
Western Baptist College	6 years	6 years	No

(Endicott College (B2) and Simpson College's (B2) appointment procedures are not). Of this group, three institutions (Allen University (B2), Florida Southern College (B2), and Liberty University (M1)) offer only one-year, annually renewable appointments. Sixteen institutions offer multiyear contracts after some type of probationary period. Probationary periods range from one year to ten years, with an average length of 5.06 years. After the initial one-year contract at Wayland Baptist University (B2), faculty are offered rolling two- or three-year contracts. Conversely, King College (B2) stipulates that faculty must have at least ten years of service before they are eligible for five-year contracts.

The length of the longest multiyear contract offered at these institutions varies from three to ten years (see Table 9-2). Professors at Lesley College (M1) can earn contracts up to ten years depending on "evidence of excellence in teaching, meritorious service, and scholarship; distinguished leadership in the institution and/or profession; and when the length is consistent with institutional need." Lesley College also offers contracts of two, three, five, and seven years. Warren Wilson College (B2) is next, awarding faculty a seven-year contract after a successful probationary period.

Notice of Nonrenewal

The majority of institutions tend not to conform to AAUP guidelines on notice of nonrenewal of appointments. AAUP policy stipulates that the institution notify faculty of nonrenewal by March 30 in the first year of employment at the college, by December 15 in the second year, and one year in advance of the expiration of the contract after faculty have been at the institution more than two years. Only five of 17 contract colleges with nonrenewal policies conform to these guidelines. Trinity College of Vermont (B2) actually exceeds the recommendation. Its policy stipulates that faculty must be notified of nonrenewal by January 15 of the penultimate contract year, 16 months before the expiration of the contract.

The other 12 colleges have briefer periods of due notice. Allen University (B2) only needs to give faculty two months notice before the end of the fiscal year. Others vary from the norm as described in Table 9-3.

Table 9-3   Notices of Nonrenewal

College of the Atlantic	September 1 of final contract year
College of the Ozarks	End of fall term of final contract year
King College	By December 31 in years 1-3; thereafter, March 15 in penultimate year of contract
Liberty University	By January 1 with no reason given. After January 1, a reason must be offered
Lourdes College	March 15 in years 1-3; January 15 afterwards
Northwest Christian College	March 1 for all
Pacific Union College	Four months before end of contract
Rust College	March 1 in first year; February 1 thereafter
Shimer College	March 15 in years 1-3. Not specified thereafter
Wayland Baptist University	March 1 for all
Western Baptist College	December 31 of last contract year

One cannot discern from faculty handbooks, of course, whether or how often nonrenewal policies are invoked, although research (Chait & Ford, 1982; Chait & Trower, 1997) suggests not very often. Nevertheless, fixed contracts, without lengthy notices of nonrenewal, theoretically afford these colleges considerable leeway to cut faculty for reasons related to individual performance or institutional circumstance.

FACULTY EVALUATION

This section concerns three questions about faculty evaluation at colleges with contracts: 1) Who is responsible for evaluating faculty? 2) What criteria and measures are used in the evaluation? and 3) How often are faculty evaluated?

Who Evaluates Faculty?

Most contract colleges rely solely on administrators to evaluate faculty. Thirteen of the 21 institutions (62%) have no provisions for faculty involvement in the evaluation of faculty performance (see Appendix 9-A.) Midlevel administrators, such as the dean or department or division chair, are responsible for faculty evaluation at these 13 sites.

The other eight colleges use committees to evaluate faculty members and make recommendations to the academic dean or vice president. The committees at five of these eight are faculty committees. None of these five explains in their policy manuals the process by which the faculty committee is formed. The other three form committees with multiple constituencies. At Prescott College (B2), administrators and faculty sit on evaluation committees—an "individual" committee is comprised of an administrator, the program coordinator, and two faculty members, one of whom is chosen by the person under review. The Promotion and Extended Contract Committee at Rust College (B2) includes the academic dean, division chairs, and faculty representatives from each division. College of the Atlantic is the most unique. It employs a three-person "Contract Review Team," comprised of a member of the Personnel Committee, one faculty member chosen by the person being evaluated, and one student.

What is Evaluated?

Criteria and measures of faculty evaluation tend to be consistent across the contract colleges. Most colleges use student, supervisor, and self-evaluations to measure faculty productivity and effectiveness. Several colleges also include other measures, such as:

- ◆ Lesley College (M1), Trinity College of Vermont (B2), Olivet College (B2), and Shimer College (B2) require classroom observation. Administrators at Lesley, Trinity, and Olivet conduct the classroom observation. At Shimer, members of the faculty evaluation committee perform the task.

- ◆ At Lesley College (M1), Endicott College (B2), and Lourdes College (B2), peer evaluation is optional. At Northwest Christian College (B2), peer evaluation consists of "two faculty members [reviewing] each other's portfolios. They share helpful ideas and make suggestions for improvement in all areas of faculty concern . . ."

- ◆ Prescott College (B2) requires advising evaluations in addition to course evaluations.

- ◆ Shimer College (B2) has two unique requirements: The evaluation committee 1) conducts interviews with students, faculty, and staff who know the candidate, and 2) distributes a questionnaire to all faculty and staff "regarding the faculty member's contributions to the Shimer community."

Most contract colleges in the FAPA CD-ROM evaluate teaching, scholarship, and service. Consistent with the aims of many smaller liberal arts colleges, all of these institutions put greatest emphasis on teaching effectiveness. These institutions typically define scholarship broadly. Endicott College's (B2) definition is a good example:

> Scholarship: Courses taken, degrees completed, attendance at workshops, trade shows and conferences, publications, papers presented to professional societies and conferences, art exhibitions and performances, research projects, grants, fellowships and any documented form

of disciplinary inquiry which furthers teaching or the development of the professional field.

Four institutions also include additional criteria beyond teaching, scholarship and professional development, and service to the college. For example, College of the Atlantic (B1) reviews "community building" and "public service, relations, and education." Northwest Christian College (B2) considers service to supporting churches. Pacific Union College (B2) evaluates dedication to the mission of its church and the quality of interpersonal relationships. Florida Southern College (B2) indicates that, in addition to teaching ability,

> [A] number of other things are of great importance such as continued academic development, progress toward the terminal degree, scholarship, advising and counseling service to students, punctuality and thoroughness in discharging college obligations, compliance with college regulations, cooperation with the college and its employees, general service to the college, character and personality, cooperation with and participation in Lakeland Church and community affairs, and the ability to meet and speak to the public as a representative of the college.

How Often Does Evaluation Occur?

For the majority of these contract institutions (11 of 21), faculty are normally evaluated annually or biannually during the probationary period and then once during the extended contract period (usually in the penultimate year of the contract) (see Appendix 9-2). Deviations from this norm include:

- ◆ One-third of the institutions (seven of 21) conduct annual evaluations for all faculty: Allen University (B2), Brenau University (M1), Florida Southern College (B2), Liberty University (M1), Lourdes College (B2), Rust College (B2), and Wayland Baptist University (B2).

- ◆ Pacific Union College (B2) indicates that faculty are evaluated "at regular intervals," but does not specify these intervals.

◆ Western Baptist College (B2) evaluates extended contract faculty twice during each six-year contract, in years three and five.

◆ Shimer College (B2) does not regularly evaluate its senior faculty. Once faculty "interns" complete a three-year probationary period and become "senior faculty," they do not go through a formal evaluation process except under "unusual circumstances."

PROMOTION AND RANK

Who Is Involved?

Four colleges do not offer promotion and rank, 14 institutions have committee structures for promotion review, and three offer promotion but have no committee structure (see Appendix 9-C). Florida Southern College (B2), which awards promotion, explains its process in one sentence: "Salary increases and promotions in rank are determined by the president on the basis of recommendations from the dean of the college and the division chairs." At Western Baptist College (B2), the faculty member and the area manager complete a portfolio review. The area manager and vice president "meet to discuss the findings of the review." The vice president then reports on the "completion of the procedures" to a faculty affairs committee, which "determines that the proper procedures have been followed." In other words, the faculty committee only ensures that procedural standards have been met; it has no substantive input on the promotion review.

What Is Required for Promotion in Rank?

All 17 institutions with rank have four standard levels: instructor and assistant, associate, and full professor. In addition to reviewing teaching ability, scholarship, and service, many colleges have flexible minimum requirements for academic credentials and length of service.

Instructor. For instructors, the 17 institutions with rank are similar. Thirteen require a minimum of a master's degree with no prior college teaching experience. Three have options for candidates without master's: Pacific Union College (B2) requires a master's or a bachelor's and one year of college teaching; Simpson College (B2) requires a master's or a bachelor's and "demonstrated abilities"; and College of the Ozarks (B2) demands a master's or "equivalent experience" or three years of full-time teaching. Lesley College (M1) is the only institution with more stringent requirements: instructors need a master's and "prior experience."

Assistant professor. Only two of the 17 institutions (Lesley (College (M1) and Endicott College (B2)) require a doctorate or equivalent terminal degree for promotion or appointment to assistant professor. Trinity College of Vermont (B2) requests a doctorate/terminal degree or "accomplishments that are considered academically equivalent." Nine colleges require a master's plus college teaching experience, varying from as little as one year to as many as five. Three institutions require graduate work beyond the master's: assistant professors at Lourdes College (B2) need a master's plus 15 semester hours and four years' experience; at Rust College (B2) and Pacific Union College (B2), they need a master's plus 30 semester hours. Two institutions—Allen University (B2) and Wayland Baptist University (B2)—only require the master's with no additional experience or graduate work.

Associate professor. Seven institutions require a doctoral or terminal degree for promotion to associate professor. The others have flexible requirements, with the length of service shortened for a faculty member with a doctorate and lengthened for a faculty member without one. For example, at Olivet College (B2), associate professors need a master's and eight years of college teaching experience or a terminal degree and six years of experience. Western Baptist College (B2) has multiple thresholds for an associate professor: 1) a master's plus 36 hours of additional graduate work and ten years' teaching, or 2) a master's plus ABD and seven years' teaching, or 3) two master's degrees plus ten years, or 4) a ThD plus ten years, or 5) a doctorate plus five years' teaching.

Professor. Sixteen of 17 colleges require a doctorate or terminal degree for promotion to full professor (Pacific Union College (B2) demands a doctorate or a master's plus 40 semester hours of graduate work). The institutions vary in how many years of college teaching are necessary to attain full professor, from as little as six (at Rust College (B2)) to as many as 17 at Liberty University (M1) (Liberty asks for seven years' experience for promotion to the associate level and ten years' experience as an associate for promotion to professor). An average of 9.58 years of experience is required for promotion to full professor at these 17 institutions.

ADEQUATE CAUSE

Adequate Cause Defined

Twenty of 21 (95%) contract colleges include statements about dismissals for cause (Endicott College (B2) does not). Fifteen of the institutions define "adequate cause" similarly as grounds for dismissal. Common examples of grounds for dismissal include professional incompetence (14 colleges), neglect of duty (12 colleges), and moral turpitude or delinquency (nine colleges). Other examples include personal misconduct, insubordination, unethical behavior, and fabrication of credentials (each of which is mentioned by five institutions). Several institutions provide unique examples of adequate cause (see Table 9-4).

The Dismissal Process

The AAUP's guidelines for dismissal procedures include an informal inquiry by an elected faculty committee, official notification of the charges to the faculty member, a hearing before the faculty committee, the opportunity for the faculty member to retain counsel and to confront witnesses, and burden of proof resting with the institution, satisfied by clear and convincing evidence (1995, pp. 26-27). Of the 20 colleges with sections on dismissals for cause, 12 (60%) have processes that include official notification, a faculty or administrative committee, hearings, and witnesses (see Appendix 9-D). Trinity College of Vermont (B2) and College of the Atlantic (B1) specifically use the

Table 9-4   Unique Definitions of Adequate Cause

King College	"Conduct of such nature as to indicate that the faculty member is unfit to continue as a member of the faculty of this institution of Christian higher education."
Lourdes College	Unacceptable job performance, moral delinquency, conviction of any crime other than a misdemeanor.
Northwest Christian College	Lack of commitment to the ideals and purposes of the college.
Pacific Union College	Gross and inexcusable inefficiency, repudiation of church standards.
Prescott College	Repeated and continued violation of college policy.
Rust College	Contumacious conduct by the faculty member, serious scandal in the community of constituency, national security or immigration problems.
Simpson College	"Differences relating to the doctrinal statement to which the faculty member is required to subscribe."
Wayland Baptist University	Absenteeism, failure to abide by rules and regulations of the university.
Western Baptist College	Failure to support doctrinal positions of the college

"clear and convincing evidence" language; the others do not.

The other eight colleges vary in due process. College of the Ozarks (B2) has no committee structure, but the faculty member has the opportunity to meet with the dean and president "to present his/her defense to the dismissal recommendation before the recommendation is made." At four colleges, the dismissal process is controlled by the president, academic vice president, or administrative committee. For example, at Lourdes College (B2), a faculty member's appointment "may be terminated at any time . . . in the judgment of the president." Brenau University's (M1) policy stipulates that "the president . . . may, at any time, remove or suspend any faculty member or other employee for adequate cause by giving written notice." The vice president for academic affairs at Liberty University (M1) makes all nonrenewal and dismissal decisions. At Prescott College (B2), dismissal recommendations come from a committee composed of the faculty chair, personnel coordinator, and program coordinator, and are approved by the dean.

Two colleges (Lesley College (M1) and Shimer College (B2)) do not explain the dismissal process in their faculty manuals. At

Florida Southern College (B2), there is no process. Instead, "when moral turpitude, professional incompetence, or violation of the principles of academic freedom and responsibility have been established, the faculty member is subject to immediate discharge and termination of employment agreement." Since the college does not define how these charges are "established," it appears that a faculty member can be summarily dismissed.

Appeals

Appeals of dismissals for cause can be made at 18 of 20 institutions (90%). At 15 of the colleges, appeals are presented to a committee comprised of either faculty, faculty and administrators, or trustees. Appeals are presented directly to the president (with no committee review) at three colleges (Olivet College (B2), Prescott College (B2), and Wayland Baptist University (B2)). Two colleges (Lourdes College (B2) and Shimer College (B2)) have no appeals process or have not defined such a process in their handbook.

FINANCIAL EXIGENCY AND PROGRAM DISCONTINUATION

AAUP policy stipulates that "there should be a faculty body which participates in the decision that a condition of financial exigency exists or is imminent." In addition, a faculty committee should "exercise primary responsibility" in determining who is to be terminated. Terminated faculty members should have a right to a full hearing before a faculty committee. Program discontinuance, too, should be "determined primarily by the faculty as a whole or an appropriate committee thereof" (1995, pp. 24-25).

Contract colleges as a group ignore AAUP guidelines. Shimer College (B2) and Florida Southern College (B2) do not define procedures for financial exigency or program discontinuation. Northwest Christian College's (B2) policy is summarized in one sentence: "Continuous appointment is contingent upon continuous need for services of the appointee and the financial ability of the institution to maintain the appointment." Ten colleges include a policy but have no provisions for faculty involvement in determining financial exigency or program discontinuance. Eight of the 21 explicitly mention the role of faculty in the process (see Appendix 9-E).

In addition, these colleges tend to define financial exigency/program discontinuance more broadly than the AAUP. The AAUP specifically prohibits program reduction based on enrollment changes: "Educational considerations do not include cyclical or temporary variations in enrollment. They must reflect long-range judgments that the educational mission of the institution as a whole will be enhanced by the discontinuance" (1995, p. 25). Five contract colleges, however, include declining enrollment as acceptable reasons for eliminating faculty positions. For example, College of the Atlantic (B1) defines a "financial or enrollment emergency" as a "situation where there is an unexpected drop in fiscal full-time student enrollment such as may occur due to outside factors such as market shifts, state or federal student aid policy changes, economic hardship in the major market area of the institution, or other similar reason."

Other institutions can terminate faculty for less severe conditions. Brenau University's (M1) policy stipulates that "the employment of any faculty member may be terminated due to a financial exigency, reduction in academic program, or need to reorganize, as determined by the administration of the university." Trinity College of Vermont (B2) can lay off faculty "as a result of a major change, including reduction or discontinuation of an academic program or department in whole or in part." Allen University (B2) "reserves the right to reduce the number of staff positions because of changes in institutional programs, decline in enrollment, decreases in revenue, and other just reasons." Faculty at Lourdes College (B2) can lose their jobs "at any time if the president and the board of trustees, in their sole discretion, determine that financial considerations warrant the reduction or reallocation of faculty." Simpson College (B2) faculty can be terminated for "changes in enrollment or other financial standings that require the elimination of a position."

SUMMARY

In total, the 21 FAPA institutions without tenure, not surprisingly, break from traditional faculty appointment policies in many other areas as well. If one scrolls through the appendices of this chapter, however, it is apparent that some institutions more than others are at variance with customary practice. College of the Atlantic (B1) and Warren Wilson College (B2) mirror AAUP policy quite often, while Allen University (B2), Brenau University (M1), Florida Southern College (B2), Liberty University (M1), and Lourdes College (B2) do not. In aggregate, though, standard practice for contract colleges deviates from standard policy as enacted by large research institutions and endorsed by the AAUP.

REFERENCES

American Association of University Professors. (1995). *Policy documents and reports* (8th ed.). Washington, DC: AAUP.

Chait, R. P., & Ford, A. T. (1982). *Beyond traditional tenure.* San Francisco, CA: Jossey-Bass.

Chait, R. P., & Trower, C. A. (1997). *Where tenure does not reign: Colleges with contract systems.* Washington, DC: American Association of Higher Education.

Leatherman, C. (1999, April 9). Growth in positions off the tenure track is a trend that's here to stay, study finds. *Chronicle of Higher Education,* p. A14.

National Center for Education Statistics. (1996). *Institutional policies and practices regarding faculty in higher education.* Washington, DC: US Department of Education.

National Center for Education Statistics. (1998). *Fall staff in postsecondary institutions, 1995.* Washington, DC: US Department of Education.

Schuster, J. (1998, January/February). Reconfiguring the professoriate: An overview. *Change,* 49-53.

APPENDIX 9-A
Faculty Evaluation Characteristics

Administrator-Directed Evaluations
1. Allen University
2. Brenau University
3. Endicott College
4. Florida Southern College
5. King College
6. Lesley College
7. Liberty University
8. Lourdes College
9. Northwest Christian College
10. Simpson College
11. Trinity College of Vermont
12. Wayland Baptist University
13. Western Baptist College

Committee-Led Evaluations

Faculty only
1. College of the Ozarks
2. Olivet College
3. Pacific Union College
4. Shimer College
5. Warren Wilson College

Multiple constituencies
1. College of the Atlantic
2. Prescott College
3. Rust College

APPENDIX 9-B
Frequency of Faculty Evaluation

Annual
1. Allen University
2. Brenau University
3. Florida Southern College
4. Liberty University
5. Lourdes College
6. Rust College
7. Wayland Baptist University

Annually or Biannually during Probationary Period, then Once during Length of Extended Contract
1. College of the Atlantic
2. College of the Ozarks
3. Endicott College
4. King College

    5. Lesley College
    6. Northwest Christian College
    7. Olivet College
    8. Prescott College
    9. Simpson College
    10. Trinity College of Vermont
    11. Warren Wilson College
Other
    1. Pacific Union College: "Regular intervals."
    2. Shimer College: Intern faculty evaluated at end of second year; senior
       faculty evaluated only in unusual circumstances.
    3. Western Baptist College: Annually for two-year contract faculty; in
       years three and five for six-year contract faculty.

APPENDIX 9-C

Promotion Review Structures

No Promotion
    1. College of the Atlantic
    2. Prescott College
    3. Shimer College
    4. Warren Wilson College

Faculty Committees
    1. Allen University
    2. Brenau University
    3. College of the Ozarks
    4. Endicott College
    5. King College
    6. Lesley College
    7. Liberty University
    8. Lourdes College
    9. Olivet College
    10. Pacific Union College
    11. Rust College
    12. Simpson College
    13. Trinity College of Vermont
    14. Wayland Baptist University

No Faculty Committees
    1. Florida Southern College
    2. Northwest Christian College
    3. Western Baptist College

APPENDIX 9-D
Procedures for DIsmissal for Cause

Standard Procedures That Include Official Notification,
Use of Committees, Hearings with Witnesses for
Presentation of Defense
1. Allen University
2. College of the Atlantic
3. King College
4. Northwest Christian College
5. Olivet College
6. Pacific Union College
7. Rust College
8. Simpson College
9. Trinity College of Vermont
10. Warren Wilson College
11. Wayland Baptist University
12. Western Baptist College

No Committee Structure but Opportunity for
Presentation of Defense
1. College of the Ozarks

Presidential/Administrative Decision
1. Brenau University (president)
2. Liberty University (vice president for academic affairs)
3. Lourdes College (president)
4. Prescott College (administrative committee, dean approves the decision)

No Dismissal Procedures Included in Handbook or No Process
Defined
1. Florida Southern College
2. Lesley College
3. Shimer College

APPENDIX 9-E
Financial Exigency and Program Discontinuation

No Policy in Faculty Handbook
1. Florida Southern College
2. Northwest Christian College
3. Shimer College

No Faculty Role in Determining Financial Exigency/Program Discontinuation
1. Allen University
2. Brenau University

3. College of the Ozarks
4. Lesley College
5. Liberty College
6. Lourdes College
7. Olivet College
8. Prescott College
9. Rust College
10. Simpson College

Faculty Role in Determining Financial Exigency/Program Discontinuation
1. College of the Atlantic
2. Endicott College
3. King College
4. Pacific Union College
5. Trinity College of Vermont
6. Warren Wilson College
7. Wayland Baptist University
8. Western Baptist College

BIBLIOGRAPHY

American Association for State Colleges and Universities. (1998). Academic freedom and responsibility, and academic tenure. Washington, DC: AASCU.

American Association of University Professors. (1995). *Policy documents and reports* (8th ed.). Washington, DC: AAUP.

American Association of University Professors. (1998). *Post-Tenure Review: An AAUP Response.* [On-line.] Washington, DC. Available: http://www.aaup .org/postten.htm.

Bloomfield College. (1997). *Agreement between Bloomfield College and Bloomfield College chapter of the American Association of University Professors.* Bloomfield, NJ: Bloomfield College.

Bowie State University. (1997). *Policy on appointment, rank, and tenure of faculty.* Adelphi, MD: Bowie State University.

Boyer, E. L. (1990). *Scholarship reconsidered: Priorities of the professoriate.* Princeton, NJ: The Carnegie Foundation for the Advancement of Teaching.

Brown University. (1998). *Brown University faculty rules and regulations* [On-line]. Available: http://facgov.brown.edu/facgov/facrulesfolder/part4/sect10/ Sect10.html#RTFToC307.

Chabotar, K. J., & Honan, J. P. (1996). *New yardsticks to measure financial distress.* Washington, DC: American Association for Higher Education.

Chait, R. P., & Ford, A. T. (1982). *Beyond traditional tenure.* San Francisco, CA: Jossey-Bass.

Chait, R. P., & Trower, C. A. (1997). *Where tenure does not reign: Colleges with contract systems.* Washington, DC: American Association of Higher Education.

Chronister, J. L., Baldwin, R. G., & Bailey, T. (1992, Summer). Full-time nontenure-track faculty: Current status, condition and attitudes. *The Review of Higher Education, 15* (4), 383-400.

Columbia University. (1987). *The faculty handbook.* New York, NY: Columbia University.

Cook, J. (1974, April 30). Information bank abstracts. *The New York Times,* p. 87.

Drew University. (1969). *Charter and bylaws and faculty personnel policy.* Madison, NJ: Drew University.

Finkin, M. W. (Ed.) (1996). *The case for tenure.* Ithaca, NY: Cornell University Press.

Gappa, J. M. (1996). Off the tenure track: Six models for full-time, non-tenurable appointments. *New Pathways Working Papers Series,* No. 10. Washington, DC: American Association for Higher Education.

Gappa, J. M., & Leslie, D. W. (1997). Two faculties or one? The conundrum of part-timers in a bifurcated work force. *New Pathways Working Papers Series,* No. 6. Washington, DC: American Association for Higher Education.

James Madison University. (1994). *Faculty handbook, 1994-1995.* Harrisonburg, VA: James Madison University.

Leatherman, C. (1999, April 9). Growth in positions off the tenure track is a trend that's here to stay, study finds. *The Chronicle of Higher Education,* A14-A16.

Licata, C. M. & Morreale, J. C. (1997). *Post-tenure review: Policies, practices, precautions.* Washington, DC: American Association for Higher Education.

Lynton, E. (1995). *Making the case for professional service.* Washington, DC: American Association for Higher Education.

National Center for Education Statistics. (1996). *Institutional policies and practices regarding faculty in higher education.* Washington, DC: US Department of Education.

National Center for Education Statistics. (1998). *Fall staff in postsecondary institutions, 1995.* Washington, DC: US Department of Education.

Northwestern University. (1993). *Northwestern University faculty handbook.* Evanston, IL: Northwestern University, University Relations.

Oklahoma State University. (1999, September 17). Appendix D: Policy statement to govern appointments, tenure, promotion, and related matters of the faculty of Oklahoma State University. Section D: Financial exigency policies and procedures. *Online faculty handbook* [On-line]. Available: www2.okstate.edu/acad/fachanind.htm.

Schuster, J. (1998, January/February). Reconfiguring the professoriate: An overview. *Change,* 49-53.

Spiro, G. (1980, Summer). Facing reductions in force in higher education. *Journal of the College & University Personnel Association, 31*(2), 18-24.

State University System of Florida. (1996). *Collective bargaining agreement between Board of Regents State University System of Florida and United Faculty of Florida.* Tallahasee, FL: State University System of Florida.

University of Colorado. (1988). *Faculty handbook.* Boulder, CO: University of Colorado.

University of Delaware. (1999). *Handbook for faculty* [On-line]. Available: www.udel.edu/provost/fachb/.

University of Hawaii, Manoa. (1997). *Procedures for evaluation of faculty at UH Manoa.* Manoa, HI: University of Hawaii, Board of Regents Bylaws and Policies.

University of Toledo. (1998). *UT-AAUP contract* [On-line]. Available: www.utoledo.edu/POLICIES-PROCEDURES-AND-CONTRACTS/UT-AAUP-CONTRACT.

University System of Georgia. (1999). *Policy manual of the Board of Regents* [On-line]. Available: www.usg.edu/admin/humex/policy/sec800.html.

INDEX

AAHE (American Association of Higher Education), 299, 304

AASCU (American Association of State Colleges and Universities), 80, 82, 84-85, 90, 103, 105, 304

AAUP (American Association of University Professors), 1, 2-7, 9, 12-13, 80, 82-85, 89-90, 103, 105, 107, 115-116, 131, 143, 149-150, 152-153, 156-157, 166, 170-171, 182-184, 186, 189, 192, 198, 215-216, 218, 226-229, 233, 245-246, 248-252, 254-256, 263, 265-270, 272-274, 282-283, 285-289, 295, 297-299; and *1940 Statement of Principles on Academic Freedom and Tenure*, 1, 3- 6, 12, 80, 246, 282, 285-287; and *Recommended Institutional Regulations on Academic Freedom and Tenure*, 245-246, 248, 254-255, 265-268, 270

Academic freedom, xiii, 1-17, 80, 82-86, 88-92, 95, 97, 102, 116, 182, 216, 247, 274; and AAUP, 1, 3-7, 9, 12-13; and adjunct faculty, 2, 9, 14; and contract institutions, 282, 284-287, 297; and guest speakers, 3, 9, 14; and librarians, 2-4, 9, 13; and nontenure-track faculty, 9, 14; and nontenured faculty, 2; and part-time faculty, 2, 9, 14; and probationary faculty, 2, 9, 14; and rank, 283-284, 293-295 and religious affiliation, 2-4, 6, 10-12, 17; and students, 1, 3, 7-9, 13, 15-17; and teaching assistants, 9

Accountability, 95-96, 182, 184, 198

Adequate/just cause for dismissal, v, xi, xiii, xv, 79, 82-83, 85-86, 93-94, 102, 183-84, 209-210, 213-243; and AAUP on, 215-216, 218, 226-229, 233; and contract institutions, 283-284, 295-298, 301-302; and contumacious conduct, 86; and criminality, 213, 216, 219-220, 234-238; and dis-

honesty, 214, 216, 222-223, 234-238; and falsification of documents, 213, 216, 222-223, 234-238; and incompetence, 213, 216-217, 219-220, 230, 234-238, 295, 297; and misconduct/misbehavior, 213, 216, 221-222, 225, 230-231, 233-238; and misrepresentation, 213, 216, 221-222, 234-238; and moral turpitude, 213, 216, 218-219, 223, 230, 233-238, 295-297; and neglect of duty, 213, 216-219, 230, 232-238, 295; and performance, 213, 216, 220-221, 231, 234-238; and personal conduct impairing duties, 214, 216, 225, 234-238; and unethical behavior, 214-216, 223-224, 233-238; and violations of rights or policies, 214, 216, 224, 228, 234-238

Annual/one-year contract, 80, 86-87, 93-94, 102, 106, 282, 288

Annual review (see evaluation)

Appointments and contract institutions, 283-284, 287-289, 294, 296-297, 299; initial appointments, 18, 23-24

Boyer, Ernest L., 156-159, 171

Chabotar, K.J., 252, 274, 281, 304

Clinical faculty, 111, 114, 117, 125-128, 130-131, 138, 152, 159, 163

Collective bargaining, xiii, xvi, 80, 83, 105, 229, 251, 253, 257-258, 260, 262-263

Compensation, 93-94, 116, 119, 260

Continuing/continuous contracts, 80, 85-86, 93, 101-102, 107; and multi-year contracts, 282, 288

Contract institutions/institutions without tenure, 282-303; and AAUP, 282-283, 285-289, 295, 297-299; and academic freedom, 282, 284-287, 297; and appointments, 283-284, 287-289,

INDEX OF
INSTITUTIONAL NAMES

310

176, 193, 194, 202, 203, 208, 225, 231, 232, 238, 243, 259, 278, 279
Saint Louis University, 15, 17, 26, 57, 59, 62, 64, 66, 107, 117, 124, 132, 134, 135, 136, 137, 138, 139, 146, 154, 171, 172, 175, 178, 217, 220, 234, 239, 264, 276, 278, 280
Saint Maryís University, 13, 15, 16, 57, 60, 63, 67, 70, 74, 76, 100, 106, 108, 109, 133, 139, 171, 173, 176, 178, 201, 204, 224, 225, 228, 236, 241, 259, 277, 279
Saint Norbert College, 58, 60, 86, 155, 158, 174, 176, 179, 202, 203, 226, 238, 243, 271, 278, 279
Saint Olaf College, 50, 56, 60, 70, 96, 108, 134, 135, 223, 231, 233, 237, 242, 281
Saint Vincent College, 14, 17, 41, 50, 58, 61, 68, 69, 71, 100, 104, 106, 107, 108, 109, 118, 134, 136, 137, 164, 172, 174, 176, 177, 179, 220, 224, 225, 232, 238, 243
Salve Regina University, 17, 56, 61, 108, 133, 139, 140, 176, 236, 241
San Francisco State University, 7, 16, 56, 61, 65, 67, 69, 77, 105, 173, 176, 201, 203, 231, 236, 241, 277, 279, 280, 299
San Jose State University, 38, 43, 56, 61, 65, 67, 69, 77, 105, 168, 173, 176, 178, 201, 203, 206, 231, 236, 241, 277, 279, 280
Santa Clara University, 40, 56, 67, 72, 104, 124, 133, 138, 139, 140, 155, 163, 171, 173, 176, 177, 197, 201, 205, 207, 211, 229, 232, 236, 241, 277, 280
Shawnee State University, 61, 69, 93, 108, 174, 176, 238, 243
Shepherd College, 46, 56, 61, 68, 69, 71, 73, 78, 106, 113, 163, 176, 223, 224, 237, 242, 281
Shimer College, 285, 288, 289, 291, 293, 296, 297, 300, 301, 302
Simpson College, 285, 288, 294, 296, 298, 300, 301, 302, 303
Smith College, 9, 61, 63, 65, 66, 73, 134, 237, 242
Southeastern Louisiana University, 57, 62, 67, 73, 76, 77, 104, 133, 135, 139, 140, 147, 167, 173, 218, 236, 241, 277
Southeastern Oklahoma State University, 56, 60, 63, 69, 78, 133, 135, 140,

173, 176, 178, 201, 202, 206, 210, 220, 232, 236, 241
Southern Arkansas University, 58, 63, 65, 106, 156, 173, 177, 237, 242
Southern Illinois University, Carbondale, 51, 57, 64, 77, 100, 109, 132, 134, 137, 138, 140, 148, 167, 172, 175, 222, 224, 229, 234, 239, 280
Southwestern University, 16, 17, 35, 47, 56, 68, 71, 73, 89, 237, 242
Springfield College, 14, 39, 40, 57, 67, 69, 108, 133, 135, 144, 171, 173, 223, 236, 241, 249, 275, 276, 277, 279, 280
Sweet Briar College, 15, 56, 61, 63, 68, 104, 114, 222, 237, 242

Taylor University, 17, 57, 60, 69, 71, 76, 143, 144, 168, 172, 174, 176, 179, 202, 204, 207, 208, 210, 238, 243
Texas Wesleyan University, 58, 60, 92, 217, 220, 236, 241
Texas Womanís University, 7, 14, 55, 84, 92, 103, 105, 109, 132, 137, 138, 139, 140, 193, 194, 200, 204, 207, 209, 232, 235, 240
Trinity College of Vermont, 285, 288, 289, 291, 294, 295, 298, 300, 301, 302, 303

Union College, 15, 16, 58, 68, 106, 108, 147, 171, 173, 179, 237, 242
United States International University, 21, 50, 55, 77, 132, 137, 139, 175, 178, 235, 240, 277, 278
University of Alaska, 52, 56, 63, 78, 100, 104, 109, 133, 135, 138, 139, 140, 186, 201, 204, 236, 241, 277, 279, 280
University of Arizona, 44, 54, 61, 64, 66, 76, 120, 121, 122, 129, 132, 134, 135, 136, 140, 193, 194, 200, 203, 207, 208, 211, 221, 222, 234, 239, 280
University of Arkansas, 34, 55, 64, 65, 72, 85, 107, 162, 222, 234, 239, 253, 276, 278
University of California, Irvine, 42, 54, 62, 64, 66, 71, 74, 103, 132, 137, 138, 139, 146, 154, 155, 172, 175, 177, 178, 200, 205, 234, 239, 280
University of California, Santa Cruz, 25, 54, 62, 64, 66, 72, 74, 103, 172, 175, 177, 178, 200, 205, 234, 239, 280
University of Central Florida, 26, 55, 62, 64, 133, 134, 137, 139, 140, 175,